Synthesis Lectures on Data, Semantics, and Knowledge

Series Editors

Ying Ding, The University of Texas at Austin, Austin, USA

Paul Groth, Amsterdam, Noord-Holland, The Netherlands

This series focuses on the pivotal role that data on the web and the emergent technologies that surround it play both in the evolution of the World Wide Web as well as applications in domains requiring data integration and semantic analysis. The large-scale availability of both structured and unstructured data on the Web has enabled radically new technologies to develop. It has impacted developments in a variety of areas including machine learning, deep learning, semantic search, and natural language processing. Knowledge and semantics are a critical foundation for the sharing, utilization, and organization of this data. The series aims both to provide pathways into the field of research and an understanding of the principles underlying these technologies for an audience of scientists, engineers, and practitioners.

Kewei Cheng · Yizhou Sun

Knowledge Graph Reasoning

A Neuro-Symbolic Perspective

Kewei Cheng
Research Scientist
Amazon
Palo Alto, CA, USA

Yizhou Sun
Department of Computer Science
University of California
Los Angeles
Los Angeles, CA, USA

ISSN 2691-2023   ISSN 2691-2031 (electronic)
Synthesis Lectures on Data, Semantics, and Knowledge
ISBN 978-3-031-72007-9   ISBN 978-3-031-72008-6 (eBook)
https://doi.org/10.1007/978-3-031-72008-6

This Springer imprint is published by the registered company Springer Nature Switzerland AG
The registered company address is: Gewerbestrasse 11, 6330 Cham, Switzerland

If disposing of this product, please recycle the paper.

Acknowledgements

Our research has been partially supported by NSF 2211557, NSF 1937599, NSF 2119643, NSF 2303037, NSF 20232551, NSF 2312501, NASA, SRC JUMP 2.0 Center, Okawa Foundation Grant, Amazon Research Awards, Cisco Research Grant, Picsart Gifts, and Snapchat Gifts. The views and conclusions expressed in this book are solely those of the authors and do not necessarily reflect the opinions of any funding agencies.

We thank our past and existing lab members who have made significant contributions in this direction, including Xuelu (Shirley) Chen, Junheng Hao, Ziniu Hu, Roshni Iyer, and Fred Xu. This book is built upon their research.

We also thank the students from UCLA taking Spring 2024 CS 249: Neuro-Symbolic Reasoning on Knowledge Graphs, who have been the first readers of this book.

Contents

Introduction

1

> *"All our knowledge begins with the senses, proceeds then to the*
> *understanding, and ends with reason. There is nothing higher than*
> *reason."—Immanuel Kant*

Knowledge graphs have received wide attention recently, and have been successfully applied
to many domains and downstream tasks. In this book, we aim at providing a novel neuro-
symbolic perspective in summarizing recent advances in a variety of knowledge graph
reasoning tasks. By bridging the gap between neural networks and symbolic reasoning, this
book offers a unique and comprehensive perspective on knowledge graph reasoning. It aims
to equip researchers, practitioners, and enthusiasts with the knowledge and tools necessary
to tackle the complex challenges posed by knowledge graphs and contribute to the continued
advancement of this exciting field.

1.1 What Are Knowledge Graphs?

On one hand, knowledge graphs (KGs) are a collection of triples storing facts about entities[1]
via relations between them, in the form of *(head entity, relation, tail entity)*. For instance,
(Mina Miller, LiveIn, USA) is a triple, where *"Mina Miller"* and *"USA"* are entities in the KG
connected by the relation *"LiveIn"*. On the other hand, as the name suggests, knowledge
graphs are essentially graphs, where nodes denote entities and links denote relationships
between those entities. A toy example of KG can be found in Fig. 1.1a, which contains 5
entities, 3 relations, and 4 observed facts denoted as triples (e.g., *(Thomas Alva Edison,
IsMarriedTo, Mary Stilwell)*).

---

[1] KGs may also contain concepts, which will be discussed in detail in Chap. 6.

© The Author(s), under exclusive license to Springer Nature Switzerland AG 2025
K. Cheng and Y. Sun, *Knowledge Graph Reasoning*, Synthesis Lectures on Data, Semantics,
and Knowledge, https://doi.org/10.1007/978-3-031-72008-6_1

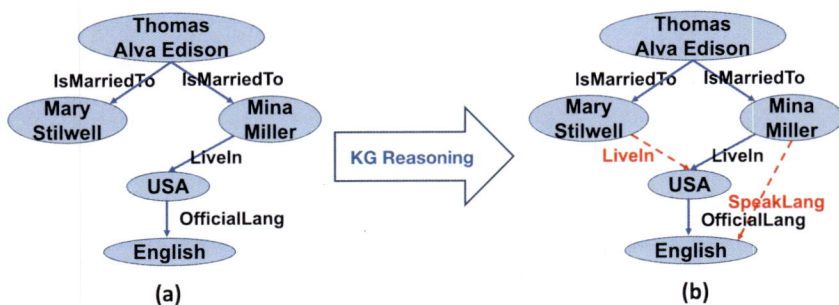

Fig. 1.1 **a** A toy example of KG containing 5 entities, 3 relations, and 4 observed facts. **b** A set of new facts denoted as the red dotted lines that can be inferred from existing facts

Various types of KGs have emerged, which include (1) general-purpose KGs such as DBpedia [1] and Freebase [2]; (2) domain-specific KGs such as STRING [3] in the biomedical domain and Amazon Product Graph [4] in E-Commerce; and (3) common sense KGs such as WordNet [5] and ConceptNet [6] that describe common sense knowledge on general concepts instead of concrete entities.

1.2   Why Are Knowledge Graphs Important?

Knowledge has played a critical role in *Human Intelligence*. The knowledge that gets accumulated over time enables humans to conduct reasoning and solve problems. A similar goal has been set for *Artificial Intelligence (AI)*, which aims to mimic actions and decisions taken by humans. Knowledge graphs have served as an important role to represent, store, and manage knowledge, which are usually collected from various sources. Bringing knowledge graphs into AI can systematically improve the performance and reasoning capabilities of AI systems, which have been widely applied to a variety of applications. For example, Google has been using KGs to power its search engine since 2012, which turns *webpage retrieval* into *knowledge retrieval* and thus significantly enhances user experiences [7]. Following Google, many companies such as Meta, Amazon, and LinkedIn, launched their own knowledge graphs, encompassing similar ideas. To this day, knowledge graphs have been gaining a lot of momentum. They have been actively explored and deployed across multiple domains, such as recommender systems in e-commerce, drug re-purposing in bio-medicine, question and answering (Q&A) systems, and dialogue systems in AI assistants. We provide a few examples of KG applications below.

- **Search engines**. KGs have been widely used in search engines, such as Google [7], Microsoft's Bing [8], and Yahoo [9]. For example, the Google search engine returns related info organized as infobox, such as education, birthplace, and spouse in a knowledge panel, when a query is about a famous person.

- **E-Commerce**. KGs have been widely adopted in E-Commerce systems, which are built to capture the behavioral relationship between products and shoppers, such as click-through and purchase. These KGs facilitate the recommender systems that are designed for personal recommendations for products and ads. Companies that are heavily relied on KGs include Amazon [4], eBay [10], and Alibaba [11].
- **Finance**. The usage of KGs has been evidenced in financial systems. One application is to construct corporate KGs to capture business relations between relevant stocks, which is used for stock price movement prediction. Another application is in finance security, where KGs can assist in financial crime prevention and investigation, allowing banking institutions to understand the flow of money across their clientele and identify non-compliant customers. Some representative financial companies using KGs include Bloomberg [12], Capital One [13], and Wells Fargo [14].
- **Biomedical science and healthcare**. KGs such as Bio2RDF [15] are also benefiting the healthcare industry by organizing and categorizing relationships within biomedical area, which assist medical providers by validating diagnoses and identifying treatment plans based on individual needs. In addition, biomedical KGs have significantly boosted the pharmaceutical industry via new drug design and drug re-purposing [16].

1.3   Knowledge Graph Reasoning Tasks

KG reasoning aims at inferring new knowledge from a knowledge graph, by using the relationships and facts encoded in the graph. For instance, we are interested in inferring missing triples or summarizing the underlying pattern of the KGs in the form of logical rules. In this book, we consider three types of reasoning tasks.

Knowledge Graph Completion.

Knowledge graph completion aims at predicting one-hop queries by reasoning with existing facts. For example, given the head entity *"Mary Stilwell"* and the relation *"LiveIn"* in Fig. 1.1, the knowledge graph completion task aims to predict the missing tail entity. As the query *(Mary Stilwell, LiveIn, ?)* can be considered as a one-hop link prediction, we call it a one-hop query, in contrast to complex queries such as multi-hop queries and first-order logic queries.

Knowledge Graph Complex Query Answering.

Similar to KG completion, KG complex queries return entities in the KG that satisfy the constraints described in the query. But different from the KG completion task, KG complex queries describe a much more complex structural pattern between entities and the target entity. For instance, as shown in Fig. 1.1, a query could be *"Which language does an American's spouse speak?"*, which can be expressed in the form of first-order logic (FOL) with entities, variables (place holder entities), and target entity from KG:

$$V?.\exists V_1, V_2 : \text{LiveIn}(V_1, \text{USA}) \wedge \text{IsMarriedTo}(V_1, V_2) \wedge \text{SpeakLanguage}(V_2, V?) \quad (1.1)$$

This type of query involves multiple relations between entities and thus requires more advanced reasoning.

Logical Rule Induction from KGs.

Logical rules in the form of *head* ← *body* are frequently used by people to conduct reasoning in daily life or specific domains. Most of these logical rules are provided by human experts summarized from their experiences, which are usually labor-intensive to obtain. Logical rule induction from KGs aims at *automatically* learning logical rules by summarizing instance-level facts in KGs to template-level rules. For example, as shown in Fig. 1.1, we may learn the following logical rule:

$$\text{SpeakLanguage}(x, y) \leftarrow \text{LiveIn}(x, z) \wedge \text{OfficialLanguage}(z, y) \quad (1.2)$$

Logical rules serve as another important form of knowledge, which enable the reasoning process to be more transparent, accountable, and trustworthy.

The first two KG reasoning tasks fall in the regime of *deductive reasoning*, and the third one falls in the regime of *inductive reasoning*. Both are critical reasoning types that human beings possess. In this book, we do not touch the third reasoning type, which is *abductive reasoning* and could be a very interesting future work.

Overall, KG reasoning aims at expanding the knowledge represented in the graph, which is a crucial step in the process of knowledge representation and management. By leveraging the relationships and facts encoded in a KG, KG reasoning can provide a powerful and flexible way of inferring new knowledge, making predictions, and supporting a variety of applications.

1.4   Two Approaches to KG Reasoning

The most studied approach to KG reasoning since the earliest days of AI is symbolic reasoning. Symbolic reasoning encodes expert knowledge as statements in a logic-based representation language and implements reasoning in the form of logical inference, which can address high-level reasoning and model thought processes. In this way, symbolic reasoning is good at reasoning abstract concepts and can be used to derive logical conclusions from premises. For example, given a logical rule *SpeakLanguage*(x, y) ← *LiveIn*(x, z) ∧

OfficialLanguage(z, y), and the observed facts *LiveIn(Mina Miller, USA)* and *OfficialLanguage(USA, English)*, we can infer the new fact *SpeakLanguage(Mina Miller, English)* as shown in Fig. 1.1.

Symbolic reasoning is based on logic and inference rules that are human-understandable, thus the inference process can be easily interpreted by human beings. Additionally, symbolic reasoning can generalize to new scenarios and unseen entities as logical rules are not limited to specific entities.

Despite its strong interpretability and generalizability, symbolic reasoning has two main limitations. First, it is very fragile and heavily relies on the quality of the KGs. In reality, unfortunately, KGs are far from complete and are full of noises and ambiguities. For example, *"USA"* and *"United States"* may refer to the same country, but symbolic reasoning approaches treat them as separate entities. Second, symbolic reasoning fails to scale to large datasets, due to the high complexity nature of the algorithms.

More recently, representation learning-based techniques have been proposed for KG reasoning. Unlike symbolic reasoning, representation learning-based techniques map entities into continuous vectors and relations into operations that are defined over entities. The reasoning tasks are then turned into learning tasks, which are usually less sensitive to noisy data and more scalable. For instance, these techniques can identify that both *"USA"* and *"United States"* refer to the same country, showcasing their capacity for flexible and robust modeling.

However, there are several disadvantages of representation learning-based approaches. First, unlike symbolic reasoning, representation learning-based techniques lack the ability to leverage logical rules, limiting their reasoning capacity. For instance, without the capability of leveraging logical rules, representation learning-based techniques cannot infer *"Mary Stilwell"* and *"Mina Miller"* speak *"English"* from Fig. 1.1. Second, these approaches are data hungry, which cannot generalize to low-resource entities/relations nor handle cold start cases. Third, similar to most neural network approaches, these approaches lack of interpretability, and the reasoning process is hard to understand by human.

In summary, symbolic logical reasoning techniques and representation-learning-based techniques are the two main directions for KG reasoning, which correspond to the first wave of AI and the second wave of AI, respectively. Both lines of research have their pros and cons. It is natural to combine these two lines, i.e., the neuro-symbolic integration, which is the focus of this book.

1.5   A New Perspective: Integrating Symbolic Reasoning and Representation Learning

When considering knowledge graph reasoning, symbolic reasoning and representation learning are often seen as distinct approaches. However, these approaches possess the potential to mutually enhance each other, leading to more comprehensive and effective KG reasoning models.

On one hand, symbolic approaches are particularly well suited for tasks that require precise, logically consistent reasoning. By leveraging logical rules, symbolic approaches offer interpretability and generalizability. They enable insightful interpretations of inferred results and facilitate straightforward generalization to unobserved objects. However, symbolic approaches encounter challenges in scaling to large datasets and navigating complex or ambiguous situations. In such cases, where clear sets of rules or logical relationships are unavailable, symbolic reasoning struggles to provide accurate predictions. On the other hand, representation learning-based techniques address the limitations of symbolic approaches by exploring complex patterns among triples. They excel at capturing intricate relationships and dependencies within knowledge graphs, enabling effective reasoning in the absence of explicit rules. By mapping entities to continuous vectors and leveraging operations to represent relations, representation learning-based techniques offer scalability in handling large datasets. Nevertheless, they lack interpretability and generalizability compared to symbolic approaches. Understanding the reasoning processes and generalizing to new, unseen instances can be challenging with representation learning alone. Furthermore, representation learning-based techniques often require substantial amounts of training data to achieve optimal performance.

By combining the strengths of symbolic reasoning and representation learning, researchers can achieve a more comprehensive approach to KG reasoning. Leveraging the interpretability and logical consistency of symbolic reasoning, while harnessing the pattern recognition and scalability of representation learning, can lead to neuro-symbolic models that deliver a more **scalable**, **generalizable**, and **interpretable** solution to perform KG reasoning.

- **Scalable**: Symbolic reasoning can be computationally expensive for large-scale problems. For example, in a large-scale knowledge graph reasoning task, traditional symbolic methods would not be suitable, as their computational complexity increases exponentially with the size of the knowledge graph. In contrast, representation learning exhibits a formidable computational advantage. This reduction in complexity allows for more efficient and scalable computations, enabling improved performance and broader applicability of neuro-symbolic models in handling complex knowledge graphs.
- **Generalizable**: The strong generalizability of symbolic logic can be leveraged to compensate for the lack of data availability for neural methods. For example, although representation learning highly rely on large amounts of high-quality training data, neuro-symbolic methods are not significantly impacted by limitations on the amount of available training data. In a few-shot learning task, a neuro-symbolic system can use symbolic knowledge as extra data to enrich the limited training samples.
- **Interpretable**: neuro-symbolic systems can provide explicit computation processes, such as a traced reasoning process or a chain of evidence of results. For example, in medical diagnosis, neuro-symbolic systems are expected not only to make a decision but also to show the reason for this decision in order to aid the doctor in the diagnosis.

Due to the advantages brought by the neuro-symbolic systems, in this book, we will focus on discussing how to seamlessly integrate the discrete symbol of symbolic systems with the continuous vector of neural systems to improve the reasoning performance, which may have the potential to revolutionize the way we interact with and utilize knowledge graphs.

1.6   Structure of the Book

This chapter provides a general introduction to the problem of KG reasoning and the unique neuro-symbolic view of this book. In Chap. 2, we cover the basic concepts and definitions that will be used in later chapters. We discuss each of the three KG reasoning tasks in Chaps. 3, 4, and 5.

- **Chapter 3: Knowledge Graph Completion**. Knowledge graph completion aims to predict missing facts by reasoning with existing facts. Specifically, this chapter only focuses on *one-hop queries* in contrast to the complex queries mentioned in the next chapter. We give a comprehensive introduction to various methods for KG completion, including (1) traditional symbolic reasoning methods, (2) recent representation learning-based methods, and (3) neuro-symbolic integration-based methods. In the end, we introduce UniKER [17], our recent advance in the line of neuro-symbolic integration, which combines logical reasoning and representation learning to enhance the KG completion task.
- **Chapter 4: Complex Query Answering**. In this chapter, we discuss a more challenging problem of answering *complex queries*, which involve multiple relations or conditions between entities to perform more advanced reasoning and inference. There are two approaches in addressing complex query answering in KG, including (1) traditional subgraph matching methods, and (2) more recent neuro-symbolic methods - logical query embedding. In the end, we introduce FuzzQE [18], which is a neuro-symbolic approach that represents FOL queries as embeddings by combining representation learning and fuzzy logic.
- **Chapter 5: Logical Rule Learning**. Logical rules are widely used to represent domain knowledge and hypothesis, which are fundamental to symbolic reasoning-based methods discussed in Chap. 3. Despite the potential benefits brought by logical rules, they are usually *labor-intensive* to obtain. In this chapter, we provide a comprehensive survey on the problem of *automatic* logic rule learning from knowledge graphs, which include two lines: (1) the traditional searching-based methods; and (2) the recent neuro-symbolic integration approaches. In the end, we introduce our RLogic [19] algorithm, which is the state-of-the-art neuro-symbolic rule learning algorithm.

Next, we introduce ontology into KG and discuss techniques for handling ontology.

- **Chapter 6: Incorporating Ontology to Knowledge Graph Reasoning**. Although many knowledge graphs represent two views: (1) an ontological view for meta-level abstraction, and (2) an instance view for instance-level instantiation, Chaps. 3–5 leverage merely instance view knowledge graphs for KG reasoning. In this chapter, we focus on methods that incorporate additional information in the ontology view with the goal of further improving KG reasoning. In particular, we survey methods that inject concept, concept hierarchies, and relation hierarchies into KG reasoning. In the end, we introduce our JOIE [20] framework in detail, which is the first KG embedding approach jointly considering the ontology view and instance view of KGs.

Finally, Chap. 7 concludes this book and lists several future research directions.

References

1. S. Auer, C. Bizer, G. Kobilarov, J. Lehmann, R. Cyganiak, and Z. Ives. Dbpedia: A nucleus for a web of open data. In *Proceedings of the International Semantic Web Conference (ISWC)*, pages 722–735. Springer, 2007.
2. K. Bollacker, C. Evans, P. Paritosh, T. Sturge, and J. Taylor. Freebase: a collaboratively created graph database for structuring human knowledge. In *Proceedings of ACM SIGMOD International Conference on Management of Data (SIGMOD)*, pages 1247–1250. ACM, 2008.
3. D. Szklarczyk, A. L. Gable, D. Lyon, A. Junge, S. Wyder, J. Huerta-Cepas, M. Simonovic, N. T. Doncheva, J. H. Morris, P. Bork, et al. String v11: protein–protein association networks with increased coverage, supporting functional discovery in genome-wide experimental datasets. *Nucleic acids research*, 47(D1):D607–D613, 2019.
4. X. L. Dong. Building a broad knowledge graph for products. In *Proceedings of the IEEE International Conference on Data Engineering (ICDE)*, pages 25–25. IEEE, 2019.
5. G. A. Miller. *WordNet: An electronic lexical database*. MIT press, 1998.
6. R. Speer, J. Chin, and C. Havasi. Conceptnet 5.5: An open multilingual graph of general knowledge. In *Proceedings of AAAI Conference on Artificial Intelligence (AAAI)*, 2017.
7. X. Dong, E. Gabrilovich, G. Heitz, W. Horn, N. Lao, K. Murphy, T. Strohmann, S. Sun, and W. Zhang. Knowledge vault: A web-scale approach to probabilistic knowledge fusion. In *Proceedings of the ACM SIGKDD International Conference on Knowledge Discovery and Data Mining (KDD)*, pages 601–610, 2014.
8. R. Qian. Understand your world with bing. https://blogs.bing.com/search/2013/03/21/understand-your-world-with-bing/, 2013. [Online; accessed 21-Mar-2013].
9. R. Blanco, B. B. Cambazoglu, P. Mika, and N. Torzec. Entity recommendations in web search. In *Proceedings of the International Semantic Web Conference (ISWC)*, pages 33–48. Springer, 2013.
10. R. Pittman. Cracking the code on conversational commerce. https://www.ebayinc.com/stories/news/cracking-the-code-on-conversational-commerce/, 2017. [Online; accessed 06-Apr-2017].
11. N. Zhang, Q. Jia, S. Deng, X. Chen, H. Ye, H. Chen, H. Tou, G. Huang, Z. Wang, N. Hua, et al. Alicg: Fine-grained and evolvable conceptual graph construction for semantic search at alibaba. In *Proceedings of the ACM SIGKDD International Conference on Knowledge Discovery and Data Mining (KDD)*, pages 3895–3905, 2021.

12. E. Meij. Understanding news using the bloomberg knowledge graph. *Invited talk at the Big Data Innovators Gathering (TheWebConf).*, 2019.

13. P. Branum and B. Sehon. Knowledge graph pilot improves data quality while providing a customer 360 view. In *Knowledge Graph Conference.(Invited talk)*, 2019.

14. D. Newman. Knowledge graphs and ai: The future of financial data. In *Knowledge Graph Conference.(Invited talk)*, 2019.

15. A. Callahan, J. Cruz-Toledo, P. Ansell, and M. Dumontier. Bio2rdf release 2: improved coverage, interoperability and provenance of life science linked data. In *Proceedings of the Extended Semantic Web Conference (ESWC)*, pages 200–212. Springer, 2013.

16. Z. Gao, P. Ding, and R. Xu. Kg-predict: a knowledge graph computational framework for drug repurposing. *Journal of Biomedical Informatics*, 132:104133, 2022.

17. K. Cheng, Z. Yang, M. Zhang, and Y. Sun. Uniker: A unified framework for combining embedding and definite horn rule reasoning for knowledge graph inference. In *Proceedings of the Conference on Empirical Methods in Natural Language Processing (EMNLP)*, 2021.

18. X. Chen, Z. Hu, and Y. Sun. Fuzzy logic based logical query answering on knowledge graphs. In *Proceedings of AAAI Conference on Artificial Intelligence (AAAI)*, volume 36, pages 3939–3948, 2022.

19. K. Cheng, J. Liu, W. Wang, and Y. Sun. Rlogic: Recursive logical rule learning from knowledge graphs. In *Proceedings of the ACM SIGKDD International Conference on Knowledge Discovery and Data Mining (KDD)*, pages 179–189, 2022.

20. J. Hao, M. Chen, W. Yu, Y. Sun, and W. Wang. Universal representation learning of knowledge bases by jointly embedding instances and ontological concepts. In *Proceedings of the ACM SIGKDD International Conference on Knowledge Discovery and Data Mining (KDD)*, pages 1709–1719. ACM, 2019.

Preliminaries on Knowledge Graph and Symbolic Logic

2

> *"Logic is the foundation of the certainty of all the knowledge we acquire." —Leonhard Euler*

2.1 Knowledge Graph Definition

In this section, we introduce the definition of knowledge graphs in the languages of both *graph* and *symbolic logic*.

2.1.1 KGs in the Language of Graph

A knowledge graph (KG) is a heterogeneous graph, where nodes denote entities and links denote the relations of different types between entities. Formally, a knowledge graph can be defined as follows.

Definition 2.1 (*Knowledge Graph*) A knowledge graph is a directed graph $G = \{\mathcal{E}, \mathcal{R}, O\}$, which consists of a set of *entities* $\mathcal{E}$, a set of *relations* $\mathcal{R}$, and a set of *facts* O. A *fact* is represented by a triple $(e_i, r_k, e_j) \in O$, where $e_i \in \mathcal{E}$ denotes the *head*, $e_j \in \mathcal{E}$ denotes the *tail*, and $r_k \in \mathcal{R}$ denotes the *relation* between the head and the tail.

Example 2.1.1 An example of a knowledge graph is given in Fig. 2.1. This KG contains 9 entities such as *"Bill Gates"* and *"Microsoft"*, 8 relations such as *"Founded"* and *"BornIn"*, and 7 facts such as (*Bill Gates, Founded, Microsoft*). □

© The Author(s), under exclusive license to Springer Nature Switzerland AG 2025
K. Cheng and Y. Sun, *Knowledge Graph Reasoning*, Synthesis Lectures on Data, Semantics, and Knowledge, https://doi.org/10.1007/978-3-031-72008-6_2

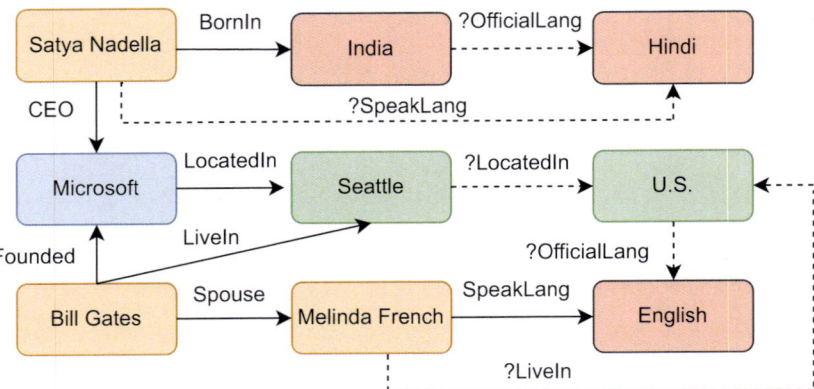

Fig. 2.1 An example of a knowledge graph. Each rectangle in the figure represents an entity in the KG and each solid line connecting two rectangles in the figure represents a relation in the KG. The dashed lines are the missing links, which can be inferred from the observed facts in KG

An interesting reasoning task for the above example might be *"which language does Satya Nadella speak"*, denoted as a query *(Satya Nadella, SpeakLanguage, ?)*. This reasoning task is called *KG completion*, which corresponds to the *link prediction* task in graph learning.

2.1.2 KGs in the Language of Symbolic Logic

In addition to the intuitive graph perspective of knowledge graphs, they can also be interpreted and reasoned in the form of symbolic logic. In the world of symbolic logic, entities can be considered as **constants** and relations are binary **predicates**. Each predicate is a function that takes a set of arguments and outputs either *True* or *False* [1]. In the KG setting, each predicate takes two arguments, which can be denoted as $r(\cdot, \cdot)$. **A ground predicate** (a.k.a. **atom** or **atomic formula**) is a predicate whose arguments are all instantiated by particular constants. For example, we may have a predicate *Founded*$(\cdot, \cdot)$. By assigning constants *"Bill Gates"* and *"Microsoft"* to it, we get a ground predicate *Founded(Bill Gates, Microsoft)*. A triple (e_i, r_k, e_j) is essentially a ground predicate, denoted as $r_k(e_i, e_j)$ in the language of logic. In the reasoning task, a ground predicate can be regarded as a binary random variable: $r_k(e_i, e_j) = 1$ when the triple (e_i, r_k, e_j) holds true, and $r_k(e_i, e_j) = 0$ otherwise. **A possible world** assigns a truth value 0 or 1 to each ground predicate. Given the observed facts O and their corresponding ground predicates $\mathbf{v}_O = \{r_k(e_i, e_j) | (e_i, r_k, e_j) \in O\}$, the task of **knowledge graph completion** is to predict the truth value for ground predicates corresponding to all **hidden triples** (i.e., unobserved triples) $H = \Omega \setminus O$, where $\Omega = \mathcal{E} \times \mathcal{R} \times \mathcal{E}$, i.e., the set of all possible triples.

2.2   Symbolic Logic

The book has a heavy component of symbolic reasoning. Considering that readers likely lack the background about symbolic logic, we provide a brief but more general introduction to it in this section. A reader who is familiar with the topic can skip this part.

Symbolic logic aims at providing a *formal* language for reasoning, in contrast to *natural* language. *Propositional logic* and *first-order logic* are the two main formal systems for symbolic logic. In the following section, we will define and compare some basic concepts in propositional logic and first-order logic which will be used later in Chaps. 3, 4, and 5. A more thorough introduction to symbolic logic can be found in [2–4].

2.2.1   Propositional Logic

In our daily life, a statement is widely used to make a declaration, which is either *True* or *False*. These statements are called propositions and are denoted with symbols such as P and Q. A famous example of a proposition is *"Socrates is a man"*, which is *True*. Propositional logic deals with propositions and relations between them, which is also called *zeroth-order logic*.

If a proposition cannot be broken down into smaller propositions, it is called **atomic proposition**. Examples of atomic propositions include *"All men are mortal"*, *"Socrates is a man"*, and *"Socrates is mortal"*, which can be denoted as P, Q, and R, respectively. Each atomic proposition is assigned a binary truth value, which is called an *interpretation*. For example, P is *True*, denoted as $I(P) = 1$.

Atomic propositions can be used to define more complex propositions via logical connectives (or logical operators), including *negation* ($\neg$), *disjunction* ($\vee$), *conjuction* ($\wedge$), and *implication* ($\rightarrow$). **Logical connectives** can be considered as functions that take propositions as arguments, and output more complex ones. The truth value of the composite proposition is determined by the truth table of each logical connective. For example, $I(\neg P) = 0$, if $I(P) = 1$. These operators are not independent, and any two of them can define the other two.

With a set of atomic propositions and logical connectives, we can recursively define all valid logical expressions, which are called **well-formed formulas**. *Atomic formulas* or *atoms* are well-formed formulas with no logical connectives. In propositional logic, *atomic formulas* are essentially atomic propositions. Formulas are usually denoted as ϕ, ψ, and χ. Given two well-formed formulas ϕ and ψ, (1) $\phi \wedge \psi$, (2) $\phi \vee \psi$, (3) $\phi \rightarrow \psi$, and (4) $\neg \phi$ are all well-formed formulas.

Based on the logical language defined above, we can leverage **a rule of inference** in propositional logic such as *Modus Ponens* to deduce new propositions from existing ones. Modus Ponens says if the premises ϕ and $\phi \rightarrow \psi$ are both *True*, then the conclusion ψ

is also *True*, which can be verified by the truth table. There are other inference rules, and Modus Ponens is the simplest and most popular one.

2.2.2 First-Order Logic (FOL)

Propositional logic is limited in its expressive power and can only deal with simple propositional statements that are either *True* or *False*. It cannot represent more complex structures, such as relationships between objects or properties of objects, and does not allow for quantification. For example, *"All men are mortal"* can only be represented as an atomic proposition P in propositional logic without further exploring its inner structure. To address the limitation, first-order logic (FOL) (also known as predicate logic) extends propositional logic by (1) enriching atom representation with objects, functions, and predicates, and (2) introducing variables and quantifiers to formulas.

Enriching Atom Representation with Objects, Functions, and Predicates

Different from propositional logic, where atomic formulas (atoms) are atomic propositions, FOL atoms have a much richer internal structure. The atoms in FOL contain three types of symbols related to *objects*, *functions*, and *predicates*, which are introduced below.

- **Objects**: Objects refer to things that are of interest, which could be persons, numbers, locations, etc. If an object is known, we use an *constant* to denote it; otherwise, we use a *variable* to denote it, which will be explained later. For example, *Socrates* is an object constant. An object, either a constant or a variable, is a *term*. Objects correspond to entities in KGs.
- **Functions**: Functions take terms as arguments and output objects. An n-ary function can be written as $f(t_1, \ldots, t_n)$, where $t_1, \ldots, t_n$ are terms. For example, the function *FatherOf(Socrates)* can be interpreted as *"the father of Socrates"*. Functional expressions are also *terms*. Functions do not typically exist in KGs.
- **Predicates**: Predicates takes terms as arguments and output *True* or *False*. An n-ary predicate is written as $P(t_1, \ldots, t_n)$, where $t_1, \ldots, t_n$ are terms. A predicate is an atom. For example, the predicate *Men(Socrates)* is an atom. It means *"Socrates is a man"*, which can only be represented as an atomic proposition Q in propositional logic. In most existing KGs, only binary predicates are considered. For example, *Founded(Bill Gates, Microsoft)* is a binary predicate. If a predicate takes object constants as the arguments, it is called a *ground predicate*. Both *Men(Socrates)* and *Founded(Bill Gates, Microsoft)* are ground predicates.

Introducing Variables and Quantifiers to Formulas

In order to accommodate the situations that *all* or *some* of the objects have some property, FOL introduces *object variables* and *quantifiers*, which are discussed below.

- **Variables.** In contrast to the object constants, variables denote any objects, which can be considered as a placeholder. A variable is also a term, which can be the arguments of functions and predicates. For example, *Men(x)* contains a variable *x*, which can be interpreted as *x* is a man. Atoms and well-defined formulas may include variables, such as *Men(x)* and *Founded(x, Microsoft)*.
- **Quantifiers.** *Universal quantifier* (denoted as ∀) and *existential quantifier* (denoted as ∃) are used to describe whether all objects or some objects make a formula *True*. Assume ϕ is a well-defined formula with a variable *x*, both $(\forall x)\phi$ and $(\exists x)\phi$ are well-defined formulas. For example, we can use $(\forall x)(Men(x) \rightarrow Mortal(x))$ to represent "All men are mortal."

Well-formed formulas in first-order logic can be recursively defined over atoms via logical connectives and quantifiers. An example of a well-formed formula is $(\exists x)$ $\big(Founded(x, Microsoft) \wedge Born(x, Seattle)\big)$, representing "there exists a person who founded Microsoft and was born in Seattle."

All the **inference rules** in propositional logic work in first-order logic. There are two additional inference rules, which are called *Universal Instantiation* (UI) and *Existential Generalization* (EG). UI allows us to infer a specific instance of a universally quantified statement. For example, from the statement $(\forall x)(Men(x) \rightarrow Mortal(x))$, we can infer *Men(Socrates)* → *Mortal(Socrates)*. EG allows us to generalize a statement about a specific instance to a statement about a whole class of instances. For example, from the statement *Mortal(Socrates)*, we can infer $(\exists x)Mortal(x)$, which means "there exists at least one person that is mortal."

In summary, propositional logic is a *simple* system for reasoning about truth values of propositions, while first-order logic is a more *expressive* system for reasoning about objects, relations between them, and properties of those objects. First-order logic is a better choice for KG reasoning due to its stronger expressivity.

2.2.3 Literal, Clause, and Other Terminologies

Some other terminologies are frequently used in symbolic logic, which are introduced below.

- **Literal**: Literals are either atomic formulas (e.g., $l_1 := P$), called positive literals, or the negation of atomic formulas (e.g., $l_2 := \neg P$), called negative literals.

- **Clause**: A Clause c is a formula defined over a set of literals with logical connectives. A *conjuctive clause* is a conjunction of literals, e.g., $c \coloneqq l_1 \wedge l_2 \wedge l_3$. A *disjunctive clause* is a disjunction of literals, e.g., $c \coloneqq l_1 \vee l_2 \vee l_3$.
- **Clausal Form or Conjuctive Normal Form**: Every formula can be represented in a clausal form, also called conjunctive normal form (CNF), which is a conjunction of disjunctive clauses, e.g., $c_1 \wedge c_2 \wedge c_3$.
- **Disjunctive Normal Form**: Every formula can be represented in a disjunctive normal form (DNF), which is a disjunction of conjunctive clauses, e.g., $c_1 \vee c_2 \vee c_3$.
- **Satisfiable**: A formula is satisfiable if there exists some truth value assignment to each ground atom that makes the formula *True*.
- **De Morgan's Law**: De Morgan's law is a fundamental concept in Boolean logic that enables the expression of conjunctions ($\wedge$) and disjunctions ($\vee$) purely in terms of each other through the use of negation ($\neg$). Symbolically, De Morgan's law can be expressed as:

$$\neg(\phi \wedge \psi) \equiv (\neg\phi \vee \neg\psi)$$
$$\neg(\phi \vee \psi) \equiv (\neg\phi \wedge \neg\psi)$$

(2.1)

These rules state that the negation of a conjunction is equivalent to the disjunction of the negations of the individual propositions, while the negation of a disjunction is equivalent to the conjunction of the negations of the individual propositions.

2.2.4 Fuzzy Logic

Classical FOL is Boolean logic, meaning each well-formed formula can only take *True* (denoted as 1) or *False* (denoted as 0). Fuzzy logic extends FOL by allowing a soft truth value in the range $[0, 1]$. Similar to Boolean logic, we call the mapping from atoms to soft truth values an *interpretation*. The interpretation of atoms x is denoted as $I(x)$. Although fuzzy logic has been widely studied in the literature, there is still no common standard for the computation of fuzzy logic. Here we present some broadly used functions to relax the logical AND, OR, and NOT in fuzzy logic.

- **Gödel Logic.** The Gödel logic is defined by [5]. It simply uses min and max to relax the logical AND and OR, respectively.

$$x \wedge y = \min\{I(x), I(y)\}$$
$$x \vee y = \max\{I(x), I(y)\}$$
$$\neg x = 1 - I(x).$$

- **Łukasiewicz Logic.** Łukasiewicz logic uses the Łukasiewicz t-norm [6] as the relaxation of the basic logical operations.

$$x \wedge y = \max\{0, I(x) + I(y) - 1\}$$
$$x \vee y = \min\{1, I(x) + I(y)\}$$
$$\neg x = 1 - I(x).$$

- **Product Logic.** The third interpretation follows the paper [7], which uses the following function to approximate the basic logical operations:

$$x \wedge y = I(x)I(y)$$
$$x \vee y = I(x) + I(y) - I(x)I(y)$$
$$\neg x = 1 - I(x).$$

Fuzzy logic provides an important direction to bring symbolic logic and learning together, which will be revisited in Sects. 3.2.3.2, 3.4.2 and 4.4.

2.3   Logical Rules

Logical rules are frequently used to represent symbolic knowledge or hypothesis, which we use heavily for reasoning. How to leverage these logical rules in a differentiable way is key to the success of neuro-symbolic integration. We thus formally introduce logical rules and connect them to knowledge graphs.

Definition 2.2 (*Logical rules*) A logical rule is given in the following standard form:

$$\psi \leftarrow \phi \tag{2.2}$$

where ψ and ϕ are well-formed formulas, ψ is called *rule head* (or *conclusion*), and ϕ is called *rule body* (or *premise*). It states that whenever the premises (or rule body) is *True*, the conclusion (or rule head) can be derived as *True*.

According to whether the rule is with variables (general knowledge) or just constants (specific knowledge), we have (1) *template rule* and (2) *ground rule*. We will illustrate the difference between them with examples.

- **Template Rule**: a template rule or a first-order logical rule, is a general statement that involves variables and quantifiers. For example, consider the template rule: $(\forall x)$ ($Mortal(x) \leftarrow Men(x)$). This is a general statement that involves only one variable x, which can take on any value. In practice, the universal quantifier can be dropped when there is no ambiguity.
- **Ground Rule**: a ground rule is a specific instance of a template rule in which all variables are replaced with concrete objects. For instance, we could make the ground

rule $Mortal(Socrates) \leftarrow Men(Socrates)$ by replacing the variable x in the template rule $(\forall x)(Mortal(x) \leftarrow Men(x))$ with a concrete object *"Socrates"* and applying the inference rule of Universal Instantiation (UI). This ground rule is a specific instance of the more general template rule.

Definition 2.3 (*Horn rules*) The most widely-used logical rules belong to the Horn rules, which are named after the logician Alfred Horn who first studied them. A Horn rule has the following form: if $P_1 \wedge P_2 \wedge \ldots \wedge P_l$, then Q. Formally, a Horn rule written in a (reverse) implication form is given below:

$$Q \leftarrow P_1 \wedge P_2 \wedge \ldots \wedge P_l \tag{2.3}$$

where $P_1, \ldots, P_l$ are positive literals. A Horn rule can also be written as a clause (a disjunction ($\vee$) of literals) with at most one positive literal, thus is also called *Horn clause*:

$$\neg P_1 \vee \neg P_2 \vee \ldots \vee \neg P_l \vee Q \tag{2.4}$$

A Horn rule is said to be *definite* or *strict* if it has exactly one positive literal. For example, the rule in Eq. (2.4) is definite if Q is a positive literal. Horn rules are widely used in the context of KGs to derive new facts from existing ones. As shown in Fig. 2.1, we have the following definite Horn rule:

$$SpeakLanguage(x, y) \leftarrow BornIn(x, z) \wedge OfficialLanguage(z, y) \tag{2.5}$$

where $BornIn(x, z)$, $OfficialLanguage(z, y)$ and $SpeakLanguage(x, y)$ correspond to P_1, P_2 and Q in Eq. (2.4), respectively. This rule states that if there is a z that satisfies two conditions: (1) "x was born in z" and (2) "z has y as an official language", then we can conclude that "x can speak language y". Note variables in a Horn rule are implicitly universally quantified with the scope being the entire Horn rule. In other words, the Horn rule in Eq. (2.5) is a simplification of the rule below:

$$(\forall x, y, z)(SpeakLanguage(x, y) \leftarrow BornIn(x, z) \wedge OfficialLanguage(z, y))) \tag{2.6}$$

Definition 2.4 (*Chain-like Horn rules*) A chain-like Horn rule is a special form of Horn rule. It requires every atom in the rule shares one variable with another atom, where the variables form a chain [8]. A chain-like horn rule in general form is given below:

$$r_h(x, y) \leftarrow r_{b_1}(x, z_1) \wedge r_{b_1}(z_1, z_2) \wedge \cdots \wedge r_{b_n}(z_{n-1}, y) \tag{2.7}$$

where $x, z_1, z_2, \ldots, z_{n-1}, y$ are variables that range over the objects in the KG and $r_{b_1}, \ldots, r_{b_n}, r_h$ are binary predicates in the KG. We can see that Horn rule shown in Eq. (2.5) is chain-like. The body of a chain-like Horn rule corresponds to a relation path starting from *x* and ending with *y* in KG.

2.3.1   Knowledge Graph Inference Using Logical Rules

Intuitively, logical rules provide high-level knowledge regarding relationships between facts. With the help of such rules, humans can make reasoning based on facts they have observed. As discussed in Sect. 2.2.1, the basic inference rule is Modus Ponens. The general form of Modus Ponens can be expressed as: if the premises ϕ and $\phi \rightarrow \psi$ are both *True*, then we can conclude that ψ is also *True*. For example, asssume we have the following logical rule:

$$\text{hasBrother(Eva, Gino)} \leftarrow \text{hasMother(Eva, Faye)} \wedge \text{hasSon(Faye, Gino)} \qquad (2.8)$$

According to Fig. 2.2, we know that its premises *hasMother(Eva, Faye)* and *hasSon(Faye, Gino)* are both *True*. Thus, we can make the conclusion that *Eva* has a brother *Gino*.

The inference process is slightly more complicated when the rules contain variables and quantifiers. Universal instantiation (UI), which involves making a specific instance of a universal quantification by replacing the variables with concrete objects, can be applied. Let us take the KG in Fig. 2.2 as an example to illustrate how to use UI with the following formula:

$$(\forall x, y, z)(\text{hasBrother}(x, y) \leftarrow \text{hasMother}(x, z) \wedge \text{hasSon}(z, y))) \qquad (2.9)$$

By replacing the variables x, y, z with concrete entities *"Eva," "Gino,"* and *"Faye,"* respectively, this general rule leads to a ground rule Eq. (2.8), which is *True* according to UI. Then we can follow the same reasoning via modus ponens to derive that *hasBrother(Eva, Gino)* is *True*.

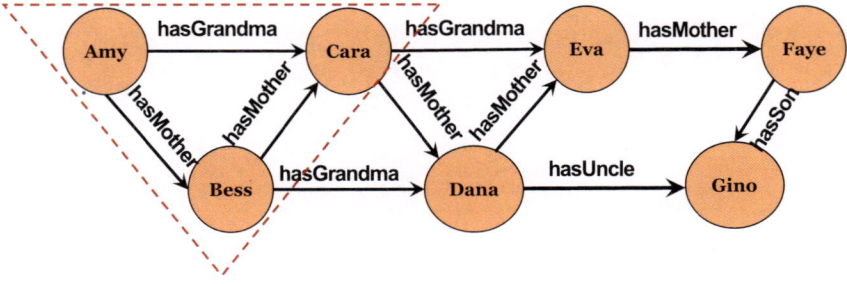

Fig. 2.2 An example of Kinship knowledge graph. A closed path in the Kinship knowledge graph corresponding to Eq. (2.8) is highlighted by a red dotted triangle

Table 2.1 Comparison of concepts in the language of symbolic logic versus KG

Symbolic logic	Knowledge graph
Constant	Entity
Predicate	Relation
Ground predicate	Triple
Rule instance	Closed path

In this example, UI allows us to move from a general statement to a specific statement about *"Eva," "Gino,"* and *"Faye."* Following the same way, we can use the same FOL formula with different instantiations of x, y, and z to infer other individuals' relations.

2.3.2 Logical Rules in the Context of Knowledge Graph

The concepts in symbolic logic, including logical rules, are closely connected to the concepts in KGs. In the previous sections, we have mentioned some of the connections. We now summarize them in this section using the example KG in Fig. 2.2.

Constants in FOL correspond to entities in KGs, e.g., *"Amy"*. Predicates correspond to relations in KGs, which are binary, e.g., *hasGrandma(x, y)*. Ground predicates correspond to triples in KGs, e.g., *hasGrandma(Amy, Cara)*, or *(Amy, hasGrandma, Cara)* in the triple form.

A chain-like Horn rule instance can be easily identified as a *"closed path"* in a graph, where the rule body corresponds to a path in the KG, and the rule head corresponds to the edge connecting the starting entity and ending entity in the rule body. For example, given the KG in Fig. 2.2, we can observe closed paths (rule instances) such as:

$$
\begin{aligned}
CP_1 &\coloneqq \text{Amy} \xrightarrow{\text{hasMother}} \text{Bess} \xrightarrow{\text{hasMother}} \text{Cara} \xleftarrow{\text{hasGrandma}} \text{Amy} \\
CP_2 &\coloneqq \text{Dana} \xrightarrow{\text{hasMother}} \text{Eva} \xrightarrow{\text{hasMother}} \text{Faye} \xrightarrow{\text{hasSon}} \text{Gino} \xleftarrow{\text{hasUncle}} \text{Dana}
\end{aligned}
\tag{2.10}
$$

Table 2.1 provides a comparison of how concepts are expressed in the languages of symbolic logic and KGs.

2.4 Notations

Throughout this book, we use a boldface lower-case letter $\mathbf{x}$ to represent a vector. Its i-th entry is denoted as $\mathbf{x}_i$. The ℓ_p norm of a vector for $p \geq 1$ is denoted as $\|\mathbf{x}\|_p$, and $\|\mathbf{x}\|_{1/2}$ means either the ℓ_1 norm or the ℓ_2 norm. Let $\text{diag}(\mathbf{x})$ be a diagonal matrix, the i-th diagonal entry of which is $\mathbf{x}_i$. $|\mathbf{x}|$ denotes the element-wise absolute value function, $\tanh(\mathbf{x})$ denotes the element-wise hyperbolic tangent function, and $\text{ReLU}(\mathbf{x})$ denotes the element-wise rectified linear unit.

A matrix is represented by a boldface upper-case letter $\mathbf{X}$ with its ij-th entry denoted as $\mathbf{X}_{ij}$. $\|\mathbf{X}\|_F$ is the Frobenius norm of a matrix, $\text{tr}(\mathbf{X})$ and $\det(\mathbf{X})$ are the trace and determinant of a square matrix.

References

1. C. I. Lewis, C. H. Langford, and P. Lamprecht. *Symbolic logic*, volume 170. Dover Publications New York, 1959.
2. A. N. Whitehead and B. Russell. *Principia mathematica to* 56*, volume 2. Cambridge University Press, 1997.
3. N. J. Nilsson and N. J. Nilsson. *Artificial intelligence: a new synthesis*. Morgan Kaufmann, 1998.
4. G. Bezhanishvili and W. Fussner. An introduction to symbolic logic. *Convergence*, 2013.
5. R. Fagin. Combining fuzzy information from multiple systems. *Journal of Computer and System Sciences*, 58(1):83–99, 1999.
6. A. Kimmig, S. Bach, M. Broecheler, B. Huang, and L. Getoor. A short introduction to probabilistic soft logic. In *Proceedings of the NIPS Workshop on Probabilistic Programming: Foundations and Applications*, 2012.
7. P. Hájek, L. Godo, and F. Esteva. A complete many-valued logic with product-conjunction. *Archive for mathematical logic*, 35(3):191–208, 1996.
8. F. Yang, Z. Yang, and W. W. Cohen. Differentiable learning of logical rules for knowledge base reasoning. In *Advances in Neural Information Processing Systems (NeurIPS)*, pages 2319–2328, 2017.

Knowledge Graph Completion

3

"Acquire new knowledge whilst thinking over the old, and you may become a teacher of others." —Confucius

3.1 Overview

A KG is a collection of facts that are believed to be true, and it provides a valuable resource for a wide range of real-world applications, such as semantic parsing, entity disambiguation, information extraction, and question answering [2–5]. Despite significant efforts to create and maintain KGs, it is impossible to capture all the knowledge in the real world, resulting in significant incompleteness in KGs. To address this issue, the KG completion task aims to predict missing information in a KG. It can be formally formulated as inferring the tail entity given the head entity and the relation (i.e., $(e_i, r_k, ?)$) or inferring the head entity given the tail entity and the relation (i.e., $(?, r_k, e_j)$). For example, in Fig. 3.1, a query in the KG completion task can be represented as *(Mary Stilwell, LiveIn, ?)*, which asks "where does Mary Stilwell live?"

KG completion can be considered as a *one-hop* query, in contrast to the *complex* queries that will be discussed in the next chapter. We divide existing methods for KG completion into (1) *traditional symbolic reasoning* methods, (2) recent *representation learning-based* methods, and (3) *neuro-symbolic integration* methods.

- **Traditional Symbolic Reasoning Methods**: These methods rely on a set of predefined rules to infer new knowledge.
- **Representation Learning-based Methods**: These methods learn low-dimensional embeddings to represent entities and relations in the KG, which can then be used to predict missing facts.

K. Cheng and Y. Sun, *Knowledge Graph Reasoning*, Synthesis Lectures on Data, Semantics, and Knowledge, https://doi.org/10.1007/978-3-031-72008-6_3

- **Neuro-symbolic Integration Methods**: These methods combine symbolic reasoning and representation learning to improve the accuracy of KG completion. They can leverage the strengths of both symbolic reasoning and representation learning.

In the following sections, we will introduce the most representative methods in each category and discuss their advantages and disadvantages.

3.2   Symbolic Reasoning-Based KG Completion

In symbolic reasoning-based KG completion, predefined logical rules are used to infer new facts based on the existing facts. These rules are typically expressed in formal logic, such as first-order logic. More discussions of logical rules can be found in Sect. 2.3. For instance, in Fig. 3.1, given a logical rule

$$\text{SpeakLanguage}(x, y) \leftarrow \text{LiveIn}(x, z) \wedge \text{OfficialLanguage}(z, y), \tag{3.1}$$

we can answer the query *SpeakLanguage(Mina Miller, ?)* via inference. Specifically, we replace the variables x, y, z in rule (3.1) with concrete entities *"Mina Miller"*, *"English"* and *"USA"* to get the ground rule

$$\text{SpeakLanguage}(\text{Mina Miller, English}) \leftarrow \text{LiveIn}(\text{Mina Miller, USA}) \\ \wedge \text{OfficialLanguage}(\text{USA, English}) \tag{3.2}$$

Since both *LivIn(Mina Miller, USA)* and *Official Language(USA, English)* are true due to the two corresponding triples observed in the KG, the rule body is true. By applying Modus Ponens, the conclusion *SpeakLanguage(Mina Miller, English)* is also *True*. Therefore *"English"* should be the answer to our query.

Symbolic reasoning-based KG completion can naturally incorporate domain knowledge in the form of logical rules into the reasoning process. The whole process is transparent and interpretable, which are particularly useful in domains where both effectiveness and interpretability are critical, such as healthcare, finance, and scientific research.

In this section, we will first formally introduce the KG completion task in the language of symbolic reasoning, and then introduce two types of symbolic reasoning approaches for knowledge completion.

3.2.1   Problem Definition

Let $\mathcal{G} = \{\mathcal{E}, \mathcal{R}, \mathcal{O}\}$ be a knowledge graph, where $\mathcal{E}$ denotes the entity set, $\mathcal{R}$ denotes the relation set, and $\mathcal{O}$ denotes the fact set. Each triple $(e_i, r_k, e_j) \in \mathcal{O}$ in KG can be regarded as a ground predicate in the context of symbolic reasoning. We denote the observed ground

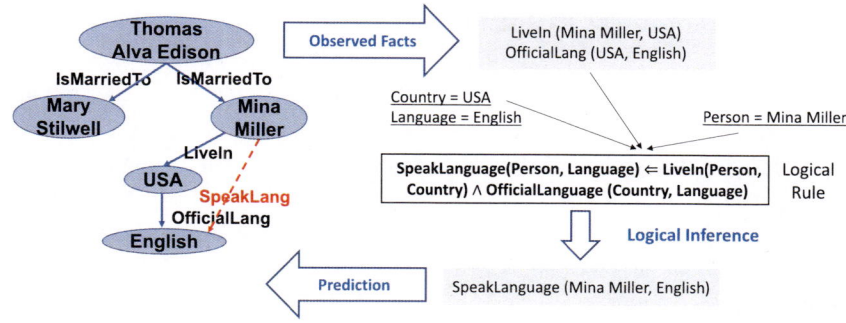

Fig. 3.1 Symbolic reasoning over a toy example of KG. **Left**: A toy example of KG. **Right**: A predefined logical rule. The new fact denoted as the red dotted line can be inferred from the logical rule and the KG

Table 3.1 Summary of notations

$r_k(e_i, e_j)$	A ground predicate
$I(r_k(e_i, e_j))$	Truth value assigned to the ground predicate $r_k(e_i, e_j)$
$\mathbf{v}_O$	The set of the observed ground predicates
$\mathbf{v}_H$	The set of the unobserved ground predicates
$\mathcal{F}$	The set of predefined logical formula
(F_i, w_i)	Logical rule F_i associated with its weight w_i

predicates as $\mathbf{v}_O = \{r_k(e_i, e_j)|(e_i, r_k, e_j) \in O\}$. For all $r_k(e_i, e_j) \in \mathbf{v}_O$, their truth value is 1. Given a set of predefined logical formulas $\mathcal{F} = \{F_i\}$, where F_i denotes a logical rule, the task of KG completion in the symbolic reasoning view is to assign the truth value for all hidden ground predicates $\mathbf{v}_H = \{r_k(e_i, e_j)|(e_i, r_k, e_j) \notin O\}$ such that the total number of satisfied logical formulas can be maximized. This is essentially the *maximum satisfiablity problem (MAX-SAT)*. More generally, we can introduce weight w_i to each of the logical formula F_i to indicate their importance. It is then turned into weighted MAX-SAT problem, i.e., to find the truth value assignment that can maximize the weighted sum of satisfied rules.

According to the truth value assigned to each ground predicate, existing symbolic methods can be roughly divided into two categories: (1) *Boolean logic-based approaches*, where the truth value assignment to predicate $r_k(e_i, e_j)$ is Boolean, i.e., $I(r_k(e_i, e_j)) \in \{0, 1\}$; and (2) *probabilistic logic-based approaches*, where either every possible world is associated with a probability or the truth value to the ground predicates $r_k(e_i, e_j)$ is in the range of $[0, 1]$, i.e., $I(r_k(e_i, e_j)) \in [0, 1]$. A summary of notations is given in Table 3.1.

3.2.2 Boolean Logic-Based Reasoning

When each predicate is assigned with either *True* (1) or *False* (0), the knowledge graph completion task is essentially a MAX-SAT problem. The standard form of MAX-SAT problem is a discrete optimization problem, which is to determine the maximum number of satisfied clauses for a given Boolean formula in *conjunctive normal form* (CNF). As introduced in Sect. 2.2.3, a CNF is a conjunction ($\wedge$) of clauses, where each clause is a disjunction ($\vee$) of literals. A literal can be either an atomic formula or its negation, such as P or $\neg P$. In the context of KG, each atom is a ground predicate of the form $r_k(e_i, e_j) \in \mathbf{v}_O \cup \mathbf{v}_H$; and each logical rule is corresponding to a clause. For example, a rule $Q \leftarrow P_1 \wedge P_2$ can be represented in the form of clause $\neg P_1 \vee \neg P_2 \vee Q$, where P_1, P_2, Q are predicates in KG.

The objective is to identify a truth value assignment (*True* or *False*) for the hidden variables $\mathbf{v}_H$ that maximizes the number of satisfied clauses. When each logical formula F_i is associated with a weight w_i, the MAX-SAT problem becomes the *weighted MAX-SAT* problem, where each clause in the given CNF formula is assigned with the corresponding positive weight. The objective is to identify a truth value assignment for the variables that maximizes the total weight of satisfied clauses. If all the weights are equal (i.e., each clause has the same importance), the weighted MAX-SAT problem reduces to the standard MAX-SAT problem.

The complexity of solving the MAX-SAT problem depends on the size of the given Boolean formula and the number of variables and clauses involved. The MAX-SAT problem is *NP-hard* [6], which means that finding an optimal solution requires exponential time in the worst case. Therefore, *exact solutions* are often infeasible for large and complex instances of the problem. Many *approximation algorithms* have been developed to solve the MAX-SAT problem efficiently in practice. These algorithms aim to find a good approximate solution that is close to the optimal solution, but with lower computational complexity.

Local search is one of the most representative approximation algorithms for solving MAX-SAT problem. The main idea behind local search is to explore the solution space by making small changes (flips) to the current assignment of variables, with the goal of finding an assignment that maximizes the number of satisfied clauses (or the total weight of satisfied clauses in the case of weighted MAX-SAT). Let us use a toy example to illustrate how a local search algorithm solves a MAX-SAT problem.

Example 3.2.1 Consider the following Boolean formula in Conjunctive Normal Form (CNF):
$$(a \vee \neg b) \wedge (\neg a \vee \neg b) \wedge (b \vee c) \tag{3.3}$$

The goal is to find an assignment of truth values to the variables a, b, and c that maximizes the number of satisfied clauses.

We start with a random assignment of truth values $a = T, b = T, c = T$. Then we calculate the number of satisfied clauses. We can see that 2 out of 3 clauses are satisfied. After that, we create neighboring assignments by flipping the truth value of a single variable: (1)

$a = F, b = T, c = T$, (2) $a = T, b = F, c = T$ and (3) $a = T, b = T, c = F$. Finally, we evaluate the neighboring assignments and choose the one with the maximum number of satisfied clauses. We can see that the best neighboring assignment is (2), where all clauses are satisfied. Since we have found an assignment that satisfies all clauses, the algorithm terminates. The solution is (2) $a = T, b = F, c = T$. $\square$

Although logical inference is difficult in general due to the NP-hard nature of MAX-SAT, more efficient algorithms (in polynomial time) can be used when restricting logical rules to definite Horn rules (see definition of definite Horn rules in Sect. 2.3). Two commonly used inference algorithms, namely *forward-chaining* and *backward-chaining*, are introduced next.

3.2.2.1 Forward-Chaining Algorithm

Forward-chaining algorithm is a *bottom-up* approach that starts with the available evidences and derives new conclusions based on those evidences. More specifically, it starts with a set of initial facts, triggers all rules whose premises are satisfied, adds their conclusion to the known facts, and repeats this process until the query is answered or no new facts can be added. Let us take the definite Horn rule in Fig. 3.2 as an example to illustrate how the forward-chaining algorithm works.

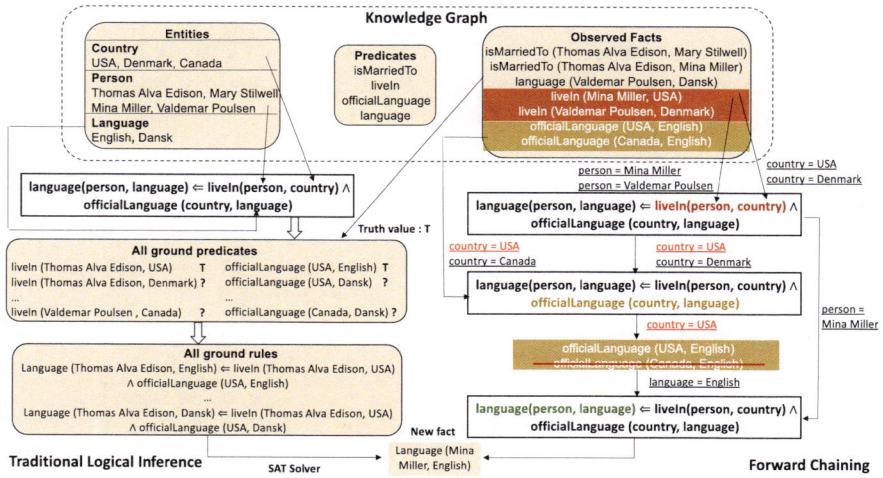

Fig. 3.2 Illustration of logical reasoning algorithms using the KG in Fig. 3.1. **Left:** using a *MAX-SAT solver* to derive new conclusions from a given set of premises. **Right:** using a *forward chaining algorithm* to iteratively derive new facts from the existing facts in the KG. Different colors are used to represent different types of relations in KG

Example 3.2.2 Given the definite Horn rule Eq. (3.1), our goal is to answer the query *SpeakLanguage(Mina Miller, ?)* using the forward chaining algorithm. We first focus on all observed triples related to the first predicate in the body, LiveIn(x, z). The variable x is fixed as *"Mina Miller"* in this case. Assuming we know z is a country, it is then limited to a small set of concrete entities { *"USA"*, *"Denmark"* }. Only *LiveIn(Mina Miller, USA)* is observed, thus *"Denmark"* can be excluded. After that, we ground the next predicate in the body OfficialLanguage(z, y) with observed triples. By restricting z as *"USA"*, the only applicable triple to ground *OfficialLanguage (z, y)* is *OfficialLanguage (USA, English)*. Finally, we get the ground rule body LiveIn$(MinaMiller, USA) \wedge$ OfficialLanguage$(USA, English)$, and infer the conclusion *SpeakLanguage (Mina Miller, English)*. □

3.2.2.2 Backward-Chaining Algorithm

As the opposite of the forward-chaining algorithm, a backward-chaining algorithm is a *top-down* approach that starts with the conclusion and works backward to find the supporting evidences and determine whether the conclusion can be satisfied. More specifically, it uses a set of rules and facts to attempt to prove the goal, recursively working backward through the rules to find a set of conditions that can satisfy the goal. Let us use the same example in Fig. 3.2 to rewrite the inference process of the backward chaining algorithm for illustration.

Example 3.2.3 Different from the forward chaining algorithm, the first step of the backward chaining algorithm is to start with the goal we want to achieve. In this case, the goal is *speakLanguage (Mina Miller, English)*. The next step is to look at the rules we have and identify which rules can achieve the goal. Here, we only have the rule (3.1). Then, with the rule (3.1), we can work backward to see if any necessary conditions are satisfied. In this example, the goal *speakLanguage (Mina Miller, English)* is achieved by substituting x and y in rule head (i.e., *speakLanguage (x, y)*) with *"Mina Miller"* and *"English"*, respectively. We then add the conditions *LiveIn (Mina Miller, z)* and *OfficialLanguage (z, English)* by replacing x with *"Mina Miller"* and y with *"English"* in the rule body. Since z is a country, it is limited to a small set of concrete entities { *"USA"*, *"Denmark"* }. By replacing z with *"USA"*, the conditions become *LiveIn (Mina Miller, USA)* and *OfficialLanguage (USA, English)*, which are *True* according to our observation. And hence the goal *speakLanguage (Mina Miller, English)* is proved *True* using backward chaining.

3.2.2.3 Comparing Forward-Chaining and Backward-Chaining

The main difference between forward-chaining and backward-chaining is the direction of reasoning. Forward-chaining works forward from the available evidences, while backward-chaining works backward from the goal (or the conclusion). Forward chaining is *data-driven*, as it starts from evidences. During the reasoning process, it will infer many conclusions, some of which might not be relevant to our question. Backward chaining is *goal-driven*, as it starts from the goal. The reasoning process only involves the evidences and rules that are in the reasoning chain, which is usually much faster than forward chaining.

3.2.3   Probabilistic Logic-Based Reasoning

Although Boolean logic shows effectiveness in capturing complex relationships and knowledge about the world, they are not able to handle the uncertainty present in many real-world applications. In other words, there might be different possible worlds to be true with different probabilities.

To address this issue, probabilistic logic provides a powerful solution by integrating both logic and probabilities. This approach allows for the simultaneous use of the expressiveness of FOL and the robustness of probabilistic approaches to better model and reason KGs with uncertainty. *Markov Logic Network (MLN)* and *Probabilistic Soft Logic (PSL)* are the two most representative probabilistic logic approaches.

3.2.3.1 Markov Logic Network (MLN)

Graphical models are a family of powerful probabilistic models to handle complex dependency among variables. Markov Logic Network (MLN) [7] is a special case of Markov Networks, which is in the family of (undirected) graphical models [8]. Markov Networks represent variables as nodes and their dependency as edges. A joint probability of all the variables can be defined according to the graph structure. In the KG completion tasks, the variables are the ground predicates ($\mathbf{v}_O \cup \mathbf{v}_H$), which are binary variables taking either 1 or 0 (*True* or *False*).

Given a set of FOL formulas $\mathcal{F}$ and their weight vector $\mathbf{w}$, MLN constructs the graph structure of a Markov network in the following way:

- A node is built for each ground predicate, including both observed and unobserved ground predicates in KG. We use $\mathbf{v}_O$ to denote all the variables that are observed, which correspond to the observed triples in KG; and use $\mathbf{v}_H$ to denote all the other ground predicates that are not observed.
- An edge is built to connect two nodes if and only if the corresponding two ground predicates participate in the same ground rule.

Example 3.2.4 An example of the graph structure of a Markov Logic Network (MLN) is given in Fig. 3.3. The MLN is composed of two formulas associated with different weights. The red formula indicates that a person who plays sports is usually healthy. The blue formula says that if two people are friends and one of them plays sports, the other person will also play sports. Two entities A and B are given in this example. In the constructed MLN graph, a node for each ground predicate is a Boolean random variable, such as Sport(A) and Healthy(B).

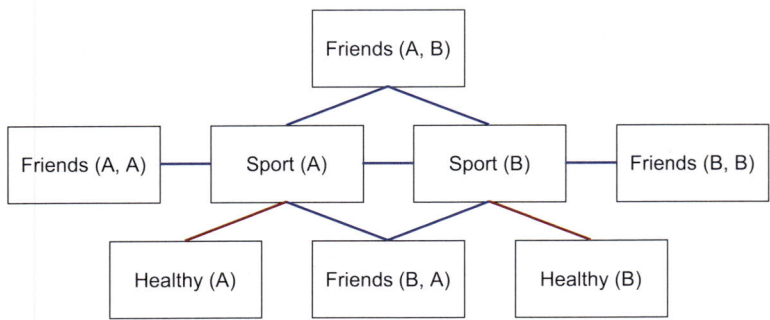

Fig. 3.3 An illustration of Markov Logic Network (MLN). The MLN is constructed based on two logical rules, which are associated with different weights. Two entities A and B are given in this example. Edges are denoted with two different colors, corresponding to the colors used in the rules they are related to

These variables are assigned to 1 if their corresponding ground predicate is observed ($\mathbf{v}_O$); and they are unknown otherwise ($\mathbf{v}_H$). An edge is built to connect two nodes if and only if the corresponding two ground predicates participate in the same ground rule. For example, an edge connecting Sport(A) and Healthy(A) is built due to their participation in the rule Sport(x) $\implies$ Healthy(x). □

A general Markov network decomposes the joint probability of all the variables according to the cliques (a complete subgraph). In the case of MLN, the cliques are corresponding to the logical rule, as the edges are defined based on whether two variables are in the same logical rules. For example, *Sport(A)* and *Healthy(A)* form a clique with size 2, which corresponds to the ground rule *Sport(A)* $\Rightarrow$ *Healthy(A)*. The joint probability of $\mathbf{v}_O$ and $\mathbf{v}_H$ under MLN is then defined as:

$$p_{\mathbf{w}}(\mathbf{v}_O, \mathbf{v}_H) = \frac{1}{Z(\mathbf{w})} \exp\Big(\sum_{i:F_i \in \mathcal{F}} w_i n_i(\mathbf{v}_O, \mathbf{v}_H) \Big) \tag{3.4}$$

where w_i is the learnable weight for the FOL formula F_i, $n_i(\mathbf{v}_O, \mathbf{v}_H)$ is the number of ground formulas of F_i that are *True* given the values of $\mathbf{v}_O$ and $\mathbf{v}_H$ (e.g., the number of times that *Sport(x)* $\Rightarrow$ *Healthy(x)* are true given the assignments of *Sport(A)*, *Sport(B)*, *Healthy(A)*, *Healthy(B)*), and $Z(\mathbf{w})$ is a normalization constant to make the probabilities of all worlds sum to one, i.e., $Z(\mathbf{w}) = \sum_{\mathbf{v}_H} \exp\big(\sum_{i:F_i \in \mathcal{F}} w_i n_i(\mathbf{v}_O, \mathbf{v}_H)\big)$.

The KG completion task then becomes the *inference problem* for $\mathbf{v}_H$ in MLNs, which involves computing the most probable assignment of values to the unseen triples in the KG, given the observed triples and the model: $\max_{\mathbf{v}_H} p_{\mathbf{w}}(\mathbf{v}_H|\mathbf{v}_O) \equiv \max_{\mathbf{v}_H} p_{\mathbf{w}}(\mathbf{v}_O, \mathbf{v}_H)$. MLN inference is computationally expensive, which is #P-complete [7]. To alleviate the burden of computing, MLN inference usually uses Markov chain Monte Carlo (MCMC), and in particular, Gibbs sampling [9, 10] to get an approximate solution. The basic idea is to sample each ground predicate in turn given its Markov blanket. A Markov blanket of a node is its neighbors in the graph. Another popular method for MLN inference is belief propagation [11, 12]. It accelerates inference in MLNs by exploiting dependencies in the network structure. The key idea behind belief propagation is to propagate beliefs, or probability distributions, through the network in a message-passing algorithm. The algorithm iteratively updates the beliefs of each node in the network based on messages received from its neighbors.

In the inference problem, we usually assume the weights for each formula w are given. The weights can actually be learned by maximizing the likelihood: $\max_w p_w(\mathbf{v}_O, \mathbf{v}_H)$, which corresponds to the *learning problem*. The weights are usually learned approximately by simplying the original objective via dropping certain dependencies, such as pseudo-likelihood [13]. The learning problem is usually not discussed in the KG completion setting.

Although MLN provides a good theoretical model in combining logic and probabilistic model, it is hard to scale to large KGs for inference, due to (1) the expensive process of grounding all the predicates and logical rules; and (2) even the approximate inference algorithm takes a long time to converge.

3.2.3.2 Probabilistic Soft Logic (PSL)

Probabilistic Soft Logic (PSL) [14] provides another way to incorporate uncertainty into the reasoning process. It relaxes the Boolean assignment to each variable to a soft probability, which allows for the underlying inference to be solved quickly as a *convex optimization problem*. We denote $I(r_k(e_i, e_j))$ the **soft truth values** in an interval between [0, 1] to a ground predicate $r_k(e_i, e_j)$, indicating how likely the ground predicate holds true. We call the mapping $I : \mathbf{v}_O \cup \mathbf{v}_H \to [0, 1]$ as an **interpretation**.

To determine the degree to which a ground rule is satisfied, PSL uses the Łukasiewicz t-norm [15] and its corresponding t-conorm as the relaxation of the logical AND and OR to non-binary variables, which has been introduced in Sect. 2.2.4:

$$I(x \wedge y) = \max\{0, I(x) + I(y) - 1\}$$
$$I(x \vee y) = \min\{1, I(x) + I(y)\}$$
$$I(\neg x) = 1 - I(x).$$

where x and y can be any well-defined formulas including ground rules (i.e., f) and ground predicates (i.e., $r_k(e_i, e_j)$). We can use the above functions to calculate the soft truth value for any ground rule f, denoted as $I(f)$, as a ground logical rule can be transformed from implication form to disjunction form as shown below:

$$r_{\text{head}} \leftarrow r_{\text{body}} \equiv r_{\text{head}} \vee \neg r_{\text{body}} \tag{3.5}$$

We define $d(f) = 1 - I(f)$ as **distance to satisfaction**. It softly measures the degree to which a ground rule is violated.

By applying the above definitions of the logical operators to a ground logical rule in disjunction form, the distance to satisfaction of the ground logical rule can be computed as:

$$
\begin{aligned}
d(f) &= 1 - I(f) \\
&= 1 - \min(1, I(r_{\text{head}}) + I(\neg r_{\text{body}})) \\
&= \max\{0, I(r_{\text{body}}) - I(r_{\text{head}})\}
\end{aligned}
$$

We can see that a ground rule f is satisfied (i.e., when $d(f) = 0$) if and only if the truth value of its head $I(r_{\text{head}})$ is the same or higher than its body $I(r_{\text{body}})$.

Given a set of ground atomic formulas (predicates), a PSL program defines a distribution over possible interpretations $I : \mathbf{v}_O \cup \mathbf{v}_H \to [0, 1]$. Let $\mathcal{F}$ be the set of all ground rules that are instances of a rule in the program, the probability density function over I is:

$$
\frac{1}{Z(\mathbf{w})} \exp\Big(\sum_{i: f_i \in \mathcal{F}} w_i (I(f_i))^p \Big) \tag{3.6}
$$

where w_i is the weight of the ground rule f_i, $Z(\mathbf{w})$ is the continuous version of the normalization term to make the probabilities of all worlds sum up to one, i.e., $Z(\mathbf{w}) = \int_{\mathbf{v}_H} \exp\big(\sum_{i: F_i \in \mathcal{F}} w_i (I(f_i))^p\big)$, and $p \in \{1, 2\}$ provides a choice of two different loss functions. Informally, the linear loss function ($p = 1$) favors interpretations that completely satisfy one rule at the expense of higher distance from satisfaction for conflicting rules, whereas the quadratic loss function ($p = 2$) favors interpretations that satisfy all rules to some degree, which typically have truth values farther away from the extreme values.

Unlike MLN, the underlying inference problem of PSL can be mathematically modeled as a convex optimization problem, making it easier to solve and more efficient than MLN. This also enables PSL to be more scalable, making it a better choice for large-scale applications. In addition, PSL's templates are designed to be flexible, allowing users to easily customize them to suit their needs, thus making them generally easier to use than MLN. For instance, PSL can be utilized to tackle the entity resolution task effectively [14]. An entity resolution task involves determining whether two entities in a dataset refer to the same real-world object. The degree to which two entities are believed to be the same depends on various factors, such as how similar their names are. In PSL, we can define a rule that expresses this dependency as follows:

$$
1.0 : \text{Same}(P_1, P_2) \leftarrow \text{Name}(P_1, N_1) \wedge \text{Name}(P_2, N_2) \wedge \text{Similar}(N_1, N_2) \tag{3.7}
$$

where P_1, P_2 denote two persons and N_1, N_2 denote their names.

Similar to MLN, PSL-based approaches still require the grounding of the logical rules, which is time-consuming for large-scale KGs.

3.3   Representation Learning-Based KG Completion

Despite the strong interpretability and generalizability of traditional symbolic methods in performing reasoning over a KG, they are not applicable to real-world KGs due to real-world KGs are usually (1) large-scale, (2) ambiguous, and (3) noisy.

- **Large-scale**. Symbolic reasoning approaches usually have high computational complexity. In the inference process of symbolic reasoning-based KG completion, logical rules need to be grounded as all ground rules are necessary for inferring missing knowledge. Considering all possible combinations of entities for each rule, the complexity of grounding a logical rule is $O(|\mathcal{E}|^n)$, where $|\mathcal{E}|$ represents the number of entities in the KG and n is the number of variables in the logical rules. For instance, in Eq.(3.1), we have three variables x, y, and z, thus the complexity of grounding Eq.(3.1) is $O(|\mathcal{E}|^3)$.
- **Ambiguous**. Symbolic reasoning approaches rely on the explicit representation of logical rules, which require a large amount of human experts' effort to create. Since logical rules may not be able to capture all the nuances of the data, symbolic reasoning-based KG completion methods also struggle to capture complex patterns in the data. For instance, symbolic reasoning approaches may struggle with handling ambiguity and capturing the correlation between entities and relations when multiple entities represent the same entity, such as "Los Angeles" and "LA".
- **Noisy**. Symbolic reasoning approaches are sensitive to the noisy triples in KG. Since KG construction usually involves automatic information extraction, some of the triples might inevitably be wrong.

To address the above issues, knowledge graph embedding (KGE) methods have been widely used recently for KG completion. The general idea of KGE methods is to represent *discrete symbols* such as entities and relations with low-dimensional *continuous vectors* [16], which are called *embeddings*, such that the KG structure can be preserved using these vectors. The embeddings then can be used to predict new facts. The idea is illustrated in Fig. 3.4.

KGE methods can be trained efficiently using stochastic gradient descent (SGD) algorithms, which can converge quickly and lead to good results with relatively few iterations. They are highly scalable and can handle real-world large KGs with millions of entities and relations. Additionally, KGE methods can capture complex patterns in the data, such as addressing entity disambiguation. For instance, KGE methods can learn distinct sub-representations for the entity "Apple" that allows them to differentiate between the two meanings of "Apple" in the two triples: *(Steve Jobs, eat, apple)* and *(Steve Jobs, co-found, Apple)*. KGE methods can also naturally handle the noises in KG and preserve the similarity between similar entities and similar relations in their embedding vectors.

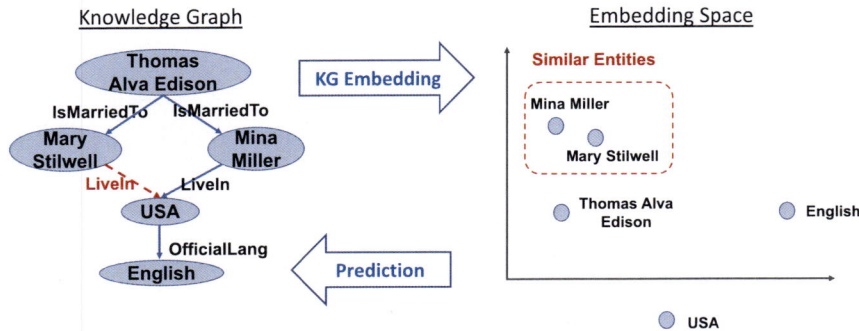

Fig. 3.4 Illustration of knowledge graph embedding. **Left**: A toy KG. **Right**: Entities are mapped into an embedding space. Two entities that are close in the embedding space are similar to each other semantically. (Relation embeddings are not shown.) Embeddings are learned from the observed facts in KG (**Left** to **Right**), and the learned embedding can be used to infer new facts, such as the dotted red line on the left panel (**Right** to **Left**)

3.3.1   Overview of Knowledge Graph Embedding Methods

Unlike traditional symbolic methods, KGE only relies on observed facts in KG without leveraging logical rules. Score functions, which measure the plausibility of triples in KGs, are the crux of KGE models. According to different score functions, existing KGE methods can be roughly divided into three categories: (1) *geometric operation-based models*, (2) *bilinear models*, and (3) *deep learning-based models*. We will introduce the most representative methods in each category in Sects. 3.3.2, 3.3.3, and 3.3.4, respectively.

A typical KG embedding method consists of three components: (1) an encoder that maps entities and relations into embeddings; (2) an embedding-based score function that measures the plausibility of every triple; and (3) a loss function that measures how good the model parameters are. We now give a brief introduction to the three components.

3.3.1.1 The Embedding Encoder

Given a knowledge graph $\mathcal{G} = \{\mathcal{E}, \mathcal{R}, \mathcal{O}\}$, the encoder maps entities $e \in \mathcal{E}$ into an low dimensional vectors and relations $r \in \mathcal{R}$ into operations defined over those vectors. Earlier embedding models use *shallow* encoders, which associate every entity and relation with a learnable embedding vector. Later embedding models use *deeper* encoders, and the embedding vectors for each entity and relation can be computed via a deep neural network, whose parameters can be learned.

3.3.1.2 The Score Function and the Properties of Relations

The next question is to decide the plausibility of a triple given the entity and relation representations, which is achieved by a score function $f : \mathcal{E} \times \mathcal{R} \times \mathcal{E} \to \mathbb{R}^+ \cup \{0\}$. It assigns a plausibility score $f_{r_k}(e_i, e_j)$ to a triple $(e_i, r_k, e_j) \in O$, where $e_i, e_j \in \mathcal{E}$ and $r_k \in \mathcal{R}$. The higher the score, the higher confidence the triple is true.

The choice of scoring function plays a crucial role in modeling a diverse spectrum of relations in KGs, which exhibit different properties based on their different semantic nature. Some important properties of relations include:

- **Symmetric**: A relation r_k is symmetric if $\forall e_i, e_j : r_k(e_i, e_j) \leftrightarrow r_k(e_j, e_i)$. For example, *Spouse* is a symmetric relation.
- **Asymmetric**: A relation r_k is asymmetric if $\forall e_i, e_j : r_k(e_i, e_j) \to \neg r_k(e_j, e_i)$. For example, *Father* is an asymmetric relation.
- **Reflexive**: A relation r_k is reflexive if $\forall e_i : r_k(e_i, e_i)$ is *True*. For example, *EqualTo* is a reflexive relation.
- **Irreflexive**: A relation r_k is ir-reflexive if $\forall e_i : r_k(e_i, e_i)$ is *False*. For example, *LessThan* is an irreflexive relation.
- **Transitive**: A relation r_k is transitive if $\forall e_i, e_j, e_z : r_k(e_i, e_z) \wedge r_k(e_z, e_j) \to r_k(e_i, e_j)$. For example, *Similar* is a transitive relation.

There are also constraints between different relations:

- **Inversion**: Two relations r_1 and r_2 are inverse to each other if $\forall e_i, e_j : r_1(e_i, e_j) \leftrightarrow r_2(e_j, e_i)$. For example, *superclass* and *subclass* are inverse to each other.
- **Composition**: a relation r_3 is a composition of relations r_1 and r_2 if $\forall e_i, e_j, e_l : r_1(e_i, e_j) \wedge r_2(e_j, e_l) \to r_3(e_i, e_l)$. For example, *MotherInLaw*(e_i, e_l) is a composition of *Spouse*(e_i, e_j) and *Mother*(e_j, e_l).

A powerful embedding method should be able to capture a wider range of relation properties. We will discuss which properties each KGE method can capture in the following subsections.

3.3.1.3 The Loss Function

The loss function aims to measure the consistency between the model-based score function and the "ground-truth" observation in KGs. There are two types of widely used loss functions. The first is to treat the problem as a classification task and tries to differentiate the positive triples and the sampled negative triples. The second is to treat the problem as a ranking task and tries to rank the positive triples higher than the sampled negative triples. More discussion will be presented later in Sect. 3.3.5.

Table 3.2 Summary of notations

(e_i, r_k, e_j)	A triple fact where e_i is head entity, e_j is tail entity and r_k is relation
$(\mathbf{e}_i, \mathbf{r}_k, \mathbf{e}_j)$	The embedding vectors corresponding to (e_i, r_k, e_j)
$f_{r_k}(e_i, e_j)$	The score function for triple (e_i, r_k, e_j)

Before we introduce the technical details of KGE methods, we first summarize notations in Table 3.2.

3.3.2 Geometric Transformation-Based KGEs

In this line, entities are treated as points in a geometric space, and relations are treated as geometric operations that transform the head entity into the tail entity. Both entities and relations are associated with learnable embedding vectors, which belong to shallow embedding. The most commonly utilized geometric operations to represent relations in KGs are the *translational* and *rotational operations*.

3.3.2.1 Translation-Based Models: TransE and Its Variants

Translation-based methods treat entities as points in a d-dimensional Euclidean space, and relations as translational operations, which can be represented as a d-dimensional vector. TransE [17] is the most representative translation-based model, which proposed the translation idea for KG embedding for the first time. A figure is provided to illustrate the translation idea in Fig. A.1a in Appendix.

Formally, TransE assumes entities are points in the $\mathbb{R}^d$ space, i.e., $\mathbf{e}_i, \mathbf{e}_j \in \mathbb{R}^d$, and relations correspond to translation operations, which are represented as d-dimensional vectors, i.e., $\mathbf{r}_k \in \mathbb{R}^d$. For a triple (e_i, r_k, e_j), the score function is defined as the negative distance between $\mathbf{e}_i + \mathbf{r}_k$ and $\mathbf{e}_j$, i.e., the distance between the projected tail entity and the true tail entity:

$$f_{r_k}(e_i, e_j) = - \left\| \mathbf{e}_i + \mathbf{r}_k - \mathbf{e}_j \right\|_2^2. \tag{3.8}$$

Despite its simplicity, TransE cannot address relations that are reflexive, symmetric, 1-to-N, N-to-1, and N-to-N due to the nature of the translation operation, which is a one-to-one mapping. Taking *"Friend"* as an example, it is a symmetric relation, i.e., if $Friend(e_i, e_j)$ then $Friend(e_j, e_i)$. But according to the translation operation, if $\mathbf{e}_i + \mathbf{r}_k = \mathbf{e}_j$, then $\mathbf{e}_j + \mathbf{r}_k \neq \mathbf{e}_i$ unless $\mathbf{r}_k = 0$. Taking *"hasSibling"* as another example, it is a 1-to-N relation, and we might observe multiple siblings for the same entity. TransE, however, can only project the entity to one point via the translation operation.

In order to overcome these limitations, different variants of TransE have been proposed, such as TransH [18], TransR [19], and TransD [20]. We have summarized these approaches in Appendix A.1.1.

3.3.2.2 Rotation-Based Model: RotatE

Other than the translation-based methods, an alternative algorithm called RotatE [21] is proposed later, which is based on the rotation operation in the complex space. RotatE defines entities in the complex space, where each embedding dimension is a complex number, i.e., $\mathbf{e}_i, \mathbf{e}_j \in \mathbb{C}^d$. Relations are defined as rotation operations on each dimension, i.e., $\mathbf{r}_k \in \mathbb{C}^d$ and each dimension has a modulus 1 (a.k.a., $|r_{k,m}| = 1$ for every dimension m). According to Euler's formula, rotation operation $r_{k,m}$ can also be written as $e^{i\theta_{k,m}} = \cos(\theta_{k,m}) + i\sin(\theta_{k,m})$, which rotates the corresponding complex number in head entities counter-clockwise with angle $\theta_{k,m}$ into a different one in tail entities. The rotation operation to a complex number can be computed as a product of the two complex numbers. Formally, given a triple (e_i, r_k, e_j), the rotation of head entity e_i with r_k is defined as $\mathbf{e}_i \circ \mathbf{r}_k$, where $\circ$ denotes the Hadamard (element-wise) product, which is expected to be close to the tail entity $\mathbf{e}_j$.

RotatE has the ability to model relations that exhibit different properties, such as *symmetry/asymmetry*, and accommodate relationships between relations such as *inversion* and *composition*. Relations with different types of properties require different $\mathbf{r}_k$. To be more precise, the requirements that need to be satisfied for each property are as follows:

- **Symmetric Relation**: Each dimension of a symmetric relation embedding satisfies $r_{k,m} = e^{0/i\pi} = \pm 1$, i.e., the corresponding $\theta_{k,m} = 0$ or π, which guarantees applying the rotation twice goes back to the same entity.
- **Asymmetric Relation**: At least one of $\mathbf{r}_k$'s dimensions does not satisfy $r_{k,m} = e^{0/i\pi} = \pm 1$.[1]
- **Inversion**: For inverse relations, their embeddings should be conjugate to each other for every element, i.e., $\forall 1 \leq m \leq d, r_{1,m} = \overline{r_{2,m}}$; or in other words, the corresponding angles $\theta_{1,m} = -\theta_{2,m}$.
- **Composition**: Given two relations r_1 and r_2, their composition's representation can be naturally computed as $\mathbf{r}_3 = \mathbf{r}_1 \circ \mathbf{r}_2$.

The score function of a triple (e_i, r_k, e_j) then can be defined as:

$$- \left\| \mathbf{e}_i \circ \mathbf{r}_k - \mathbf{e}_j \right\|_p \tag{3.9}$$

---

[1] In the original paper, it was referred as anti-symmetric relation. Since anti-symmetric relation could be reflexive, which is not satisfied here, we use asymmetric relation instead.

where the p-norm of a complex vector is defined as $\|v\|_p = \sqrt[p]{\sum_m |v_m|^p}$.

Note similar to TransE, RotatE is not able to handle reflexive, 1-to-N, N-to-1, and N-to-N relations. Table A.2 presents a summary of RotatE's capabilities in modeling various types of relation properties.

3.3.2.3 Summary

Table A.1 in Appendix A.1.1 summarizes entity and relation embeddings and score functions of geometric operation-based models. In addition, we also provide an analysis of these models on their abilities in modeling different relation properties in Table A.2. Geometric operation-based models are typically more intuitive and interpretable compared to other KGE methods as they model relations between entities as geometric transformations. However, they may face difficulties when modeling complex relations that do not have a clear geometric interpretation.

3.3.3   Bilinear KGE Models

Instead of explicitly designing geometric transformations for relations and thus deriving a distance-based score function, we can directly define the score function for a triple using the bilinear models:

$$f_{r_k}(e_i, e_j) = \mathbf{e}_i^\mathsf{T} \mathbf{M}_{r_k} \mathbf{e}_j$$

where $\mathbf{M}_{r_k}$ is a $d \times d$ matrix that models the specific pair-wise interactions between the dimensions in entity embedding space for the relation r_k. The bilinear model can also be considered as projecting e_i via a relation-specific linear transformation $\mathbf{M}_{r_k}$ and then the score function is calculated as the inner product of $\mathbf{M}_{r_k}^\mathsf{T} \mathbf{e}_i$ and entity $\mathbf{e}_j$. Linear transformation subsumes different types of geometric operations, including rotation, reflection, scaling, and shear, thus theoretically it is more powerful than the operators seen in the previous section.

3.3.3.1 RESCAL and Its Variants

RESCAL [22] is the first work that proposed the bilinear models. A vector $\mathbf{e}_i \in \mathbb{R}^d$ is used to capture the latent semantics of an entity e_i and a relation r_k is represented as a matrix $\mathbf{M}_{r_k} \in \mathbb{R}^{d \times d}$ to model pairwise interactions between latent factors. The score function for a triple (e_i, r_k, e_j) is then defined as:

$$f_{r_k}(e_i, e_j) = \mathbf{e}_i^\mathsf{T} \mathbf{M}_{r_k} \mathbf{e}_j = \sum_p \sum_q [\mathbf{M}_{r_k}]_{pq} [\mathbf{e}_i]_p [\mathbf{e}_j]_q$$

Due to the expressivity of the matrix $\mathbf{M}_{r_k}$, bilinear model can model relations that are reflexive, irreflexive, transitive, symmetric, asymmetric, 1-N, N-1, and N-N, making the model very flexible and powerful. The downside of the approach is also caused by the matrix representation of relations, which is computationally expensive. Its variants are exploring a good trade-off between *expressivity* and *efficiency*.

DistMult [23], which is the most popular bilinear model, simplifies RESCAL by restricting $\mathbf{M}_{r_k}$ to diagonal matrices, where the score function can be computed as:

$$f_{r_k}(e_i, e_j) = \sum_p [\mathbf{r}_k]_p [\mathbf{e}_i]_p [\mathbf{e}_j]_p$$

In this case, it reduces the time complexity from quadratic to linear with respect to the dimensionality of the embedding vectors. However, it can no longer model asymmetric relations, as for any relation r_k we always have:

$$f_{r_k}(e_i, e_j) = \sum_p [\mathbf{r}_k]_p [\mathbf{e}_i]_p [\mathbf{e}_j]_p = \sum_p [\mathbf{r}_k]_p [\mathbf{e}_j]_p [\mathbf{e}_i]_p = f_{r_k}(e_j, e_i)$$

To address the limitations of DistMult, ComplEx [24] extends DistMult by defining entities as well as relations in the complex vector space to model asymmetric relations, where the score function is defined as:

$$f_{r_k}(e_i, e_j) = \text{Re}(\sum_p [\mathbf{r}_k]_p [\mathbf{e}_i]_p [\overline{\mathbf{e}_j}]_p)$$

where $\overline{\mathbf{e}_j}$ is the conjugate of $\mathbf{e}_j$. In this way, the asymmetric relations can receive different scores due to the difference between head and tail entities when switching the order of the two. Note ComplEx can still model symmetric relations when only real part exists in those matrices.

There are other variants of bilinear models that have been proposed, such as SimplE [25] and HolE [26]. We have summarized these approaches in Appendix A.1.2.

3.3.3.2 ANALOGY: Introducing Constraints to Relation Matrices

Motivated by analogical reasoning, instead of using arbitrary linear maps to represent relations, ANALOGY [27] considers a special family of matrices called *normal matrices* and introduce additional constraints to capture the relation commutativity. Normal matrices satisfy $\mathbf{M}_{r_k} \mathbf{M}_{r_k}^\mathsf{T} = \mathbf{M}_{r_k}^\mathsf{T} \mathbf{M}_{r_k}$, and representative normal matrices include:

- Symmetric matrices, i.e., $\mathbf{M}_{r_k} = \mathbf{M}_{r_k}^\mathsf{T}$ (diagonal matrices as a special case), which can be used to model symmetric relations. An example of symmetric matrix is: $\begin{pmatrix} 1 & 2 \\ 2 & 1 \end{pmatrix}$.

- Anti-symmetric matrices, i.e., $\mathbf{M}_{r_k} = -\mathbf{M}_{r_k}^{\mathsf{T}}$, which can be used to model asymmetric relations. An example of anti-symmetric matrix is: $\begin{pmatrix} 0 & -1 \\ 1 & 0 \end{pmatrix}$.

- Rotation matrices, i.e., $\mathbf{M}_{r_k}\mathbf{M}_{r_k}^{\mathsf{T}} = I$, which can be used to model 1–1 mapping relations. An example of rotation matrix is: $\begin{pmatrix} 1/2 & -\sqrt{3}/2 \\ \sqrt{3}/2 & 1/2 \end{pmatrix}$.

- Circulant matrices, where each row contains the same set of elements, and the next row is to shift the rightmost element in the previous row to the leftmost. It can be used to model asymmetric relations with much fewer parameters than a full matrix. The form of a circulant matrix is: $\begin{pmatrix} x_1 & x_d & \dots & x_2 \\ x_2 & x_1 & \dots & x_3 \\ \vdots & \vdots & \vdots & \vdots \\ x_d & x_{d-1} & \dots & x_1 \end{pmatrix}$.

To model the analogical structures, ANALOGY requires *commutativity* for the composition of two relations, which translates to the commutativity for the two corresponding matrices under multiplication operation: $\mathbf{M}_{r_k}\mathbf{M}_{r_{k'}} = \mathbf{M}_{r_{k'}}\mathbf{M}_{r_k}$. The normal matrix constraint and the commutativity constraint are then incorporated into the standard loss function, which makes it an optimization problem with constraints.

It has been shown that the previously introduced methods, such as DistMult, ComplEx, and HolE, can all be subsumed by ANALOGY as special cases in a principled manner.

3.3.3.3 Summary

Table A.3 in Appendix A.1.2 presents a summary of entity and relation embeddings and score functions of various bilinear models. Bilinear models have higher expressive power compared to geometric models as they can capture complex interactions between entities through a bilinear function. However, they may be more challenging to interpret than geometric models.

3.3.4 Deep Representation Learning-Based KGE Models

All the previous embedding models belong to the category of shallow embedding, where the learnable embeddings for entities and relations are directly used to feed into the score function (the decoder). With the development of different deep learning models, such as convolutional neural networks (CNNs) [28], recurrent neural networks (RNNs) [29], Transformers [30] and graph neural networks (GNNs) [31], more complicated encoders are designed to further transform the initial learnable embeddings to deeper representations. They can be categorized based on their underlying neural network architectures, including (1) *general neural networks-based models*, (2) *convolutional neural networks (CNNs)-based models*, (3) *sequence models*, and (4) *graph neural networks (GNNs)-based models*.

3.3.4.1 General Neural Networks-Based Models

The general idea of neural network-based KGE models is to use neural networks to define the score function, which takes learnable embedding vectors as input and the plausible score as the output. This introduces more complicated interactions, such as non-linear transformations, between entities and relations.

Multi-Layer Perceptron (MLP)

Multi-Layer Perceptron (MLP) [32] is the most straightforward neural architecture. Given a triple (e_i, r, e_j), the vector embeddings $\mathbf{e}_i$, $\mathbf{r}$, and $\mathbf{e}_j$ are concatenated in the input layer and mapped to a non-linear hidden layer. The score is computed by a linear output layer.

$$f_{r_k}(e_i, e_j) = \sigma(\mathbf{w}^\mathsf{T} \tanh(\mathbf{M}[\mathbf{e}_i; \mathbf{r}; \mathbf{e}_j]))$$

The mapping matrices $\mathbf{M} \in \mathbb{R}^{k \times (3d)}$ are responsible for projecting the embedding vectors, where the $3d$ term comes from concatenating the d-dimensional vectors $\mathbf{e}_i$, $\mathbf{r}$, and $\mathbf{e}_j$. The final layer weights are represented by $\mathbf{w} \in \mathbb{R}^{k \times 1}$.

Neural Tensor Network (NTN)

Neural Tensor Network (NTN) [33] proposes another neural network architecture for KG embedding learning. For each triple (e_i, r, e_j), NTN combines entities $\mathbf{e}_i, \mathbf{e}_j \in \mathbb{R}^d$ by a 3d relation-specific tensor $\mathbf{W}_r^{[1:k]} \in \mathbb{R}^{d \times d \times k}$ via $\mathbf{e}_i^\mathsf{T} \mathbf{W}_r^{[1:k]} \mathbf{e}_j \in \mathbb{R}^k$, together with linear projections to entities. Then a relation-specific linear output layer gives the final score of the triple. NTN essentially can be regarded as a combination of MLPs and bilinear models:

$$f_r(e_i, e_j) = \mathbf{r}^\mathsf{T} \tanh(\mathbf{e}_i^\mathsf{T} \mathbf{W}_r^{[1:k]} \mathbf{e}_j + \mathbf{M}_r^1 \mathbf{e}_i + \mathbf{M}_r^2 \mathbf{e}_j + \mathbf{b}_r)$$

where $\mathbf{M}_r^1, \mathbf{M}_r^2 \in \mathbb{R}^{k \times d}$ denote relation-specific projection matrices, $\mathbf{b}_r \in \mathbb{R}^k$ denotes relation-specific bias vector, and $\mathbf{r} \in \mathbb{R}^k$ denotes the final linear weights.

3.3.4.2 Convolutional Neural Networks (CNNs)-Based Model

Some studies aim to leverage the Convolutional Neural Networks (CNNs) to achieve better expressivity and thus higher performance.

ConvE

ConvE [34] makes the first attempt to use the CNN framework for KG embedding learning. ConvE reshapes the head entity embedding and relation embedding into 2D embeddings and stacks them as the input matrix for the 2D convolution layer. Then, ConvE vectorizes and projects the output feature map tensor through a linear transformation. The score of a triple is defined as matching the output of the linear transformation and the tail entity embedding by their inner product:

$$f_{r_k}(e_i, e_j) = f(\text{vec}(f([\overline{\mathbf{e}_i}; \overline{\mathbf{r}_k}] * \omega))\mathbf{W})\mathbf{e}_j$$

where ω is the convolutional filters and $*$ denotes convolution operation, vec is the vectorization operation reshaping a tensor into a vector, f denotes a non-linear function, and $\overline{\mathbf{e}_i}$ and $\overline{\mathbf{r}_k}$ denote a 2D reshaping of vectors $\mathbf{e}_i$ and $\mathbf{r}_k$, respectively.[2]

There are several extensions to ConvE, including ConvKB [35], ConvR [36], and InteractE [37], to further enhance the performance. More details of these models can be found in Appendix A.1.3.

3.3.4.3 Sequence Models

Most KGE methods learn KG embeddings mainly based on triple-level observation, which lacks the capability of capturing long-range relational dependencies of entities. To address this issue, several studies are proposed to integrate sequence models for long-term relational dependencies learning.

Recurrent Neural Networks (RNNs)

A conventional choice to use recurrent neural networks (RNNs) to model long-range relational dependencies. Recurrent skipping networks (RSNs) [38] is the most representative work that integrates RNNs with residual learning for KG embedding. It utilizes a random walk sampler to sample an entity-relation chain $(e_{i_1}, r_{k_1}, e_{i_2}, r_{k_2}, \ldots, e_{i_l}, r_{k_l}, e_{i_{l+1}})$ from the KG as input. For example, (*"Thomas Edison"*, *IsMarriedTo*, *"Mina Miller"*, *LiveIn*, *"USA"*) is an entity-relation chain in Fig. 3.4. The chain is abstracted into $(x_1, x_2, \ldots, x_n)$ by ignoring the entity and relation type. The recurrent hidden state for each element in the entity-relation chain is calculated as $\mathbf{h}_t = \tanh(\mathbf{W}_h \mathbf{h}_{t-1} + \mathbf{W}_x \mathbf{x}_t + \mathbf{b})$ following typical RNN architecture, where t denotes t_{th} element in the sequence.

Note that the elements in an entity-relation chain do have two different types: entity and relation, which carry different semantic information. For example, if x_t is a relation, then (x_{t-1}, x_t, x_{t+1}) is a triple in KG, where x_{t-1} is the head entity and x_{t+1} is the tail entity. Since the head entity is significant in predicting its tail entity, RSN proposes a skipping operation to shortcut the head entity to let it directly participate in predicting its tail entity, which is conducted as:

$$\mathbf{h}'_t = \begin{cases} \mathbf{h}_t & \text{if } x_t \in \mathcal{E} \\ \mathbf{S}_1 \mathbf{h}_t + \mathbf{S}_2 \mathbf{x}_{t-1} & \text{if } x_t \in \mathcal{R} \end{cases}$$

where $\mathbf{h}'_t$ denotes the output hidden state of the skipping operation at time step t, and $\mathbf{h}_t$ denotes the corresponding RNN output. $\mathbf{S}_1, \mathbf{S}_2$ are the weight matrices that are shared at different time steps. In this way, both head entity (x_{t-1}) and relation (x_t) determine the latent representation of a relation element (x_t), which will be used to update the latent representation of the next tail entity (x_{t+1}).

---

[2] If $\mathbf{e}_i, \mathbf{r}_k \in \mathbb{R}^d$, then $\overline{\mathbf{e}_i}, \overline{\mathbf{r}_k} \in \mathbb{R}^{d_w \times d_h}$, where $d = d_w d_h$.

Transformer-based Models

Transformer-based models have been proven to be a more powerful architecture for sequence modeling, and have also been leveraged to embed KG entities and relations. CoKE [39] is one of such examples. Different from the entity-relation chain sequence used in RSN, the sequence used in CoKE $(x_1, x_2, \ldots, x_n)$ is a path connecting two entities, where the first and last elements are entities and the others in between are relations, in the form of $(e_{i_1}, r_{k_1}, r_{k_2}, \ldots, r_{k_l}, e_{i_{l+1}})$. Each element has an initial representation $\mathbf{h}_i^0 = \mathbf{x}_i^{\text{ele}} + \mathbf{x}_i^{\text{pos}}$, where $\mathbf{x}_i^{\text{ele}}$ is the element embedding and $\mathbf{x}_i^{\text{pos}}$ is the position embedding. CoKE feeds the sequence into a stack of L successive Transformer encoders to encode the sequence, where $\{\mathbf{h}_i^l\} = \text{Transformer}(\{\mathbf{h}_i^{l-1}\})$ for $l = 1, \ldots, L$. Motivated by the masked language model (MLM) [40], CoKE proposes an entity prediction task to train the model, i.e., to predict the masked entities given a sequence. Different from the general mask strategy, CoKE only masks entities in a sequence. For instance, given a sequence $(x_1, x_2, \ldots, x_n)$ where x_1 and x_n are two entities, CoKE associates the sequence with two training instances $(?, x_2, \ldots, x_n)$ and $(x_1, x_2, \ldots, ?)$ to predict the missing entities.

3.3.4.4 Graph Neural Networks (GNNs)-Based Models

Graph Neural Networks (GNNs) [41] are a class of deep learning models that are designed for graphs, which leverage message passing to aggregate information from neighbors of a node. Graph Convolutional Network (GCN) [31] is the most cited GNN, which contains two steps in each layer: (1) feature propagation from neighbors; and (2) feature transformation with a linear weight matrix followed by a non-linear activation. Naturally, KGs are a special case of a graph, which contain different types of relations and can benefit from GNNs to capture the graph structure. One of the most popular GNN-based KGE model is RGCN [42]. RGCN extends GCN to relation-aware. Specifically, RGCN associates each relation type with a relation-specific weight matrix W_r for the transformation:

$$\mathbf{h}_i^{(l+1)} = \sigma(\sum_{r \in \mathcal{R}} \sum_{j \in \mathcal{N}_i^r} \frac{1}{|N_i^r|} W_r^{(l)} \mathbf{h}_j^{(l)} + W_0^{(l)} \mathbf{h}_i^{(l)})$$

where $\mathbf{h}_i^l \in \mathbb{R}^{d^{(l)}}$ is the hidden state of the i-th entity in l-th layer, $\mathcal{N}_i^r$ is the set of neighbors of i-th entity within relation $r \in \mathcal{R}$, $W_r^{(l)}$ and $W_0^{(l)}$ are the weight matrices for relation r and self-influence at layer l. To predict the relationship between two entities, RGCN uses DistMult [23] as the decoder to score a triple.

Some other studies for GNN-based KGE model such as SACN [43] are discussed in Appendix A.1.3.

3.3.4.5 Summary

In general, deep learning-based models are powerful and can model complex patterns and dependencies in KGs. However, they typically demand a large amount of data to obtain good performance. In addition, these models are less interpretable compared to earlier carefully designed transformations for relations.

3.3.5 Model Training

Once the KGE models have been constructed, meaning the score function is well defined, the model parameters can be learned following standard machine learning training. We now discuss the commonly used loss functions and typical negative sampling strategies used in KGE model training.

3.3.5.1 Training Objective

Let O be the set of observed triples in KG, let (e'_i, r_k, e'_j) denote a negative triple to the positive triple (e_i, r_k, e_j), and let the set of negative triples corresponding to (e_i, r_k, e_j) be $\mathcal{N}(e_i, r_k, e_j)$, the general idea of training objective is either (1) differentiate the positive triples from the negative ones; or (2) rank the positive triples higher than the negative ones.

Classification-based Loss

The simplest loss function is cross-entropy loss, which aims to distinguish positive triples from negative ones:

$$- \sum_{(e_i, r_k, e_j) \in O} \left(\log \sigma(f_{r_k}(e_i, e_j)) + \sum_{\substack{(e'_i, r_k, e'_j) \\ \in \mathcal{N}(e_i, r_k, e_j)}} \frac{1}{|\mathcal{N}(e_i, r_k, e_j)|} \log \sigma(-f_{r_k}(e'_i, e'_j)) \right)$$

(3.10)

For instance, the bilinear models such as DistMult [23] and ANALOGY [27] employ this loss for model training. An extension to cross-entropy loss is to add a margin term $\gamma > 0$ to adjust the probability:

$$- \sum_{(e_i, r_k, e_j) \in O} \left(\log \sigma(f_{r_k}(e_i, e_j) + \gamma) + \sum_{\substack{(e'_i, r_k, e'_j) \\ \in \mathcal{N}(e_i, r_k, e_j)}} \frac{1}{|\mathcal{N}(e_i, r_k, e_j)|} \log \sigma(-f_{r_k}(e'_i, e'_j) - \gamma) \right) \quad (3.11)$$

For instance, RotatE [21] employs this loss for model training.

Ranking-based Loss

The most frequently used loss function is *margin-based pairwise ranking loss*:

$$\sum_{(e_i, r_k, e_j) \in O} \sum_{(e'_i, r_k, e'_j) \in \mathcal{N}(e_i, r_k, e_j)} \max(0, \gamma - f_{r_k}(e_i, e_j) + f_{r_k}(e'_i, e'_j))$$

(3.12)

where $\gamma > 0$ is a hyperparameter denoting the margin. The basic idea of pairwise ranking loss is to make the scores of positive triples higher than their corresponding negative ones with at least γ; otherwise, it will receive a penalty. For instance, TransE and its variants employ this loss for model training.

3.3.5.2 Creating Negative Triples

We can see that negative triples play a critical role in defining the training objective. But KGs contain only positive triples. Conventional embedding models follow *Closed World Assumption* (CWA) (i.e., all triples that are not contained in the knowledge graph are *False*) to construct negative triples. As shown in Eq. (3.13), the set of negative triples of a positive triple (e_i, r_k, e_j), denoted as $\mathcal{N}(e_i, r_k, e_j)$, is constructed by corrupting the head or tail entities of the positive triple.

$$\mathcal{N}(e_i, r_k, e_j) = \{(e_i', r_k, e_j) | (e_i', r_k, e_j) \notin O\} \cup \{(e_i, r_k, e_j') | (e_i, r_k, e_j') \notin O\} \quad (3.13)$$

Given the fact that $\mathcal{N}(e_i, r_k, e_j)$ usually contains thousands of negative triples, it is impractical to include all of them in the computation. To alleviate the computational complexity, only a small portion of negative triples will be randomly sampled. However, some of the randomly generated negative samples might be too easy to be discriminated against from positive triples and thus make a little contribution towards the training.

Some recent work has proposed to incorporate adversarial learning idea, such as Generative Adversarial Network (GAN) [44] for better negative sampling. For example, KBGAN [45] proposes to employ GAN on knowledge representation learning for high-quality negative triplets sampling. The discriminator is trained to minimize the margin-based ranking loss in Eq. (3.12) as in the previous models, where negative samples are from the triple generator: $(e_i', r_k, e_j') \sim p_G(e_i', r_k, e_j' | e_i, r_k, e_j)$. The generator learns to generate high-quality negative triplets that can fool the discriminator, i.e., maximize the expectation of scores for generated triples or minimize the following loss:

$$\sum_{(e_i, r_k, e_j) \in O} \mathbb{E}[-f_D(e_i', r_k, e_j')] \quad (3.14)$$

where $f_D(e_i', r_k, e_j)$ is the score function of the discriminator. It is equivalent to maximizing the loss for the best discriminator and thus fooling the discriminator. For example, given an observed triple (Google, LocatedIn, Mountain View), it can be corrupted by replacing its tail entity, i.e., (Google, LocatedIn, Apple). However, most of the corrupted triples are usually "too easy" to recognize. The generator generates the probability distribution over all candidate negative triples to select the "most confusing" triple. For instance, (Google, LocatedIn, Phoenix) is a very useful negative triple because it cannot be proved wrong without understanding the context. Then, the discriminator takes the generated negative triple (Google, LocatedIn, Phoenix) as well as the original triple (Google, LocatedIn, Mountain View) as the input and distinguish the generated one from the observed one to improve the embedding performance.

RotatE [21] also proposes self-adversarial negative sampling for generating negative samples, which samples negative triples according to the embedding model. Specifically, RotatE samples negative triples from the following distribution:

$$p((e_i', r_k, e_j')|(e_i, r_k, e_j)) = \frac{\exp\{\alpha f_{r_k}(e_i', e_j')\}}{\sum_{(e_i', r_k, e_j') \in N(e_i, r_k, e_j)} \exp\{\alpha f_{r_k}(e_i', e_j')\}} \tag{3.15}$$

where α is the temperature of sampling. The probability $p((e_i', r_k, e_j')|(e_i, r_k, e_j))$ is taken as the weight of the negative sample.

Therefore the final loss with self-adversarial training is given below:

$$-\sum_{(e_i, r_k, e_j) \in O} \left(\log \sigma(\gamma + f_{r_k}(e_i, e_j)) + \sum_{\substack{(e_i', r_k, e_j') \\ \in N(e_i, r_k, e_j)}} p((e_i', r_k, e_j')) \log \sigma(-f_{r_k}(e_i', e_j') - \gamma) \right)$$

$$\tag{3.16}$$

3.4   Neuro-Symbolic Integration for KG Completion

Previous sections have introduced two main directions in solving the KG completion problem, i.e., traditional logical inference approaches in Sect. 3.2 and knowledge graph embedding (KGE) approaches in Sect. 3.3.

Traditional logical inference approaches attempt to implement reasoning via logic rules. They have shown great interpretability and generalizability due to the power of symbolic representation. However, the discrete symbolic representation causes severe scalability issues and is unable to explore inherent correlations among entities and relations. Instead, KGE methods embed entities into continuous vector representations to encode the network structure of KGs. A score function can be learned by the neural network to make predictions of the missing knowledge. Although KGE methods have demonstrated their good scalability and strong ability in capturing correlation among atoms, most of them cannot model higher-order dependency of KG relations or take additional knowledge in terms of logical rules into consideration. As presented in Fig. 3.5, by integrating both techniques into a unified framework, neuro-symbolic reasoning provides a more efficient, generalizable, and interpretable way to perform KG reasoning.

In this chapter, we aim to introduce several studies that attempt to combine both approaches. Since the score function of KGE provides a soft truth value to triples in KG, *probabilistic programming frameworks* are widely used to combine the embedding model with pre-defined logic rules. Based on the types of probabilistic programming frameworks introduced in Sect. 3.2, existing neuro-symbolic integration studies can be roughly divided into two categories: (1) *embedding-based variational distribution for variational inference*

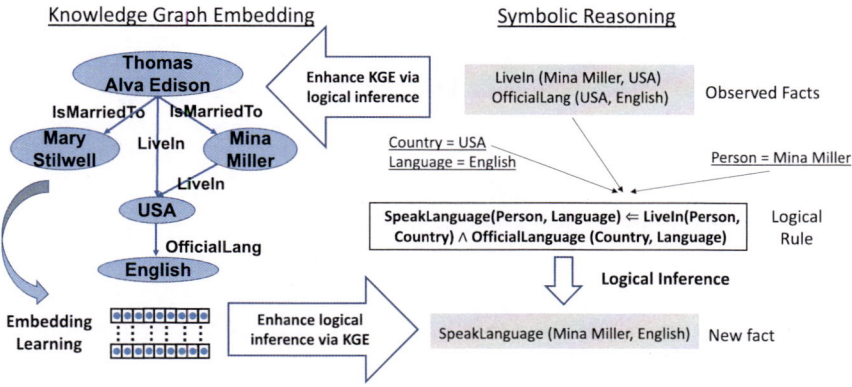

Fig. 3.5 Neuro-symbolic reasoning over a toy example of KG. **Left**: KG embedding model. **Right**: Traditional logical inference model. Integrating both approaches can lead to enhanced reasoning capabilities

of Markov Logic Network (MLN); and (2) *Fuzzy logic-based regularization to regularize embedding models.*

3.4.1 Embedding-Based Variational Inference for Markov Logic Network (MLN)

Markov Logic Network (MLN) [7] combines probabilistic graphical model and FOL, which is able to define the joint probability for all the ground predicate variables. The knowledge graph completion task then becomes the inference problem in a probabilistic model. Unfortunately, constructing MLN involves the grounding for predicates and logical rules, and MLN inference subsumes probabilistic inference, which is #P-complete. Both the construction complexity and the inference complexity prevent the application of MLN in large-scale datasets.

Recently, variation inference [46] has been proposed to provide approximate solutions to the inference problem in a much more efficient way, where the key is to design a variational distribution to approximate the original posterior distribution. In the KG setting, KG embedding can be used to define the probability for each triple (e_i, r_k, e_j) to be *True*. Embedding-based distributions are then naturally proposed to serve as variational distributions to conduct variational inference of MLN. Earlier studies consider each triple independently with each other. Later studies use *graph neural network* as the KG embedding model to capture the dependency, which lead to more effective relational data modeling.

3.4.1.1 pLogicNet: An Embedding-Based Variational Inference Approach

pLogicNet [47] is the most representative embedding-based variational inference algorithm for MLN. According to MLN, the joint probability of all the predicate variables is $p_{\mathbf{w}}(\mathbf{v}_O, \mathbf{v}_H)$, where $\mathbf{v}_O$ denotes all the observed triples that take the value *True* and $\mathbf{v}_H$ denotes all the unseen triples that take either *True* or *False*. The KG completion task is to find the assignment $\mathbf{v}_H$ that maximizes the posterior probability $p_{\mathbf{w}}(\mathbf{v}_H | \mathbf{v}_O)$, i.e., to find the best truth values for the unobserved triples based on the observed ones. As discussed earlier, the inference problem is nontrivial to solve, and the approximation solutions are needed.

Variational inference is one of such approximation algorithms. The main idea is to find a simpler distribution denoted as $q_\theta(\mathbf{v}_H)$ that is close to the true posterior distribution $p_{\mathbf{w}}(\mathbf{v}_H | \mathbf{v}_O)$, where the distance of the two can be measured as the KL divergence between the two distributions: $D_{KL}(q_\theta(\mathbf{v}_H) || p_{\mathbf{w}}(\mathbf{v}_H | \mathbf{v}_O)) = \mathbb{E}_{q_\theta(\mathbf{v}_H)}(\log q_\theta(\mathbf{v}_H) - \log p_{\mathbf{w}}(\mathbf{v}_H | \mathbf{v}_O))$. KL-divergence is difficult to be minimized directly, as the true posterior distribution is unknown. Fortunately, we can maximize another term called Evidence Lower Bound (ELBO) denoted as $\mathcal{L}(q_\theta, p_{\mathbf{w}})$, which is defined as:

$$\mathcal{L}(q_\theta, p_{\mathbf{w}}) = \mathbb{E}_{q_\theta(\mathbf{v}_H)}[\log p_{\mathbf{w}}(\mathbf{v}_O, \mathbf{v}_H) - \log q_\theta(\mathbf{v}_H)] \qquad (3.17)$$

It can be proven that KL-divergence of the distribution plus ELBO equals to the log of the marginal distribution $\log p_{\mathbf{w}}(\mathbf{v}_O)$, which is a constant with respect to the parameters in the variational distribution q_θ, i.e., $D_{KL}(q_\theta(\mathbf{v}_H) || p_{\mathbf{w}}(\mathbf{v}_H | \mathbf{v}_O)) + \mathcal{L}(q_\theta, p_{\mathbf{w}}) = \log p_{\mathbf{w}}(\mathbf{v}_O)$. Therefore, minimizing the KL-divergence between the two distributions is equivalent to maximizing the ELBO.

In pLogicNet, the variational distribution $q_\theta(\mathbf{v}_H)$ is defined using a KGE model, by assuming the truth value of each triple independently follows a Bernoulli distribution, with parameters specified by the embedding score function:

$$
\begin{aligned}
q_\theta(\mathbf{v}_H) &= \prod_{(e_i, r_k, e_j) \in H} q_\theta(r_k(e_i, e_j)) \\
&= \prod_{(e_i, r_k, e_j) \in H} f_{r_k}(r_k(e_i, e_j))
\end{aligned}
\qquad (3.18)
$$

where $r_k(e_i, e_j) \sim \mathrm{Ber}(f_{r_k}(e_i, e_j))$ follows the Bernoulli distribution and $f_{r_k}(e_i, e_j)$ is an embedding score denoting the probability of triple (e_i, r_k, e_j) to be *True*. For example, in DistMult, $f_{r_k}(e_i, e_j)$ can be defined as $\sigma(\mathbf{e}_i^{\mathsf{T}} \mathrm{diag}(\mathbf{r}_k) \mathbf{e}_j)$.

ELBO can be effectively optimized using variational EM algorithm [48], where (1) the variational E-step is corresponding to the inference problem when rule weights $\mathbf{w}$ are fixed and (2) the M-step can be considered as the learning for $\mathbf{w}$ when the assignments to $\mathbf{v}_H$ are fixed.

- In variational E-step, $p_{\mathbf{w}}$ is fixed and q_θ is updated to maximize ELBO. In pLogicNet, it is done by minimizing the KL divergence between $q_\theta(\mathbf{v}_H)$ and $p_{\mathbf{w}}(\mathbf{v}_H | \mathbf{v}_O)$ in an approximate way. Since exact inference is intractable, pLogicNet approximates the true posterior with a mean-field distribution. Alternative approaches such as stochastic variational inference can also be considered here [49].

- In M-step, q_θ is fixed and the weights of the rules w are updated to maximize the joint probability of both observed and hidden triples (i.e., $\mathbb{E}_{q_\theta(\mathbf{v}_H)}[\log p_\mathbf{w}(\mathbf{v}_O, \mathbf{v}_H)]$).

During training, pLogicNet iteratively performs the E-step and the M-step until convergence.

It is important to note that in real-world KG, there are numerous hidden triples (i.e., $|\mathcal{E}| \times |\mathcal{R}| \times |\mathcal{E}| \setminus |O|$). Optimizing all of them is not feasible due to computational constraints. To alleviate this burden, a smaller subset of hidden triples is sampled to construct the hidden set $\mathcal{H}$. One sampling approach is to select unobserved triples (e_i, r_k, e_j) that serve as the head of a ground rule $head \leftarrow body$, where the rule body is fully observed.

Other extensions to pLogicNet have been proposed to utilize Graph Neural Networks (GNNs) as the KG embedding model. Examples of such extensions include Express-GNN [50] and pGAT [51]. Further details on these approaches are provided in Appendix A.2.1.

3.4.1.2 Summary
While embedding-based variational inference for MLN offers an elegant solution to integrating embedding models and logical rules, inference efficiency remains a significant challenge. Optimizing over all the hidden triples is impractical, so approaches in this category only sample a small subset of hidden triples to reduce computational complexity. However, this reduction in computational complexity also leads to information loss from the logical rule side.

3.4.2 Fuzzy Logic-Based Regularization

Fuzzy logic provides an alternative approach to Markov logic networks (MLNs). Instead of constructing Markov networks based on KG and ground logical rules, PSL uses logical rules as additional constraints and forms regularization terms to the original KGE loss.

This idea is closely connected to probabilistic soft logic discussed in Sect. 3.2.3.2. Each predicate-based atom is associated with a soft truth value in the range of [0, 1], which can be defined via embeddings. Each ground logical rule is corresponding to a logical formula, and the truth value can be evaluated based on fuzzy logic. Intuitively, the embeddings should be consistent with the logical rules, leading to higher truth values for the corresponding ground rules.

3.4.2.1 Regularizing over Ground Rules

The bridge between the embedding-based approach and fuzzy logic is the soft truth value assignment to each ground predicate: $I(r_k(e_i, e_j))$. From embedding perspective, we can turn the score function for each triple $f_{r_k}(e_i, e_j)$ into the range $[0, 1]$. From fuzzy logic perspective, once we have $I(r_k(e_i, e_j))$ for each ground atomic formula, the truth value for any rule f can be evaluated based on fuzzy logic introduced in Sect. 2.2.4. The goal is to find the embeddings that also give high truth values for the given rules.

We start by introducing the methods which add regularization to the entity and relation representations by instantiating the FOL rules. A typical integration is defined as follows: (1) mapping each related triple (i.e., ground predicate) into a soft truth value (i.e., $I(r_k(e_i, e_j))$); (2) sampling ground logical rules given the template logical rules; (3) computing satisfaction of each ground rule based on the soft truth value of ground predicates in it; and (4) defining proper loss based on the satisfaction of all the ground rules.

The first attempt

Rocktäschel [52] is among the first integration attempts in this line. Embedding-wise, instead of learning entity embeddings for the individual entity, they utilize matrix factorization to learn joint embeddings of pairs of entities $\mathbf{v}_{e_i, e_j}$ as well as embeddings of relations $\mathbf{v}_{r_k}$. For each triple (e_i, r_k, e_j), the score function is defined as $\sigma(\mathbf{v}_{r_k} \cdot \mathbf{v}_{e_i, e_j})$, where $\sigma(\cdot)$ denotes the sigmoid function.

From embedding perspective, the likelihood of a possible world given embeddings $\mathbf{v}_{e_i, e_j}$ and $\mathbf{v}_{r_k}$ can be defined as:

$$\prod_{r_k(e_i, e_j) \in \mathbf{v}_O} I(r_k(e_i, e_j)) \prod_{r_k(e_i, e_j) \in \mathbf{v}_H} (1 - I(r_k(e_i, e_j))) \tag{3.19}$$

By maximizing the likelihood of all observed triples in KG with ℓ_2 regularization [53], the method learns entity-pair and relation embeddings that reconstruct observed facts that are able to generalize to missing facts. This objective is equivalent to to the classification-based loss in KGE (Eq. 3.10).

To inject logical rules $\mathcal{F}$ into the embeddings of relations and entity pairs, the logistic loss is defined as the negation of logarithmic transformation of the likelihood that the formulas in $\mathcal{F}$ are true under the model:

$$- \sum_{f \in \mathcal{F}} \log(I(f)) \tag{3.20}$$

where the soft truth value of a ground rule $f \in \mathcal{F}$, $I(f)$, is computed following the *product logic*. The integration of the two losses can hence be written as:

$$- \sum_{r_k(e_i, e_j) \in \mathbf{v}_O} \log(I(r_k(e_i, e_j))) - \sum_{r_k(e_i, e_j) \in \mathbf{v}_H} \log(1 - I(r_k(e_i, e_j))) - \sum_{f} \log(I(f))$$
$$\tag{3.21}$$

KALE

Compared to the first attempt, KALE [54] proposes to (1) use a different score function to assign truth values to each triple; and (2) introduce negative ground rules in addition to the positive ground rules.

KALE uses TransE-based score function for the truth value, i.e., $I(r_k(e_i, e_j)) = 1 - \frac{1}{3\sqrt{d}} \left\| \mathbf{e}_i + \mathbf{r}_k - \mathbf{e}_j \right\|_1$, where $\mathbf{e}_i$, $\mathbf{r}_k$, and $\mathbf{e}_j$ are embedding vectors to the corresponding entities and relations and d is the dimensionality of the embeddings.

Then, a set of positive and negative ground rules (i.e., f^+ and f^-) are sampled given the template logical rules. For instance, consider a positive ground rule from Fig. 3.5 as shown below:

$$f^+ : \text{liveIn(Edison, USA)} \leftarrow \text{isMarriedTo(Edison, Miller)} \wedge \text{liveIn(Miller, USA)}$$

A negative ground rule can be constructed by replacing the relation in the conclusion of the positive ground rule with a random relation $r \in \mathcal{R}$. For example:

$$f^- : \text{bornIn(Edison, USA)} \leftarrow \text{isMarriedTo(Edison, Miller)} \wedge \text{liveIn(Miller, USA)}$$

Similar to Rocktäschel [52], the truth value for rules is computed based on product logic, denoted as $I(f^+)$ and $I(f^-)$.

In addition to the sample rules, the positive and negative triples are also sampled similarly to traditional KGE approaches, which are atomic formulas. Both categories are unified under the concept of *logic formulas*, and are denoted as f^+ and f^-.

KALE defines a loss function over all sampled formulas following margin-based classification loss, with the goal to differentiate positive formulas from negative ones:

$$\sum_{f^+} \sum_{f^- \in \mathcal{N}_{f^+}} [\gamma - I(f^+) + I(f^-)]_+ \qquad (3.22)$$

where $\mathcal{N}_{f^+}$ denotes a set of negative rules constructed for the positive rule f^+, $[x]_+$ denotes $max(x, 0)$, and γ denotes the margin. Note that, by removing ground rules from the whole set of sampled formulas, the loss degenerates to regular TransE-based embedding loss.

UKGE: Modeling Probabilistic KG

Most of the existing methods focus on modeling deterministic KG while UKGE [55] extends existing methods so as to model probabilistic KG, where each triple is associated with a weight $c_{r_k(e_i, e_j)}$ indicating the confidence score of the triple to be *True*. UKGE employs two different mapping functions to transform the KGE score function to a confidence value in the range of [0, 1]. Formally, let a transformation function $\phi(\cdot)$ denote the mapping from $f_{r_k}(e_i, e_j)$ to $I(r_k(e_i, e_j))$, the truth value of the triple is then:

$$I(r_k(e_i, e_j)) = \phi(f_{r_k}(e_i, e_j)), \phi : \mathbb{R}^+ \cup \{0\} \rightarrow [0, 1] \qquad (3.23)$$

where ϕ can be defined as a logistic function:

$$\phi(x) = \frac{1}{1 + e^{-(\mathbf{w}x + \mathbf{b})}} \tag{3.24}$$

or a bounded rectifier:

$$\phi(x) = \min(\max(\mathbf{w}x + \mathbf{b}, 0), 1) \tag{3.25}$$

Specifically, DistMult score function is used in UKGE, i.e., $f_{r_k}(e_i, e_j) = \mathbf{r}_k \cdot (\mathbf{e}_i \circ \mathbf{e}_j)$.

To summarize, the interpretation of triples in KG can be defined as:

$$I(r_k(e_i, e_j)) = \begin{cases} c_{r_k(e_i, e_j)} & \text{if } r_k(e_i, e_j) \in \mathbf{v}_O \\ \phi(f_{r_k}(e_i, e_j)) & \text{if } r_k(e_i, e_j) \in \mathbf{v}_H \end{cases} \tag{3.26}$$

For each unseen triple, if it is covered by some logical rule, we can sample a set of ground rules with the unseen triple as the rule head. According to probabilistic soft logic introduced in Sect. 3.2.3.2, the distance to satisfaction of a rule is $d(f) = 1 - I(f)$, where $I(f)$ is computed based on Łukasiewicz logic. We wish the embedding-based interpretation for unseen triples could lead to a small distance to satisfaction for the sampled rules.

The goal of UKGE contains two parts: (1) to minimize the MSE between the ground truth weight $c_{r_k(e_i, e_j)}$ and the predicted soft truth value $I(r_k(e_i, e_j))$ of observed triples; (2) to minimize the weighted distance to satisfaction of sampled ground rules, in which unseen triple $r_k(e_i, e_j)$ is the rule head. The final loss can be written as:

$$\sum_{r_k(e_i, e_j) \in \mathbf{v}_O} |I(r_k(e_i, e_j)) - c_{r_k(e_i, e_j)}|^2 + \sum_{r_k(e_i, e_j) \in \mathbf{v}_H} \sum_{f \in \Gamma_{r_k(e_i, e_j)}} |w_f d(f)|^2 \tag{3.27}$$

where $\Gamma_{r_k(e_i, e_j)}$ is a set of ground rules with $r_k(e_i, e_j)$ as the head, and w_f is the given weight associated with each rule.

3.4.2.2 Regularizing over Template Rules

The above methods regularize relation and entity representations using the grounding of first-order logic rules. Nonetheless, scaling the grounding of first-order logic rules becomes challenging for large-scale KGs. To improve the scalability and generalizibility, several methods are proposed to add regularization at the template rule level. FSL [56] is one of the most representative models, which is an extension to Rocktäschel [52]. For any rule f : $r_h(x, y) \leftarrow r_b(x, y)$, such as $employeeAt(x, y) \leftarrow professorAt(x, y)$, the truth assignment for the head must be higher than or equal to the the body to make the rule satisfied, namely, for any $e_i, e_j, I(r_h(e_i, e_j)) \geq I(r_b(e_i, e_j))$. This can be easily checked for Boolean logic via truth table as well as three types of fuzzy logic mentioned in Sect. 2.2.4. A simple discussion has been provided for Łukasiewicz logic in probabilistic soft logic (Sect. 3.2.3.2). We will see this again when discussing logical laws in Sect. 4.4.1.

Let $\mathbf{v}_{r_b}$ and $\mathbf{v}_{r_h}$ be the learnable embeddings of the rule body and rule head, enforcing the implication rule to be true requires $\forall \mathbf{v}_{e_i, e_j} : \mathbf{v}_{r_b}{}^\mathsf{T} \mathbf{v}_{e_i, e_j} \leq \mathbf{v}_{r_h}{}^\mathsf{T} \mathbf{v}_{e_i, e_j}$, where $\mathbf{v}_r^\mathsf{T} \mathbf{v}_{e_i, e_j}$ is the score function for triple (e_i, r, e_j) used in FSL. The constraint can be turned into a (soft) loss, following Bayesian Personalized Ranking (BPR) loss [57] used in recommender systems:

$$- \sum_{(e_i, *, e_j) \in \mathbf{v}_O} \log \sigma(-[\mathbf{v}_{r_b} - \mathbf{v}_{r_h}]^\mathsf{T} \widetilde{\mathbf{v}}_{e_i, e_j}) \tag{3.28}$$

where $\widetilde{\mathbf{v}}_{e_i, e_j} = \mathbf{v}_{e_i, e_j} / \left\| \mathbf{v}_{e_i, e_j} \right\|_1$, and $(e_i, *, e_j) \in \mathbf{v}_O$ denotes all the entity pairs that are observed in KG.

But how can we drop the entities so that there is no need to go through all the entity pairs? FSL smartly leverages Jensen's inequality to generate an upper bound of the above loss:

$$- \sum_{(e_i, *, e_j) \in \mathbf{v}_O} \log \sigma(-[\mathbf{v}_{r_b} - \mathbf{v}_{r_h}]^\mathsf{T} \widetilde{\mathbf{v}}_{e_i, e_j})$$

$$\leq - \sum_{(e_i, *, e_j) \in \mathbf{v}_O} \sum_d (\widetilde{\mathbf{v}}_{e_i, e_j})_d \log \sigma(-[\mathbf{v}_{r_b} - \mathbf{v}_{r_h}]_d) \tag{3.29}$$

$$\leq - \sum_d \log \sigma(-[\mathbf{v}_{r_b} - \mathbf{v}_{r_h}]_d) \sum_{(e_i, *, e_j) \in \mathbf{v}_O} (\widetilde{\mathbf{v}}_{e_i, e_j})_d$$

where d is used to the denote the d_{th} dimension of the corresponding vector. Let β be the upper bound of $\sum_{(e_i, *, e_j) \in \mathbf{v}_O} (\widetilde{\mathbf{v}}_{e_i, e_j})_d$, say $|\mathbf{v}_O|$, the upper bound can be written as: $-\beta \sum_d \log \sigma(-[\mathbf{v}_{r_b} - \mathbf{v}_{r_h}]_d)$, which is called *lifted loss* and has dropped all the concrete triples successfully.

Combining the lifted loss with the matrix factorization model for KG embedding learning, the overall loss can hence be written as

$$- \sum_{\substack{r_k(e_i, e_j) \in \mathbf{v}_O, \\ r_k(e_i', e_j') \in \mathbf{v}_H}} \log \sigma(-\mathbf{v}_{r_k}^\mathsf{T} [\mathbf{v}_{e_i', e_j'} - \mathbf{v}_{e_i, e_j}]) - \beta \sum_{(r_b, r_h) \in \mathcal{F}} \sum_d \log \sigma(-[\mathbf{v}_{r_b} - \mathbf{v}_{r_h}]_d) \tag{3.30}$$

where the first term learns the KG embedding such that positive triples receive higher scores than negative ones, while the second term denotes a lifted loss for every rule in a set $\mathcal{F}$ of implication rules.

3.4.2.3 Regularizing over Unseen Triples

Different from the methods which define loss over the logical rules, RUGE [58] directly defines a loss function over triples. It employs the score function in ComplEx [24]

$$\sigma(\text{Re}(\langle \mathbf{e}_i, \mathbf{r}_k, \overline{\mathbf{e}}_j \rangle)) \tag{3.31}$$

to model triples. Triples are divided into two categories, the observed triples (i.e., $\mathbf{v}_O$) and the hidden triples (i.e., $\mathbf{v}_H$). Observed triples have hard labels $y_{r_k(e_i, e_j)} = 1$ whereas sampled negative triples used to have labels $y_{r_k(e_i, e_j)} = 0$. To inject logical rules, RUGE uses product logic to predict the soft label of hidden triples $s_{r_k(e_i,e_j)} \in [0, 1]$ in the sampled rule instances by maximizing the soft truth value of the sampled rules. With the ground truth labels $y_{r_k(e_i,e_j)}$ of the observed triples and soft label $s_{r_k(e_i,e_j)}$ of the hidden triples, RUGE learns embedding by enforcing triples to be consistent with their labels.

$$\frac{1}{|O|} \sum_{r_k(e_i,e_j) \in \mathbf{v}_O} l(I(r_k(e_i, e_j)), y_{r_k(e_i,e_j)}) + \frac{1}{|H|} \sum_{r_k(e_i,e_j) \in \mathbf{v}_H} l(I(r_k(e_i, e_j)), s_{r_k(e_i,e_j)})$$

$$(3.32)$$

where $l(x, y) = -y \log x - (1 - y) \log(1 - x)$ is the cross entropy.

3.4.2.4 Summary

The logical rule-based regularization methods typically separate the loss into two parts: the embedding-based loss and the logic-based loss. Although logical rule-based regularization approaches provide an efficient and effective way to combine embedding and logical rules, they also suffer from information loss from the logical rule side, as most of them sample only a small portion of ground rules to approximate the inference process. In addition, most methods in this category make only a one-time injection of logical rules to enhance embedding, ignoring the interactive nature between embedding learning and logical inference [52, 54].

3.5   UniKER: A Recent Advance of Neuro-Symbolic Integration for KG Completion

Despite several attempts made to combine KGE and logical rules for KG reasoning, they either use a probabilistic model to approximate the exact logical inference (i.e., MAX-SAT) [47, 50, 51] (i.e., embedding-based variational inference of MLN) or simply treat logical rules as additional constraints into KGE loss [52, 54, 56] (i.e., logical rule-based regularization approaches). Moreover, these methods rely on ground rules, the total number of which can be intractable in practice as logical rules with n variables can result in $|\mathcal{E}|^n$ possible combinations of entities for grounding the rule. To tackle the scalability issue, only a small portion of ground predicates/ground rules are sampled to approximate the inference process, which causes further *information loss from the logic side*.

To overcome the above issues, we introduce a state-of-the-art **Uni**fied framework for combining **K**nowledge graph **E**mbedding with logical **R**ules (**UniKER**) [1], to handle a special type of first-order logic, i.e., the definite Horn rules. First, UniKER combines logical rule reasoning and KG embedding in an iterative manner, to make sure the inferred knowledge via both techniques can benefit each other as shown in Fig. 3.6. Second, UniKER proposes an iterative grounding algorithm to extend the classic forward chaining algorithm that is designed for definite Horn rule reasoning in an extremely efficient way. Consequently, UniKER can fully exploit the knowledge contained in logical rules and enrich KGs for better embedding. Meanwhile, KGE enhances the forward chaining by including more potentially

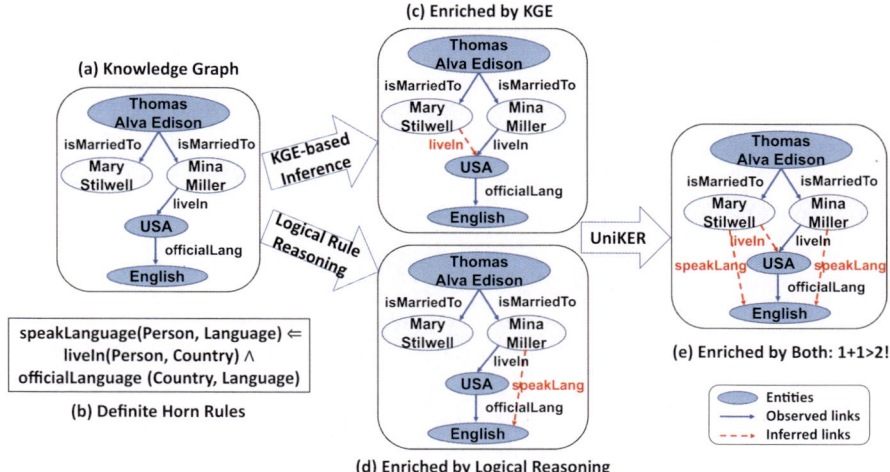

Fig. 3.6 Given **a** a KG with observed facts and **b** a set of definite Horn rules, different inference results can be obtained using **c** KGE, **d** logical inference, and **e** the proposed UniKER approach. The synergy of KGE and logical reasoning via UniKER is more powerful than a simple union of (**c**) and (**d**)

useful hidden facts (See Fig. 3.6c). In this way, the two procedures mutually enhance each other.

3.5.1   Framework of UniKER

Rather than follow probabilistic logic to integrate logical rules and KGE, UniKER shows that by leveraging the nice properties of definite Horn rules, there is a much simpler way to directly derive an optimal boolean solution for MAX-SAT problem. Definite Horn rules have been introduced previously in Sect. 2.3. Their nice properties and two efficient inference algorithms, forward chaining and backward chaining, have been discussed in Sect. 3.2.2.1. To capture the mutual interaction between KGE and logical inference, UniKER proposes an iterative mechanism, which ensures that it is more potent than a simple union of KGE and logical rules.

3.5.1.1   Enhance KG via Forward Chaining-Based Logical Reasoning for KGE

Note that there exists a truth assignment that satisfies all ground rules when restricting logical rules to be definite Horn rules [59]. The question is how to conduct such an assignment efficiently. Let $\mathbf{v}_H^{T\,*}$ (hidden triples that are true) and $\mathbf{v}_H^{F\,*}$ (hidden triples that are false) denote the satisfying truth assignment, i.e., $\mathbf{v}_H^{T\,*} = \{r_k(e_i, e_j) = 1 \mid r_k(e_i, e_j) \in \mathbf{v}_H\}$ and $\mathbf{v}_H^{F\,*} =$

$\{r_k(e_i, e_j) = 0 \mid r_k(e_i, e_j) \in \mathbf{v}_H\}$. An existing algorithm called **forward chaining** [60] can derive $\mathbf{v}_H^{T*}$ efficiently, which has been discussed previously in Sect. 3.2.2.1.

Starting from known facts (e.g., *liveIn (Mina Miller, USA)*, *officialLanguage (USA, English)*), the forward chaining algorithm triggers all ground rules whose premises are satisfied (e.g., *speakLanguage (Mina Miller, English)* ← *liveIn (Mina Miller, USA)* ∧ *officialLanguage (USA, English)*), and adds their conclusion (e.g., *speakLanguage (Mina Miller, English)*) to the known facts until no facts can be added anymore.

As illustrated in Fig. 3.2, unlike other neuro-symbolic integration algorithms, which require all ground predicates (including both observed and unobserved ground predicates) into the calculation, forward chaining adopts "lazy inference" instead. It involves only a small subset of "active" ground predicates/rules, and activates more if necessary as the inference proceeds. The mechanism dramatically improves inference efficiency by avoiding the computation for massive ground predicates/rules that are never used. Moreover, considering that definite Horn rules which can be extracted efficiently via modern rule mining systems are usually chain-like Horn rules. The conjunctive body of a ground chain-like Horn rules is essentially a path in a KG, which can be extracted efficiently using sparse matrix multiplication. To illustrate, let us consider the logical rule $r_0(x, y) \leftarrow r_1(x, z) \wedge r_2(z, y)$. We can represent relations r_1 and r_2 as sparse matrices $\mathbf{M}_1$ and $\mathbf{M}_2$, respectively. In these matrices, each row and column represent an entity in the KG, and the non-zero entries represent the existence of a relation between two entities. To find all the entity pairs (x, y) that satisfy the body of the rule (i.e., $r_1(x, z) \wedge r_2(z, y)$), we perform sparse matrix multiplication between $\mathbf{M}_1$ and $\mathbf{M}_2$, which give us new facts in the form of (x, r_0, y).

The newly generated facts denoted as $\mathbf{v}_H^{T*}$ then will be added to KG. Since $\mathbf{v}_H^{T*}$ and $\mathbf{v}_H^{F*}$ are satisfying truth assignments derived by forward chaining, the knowledge contained in definite Horn rules is guaranteed to be fully exploited.

3.5.1.2 Enhance KG via Embedding-Based Inference for Logical Reasoning
Although forward chaining can find the satisfying truth assignment for all hidden triples efficiently, its reasoning ability is severely limited by the coverage of rules, the incompleteness of KGs, and the errors/noise contained in KGs. Considering its strong reasoning ability and robustness, KGE models are not only useful to (1) prepare a more complete KG by adding useful hidden triples but also helpful to (2) eliminate incorrect triples in both KGs and inferred results.

Update the KGE model
Once the KG has been updated by logical reasoning, UniKER updates KGE by (1) treating both observed triples O and the newly inferred triples $\mathbf{v}_H^{T*}$ as positive triples and (2) treating $\mathbf{v}_H^{F*}$ as negative triples to form the objective function of KGE model: Following the margin-based cross entropy loss discussed in Sect. 3.3.5, the new KGE loss can be defined as:

$$- \sum_{\substack{(e_i, r_k, e_j) \\ \in \{O \cup \mathbf{v}_H^{T\,*}\}}} \left(\log \sigma(\gamma + f_{r_k}(e_i, e_j)) + \sum_{\substack{(e_i', r_k, e_j') \\ \in \mathcal{N}(e_i, r_k, e_j)}} \frac{\log \sigma(-f_{r_k}(e_i', e_j') - \gamma)}{|\mathcal{N}(e_i, r_k, e_j)|} \right) \qquad (3.33)$$

where $\mathbf{v}_H^{T\,*}$ denotes the inferred triples derived by forward chaining, (e_i', r_k, e_j') denotes their corresponding negative samples, and γ is a margin to separate them. The score $f_{r_k}(e_i, e_j)$ of a triple (e_i, r_k, e_j) can be calculated following any score functions of KGE models. To reduce the effects of randomness, UniKER samples multiple negative triples for each positive sample, which is denoted as $\mathcal{N}(e_i, r_k, e_j)$. To ensure *True* but unseen triples not be sampled, the selection of $\mathcal{N}(e_i, r_k, e_j)$ is restricted to $\mathbf{v}_H^{F\,*}$.

Update the KG

Now let us discuss how to use the embeddings to efficiently and effectively update the KG, by adding high-quality new triples and removing noisy triples.

(1) Including Potential Useful Hidden Triples ($\Delta+$). A straightforward solution to adding hidden true triples would be computing the score for *every* hidden triple and adding the most promising ones with the highest scores to the KG. Unfortunately, the number of hidden triples is quadratic to the number of entities (i.e. $O(|\mathcal{R}||\mathcal{E}|^2)$), thus it is too expensive to compute scores for all of them. Instead, UniKER adopts the "lazy inference" strategy to select only a small subset of "potentially useful" triples.

Considering the ground rule below:

$$r_0(e_i, e_j) \leftarrow r_1(e_i, e_p) \wedge r_2(e_p, e_q) \wedge r_3(e_q, e_j), \qquad (3.34)$$

if $r_1(e_i, e_p) \in \mathbf{v}_O$, $r_3(e_q, e_j) \in \mathbf{v}_O$, and $r_2(e_p, e_q) \in \mathbf{v}_H$, we would not be able to infer the head $r_0(e_i, e_j)$ as whether $r_2(e_p, e_q)$ is *True* or not is unknown. Thus, $r_2(e_p, e_q)$ becomes the crux to determine the truth value of the head, which is called "potentially useful". In general, given a ground rule whose body includes only one unobserved ground predicate, this unobserved ground predicate can be regarded as a "potentially useful" triple. The set of all "potentially useful" triples is denoted as Δ_+. According to their positions, "potentially useful" triples can be divided into two categories: (1) triples that are the first or the last predicate in a ground rule; and (2) triples that are not in the two ends of the rule (neither the first nor the last).

UniKER identifies both types of "potentially useful" triples as illustrated in Fig. 3.7 by taking the above logical rule (Eq. 3.34) with length 3 as an example. Let every relation r_k in KG associate with an $|E| \times |E|$ matrix $\mathbf{M}^{(k)}$, in which the element $\mathbf{M}_{ij}^{(k)} = 1$ if the triple $(e_i, r_k, e_j) \in O$, and 0 otherwise. The algorithms to identify both types of "potential useful" triples are sketched as follows.

- When the "potential useful" triple is the first or the last predicate in a ground rule, other observed triples in a chain-like definite Horn rule still constitute a complete path, which can be extracted efficiently by sparse matrix multiplication. Take Fig. 3.7c as an

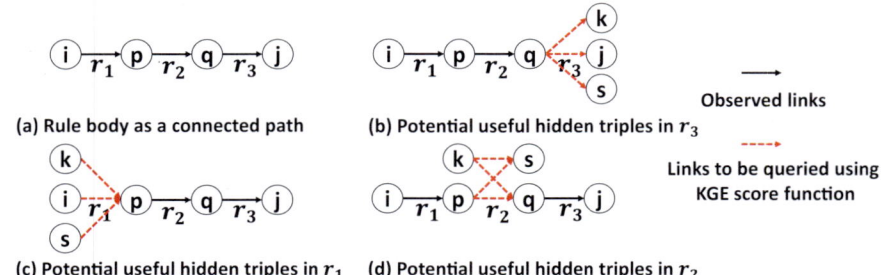

(a) Rule body as a connected path   (b) Potential useful hidden triples in r_3

Observed links

Links to be queried using KGE score function

(c) Potential useful hidden triples in r_1 (d) Potential useful hidden triples in r_2

Fig. 3.7 Illustration of potential useful hidden triples by taking Eq.(3.34) as an example

example, to identify the "potential useful" triple $r_1(e_i, e_p)$, we have to first extract all connected path $r_2(e_p, e_q) \wedge r_3(e_q, e_j)$ by calculating $\mathbf{M} = \mathbf{M}^{(2)}\mathbf{M}^{(3)}$, where $\mathbf{M}^{(2)}$ and $\mathbf{M}^{(3)}$ are adjacency matrices corresponding to relations r_2 and r_3. Each nonzero element $\mathbf{M}_{pj}$ indicates a connected path between e_p and e_j. We denote all indexes correspond to nonzero rows in $\mathbf{M}$ as $\delta = \{p|(\sum_j \mathbf{M}_{pj}) \neq 0\}$, which indicates that there is always a connected path starting at p. For specific $p \in \delta$, $\Delta_p = \{(e_i, r_1, e_p)|e_i \in E\}$ defines a set "potential useful" triples. If (e_i, r_1, e_p) in Δ_p is predicted to be true via KGE, the head predicates $r_0(e_i, e_j)$ can be inferred.

- Otherwise, the path corresponds to the conjunctive body of the ground rule get broken into two paths by the "potential useful" triple, which we have to extract separately. As shown in Fig. 3.7d, when identifying "potential useful" triple $r_2(e_p, e_q) \in v_H$, two paths to be extracted are essentially two single relations r_1 and r_3, whose corresponding matrices are $\mathbf{M}^{(1)}$ and $\mathbf{M}^{(3)}$, respectively. We denote all indexes correspond to nonzero columns in $\mathbf{M}^{(1)}$ as $\delta_1 = \{p|(\sum_i \mathbf{M}^{(1)}_{ip}) \neq 0\}$ and all indexes correspond to nonzero rows in $\mathbf{M}^{(3)}$ as $\delta_2 = \{q|(\sum_j \mathbf{M}^{(3)}_{qj}) \neq 0\}$. $\Delta_{12} = \{(e_p, r_2, e_q)|p \in \delta_1, q \in \delta_2\}$ defines a set "potential useful" triples. If (e_p, r_2, e_q) in Δ_{12} is predicted to be true via KGE, the head predicates $\{r_0(e_i, e_j)|\mathbf{M}^{(1)}_{ip} \neq 0, \mathbf{M}^{(3)}_{qj} \neq 0\}$ can be inferred.

The score $f_{r_k}(e_i, e_j)$ will be computed by KGE model to predict whether a "potentially useful" triple is *True*. If $f_{r_k}(e_i, e_j)$ is larger than the given threshold Ψ, the triple is classified as *True*. Otherwise, the triple is classified as *False*.

(2) Excluding Potential Incorrect Triples ($\Delta-$). In addition, due to their symbolic nature, logical rules cannot handle noisy data as well. If the KGs contain any error, based on incorrect observations, forward chaining will not be able to make the correct inference. Even worse, it may contribute to the propagation of the errors by including incorrectly inferred triples into KGs. Therefore, a clean KG is significant for logical inference. Since KGE models show great power in capturing the network structure of KGs, incorrect triples usually result in contradictions and get lower prediction scores in KGE models compared to correct ones. Therefore, the score $f_{r_k}(e_i, e_j)$ computed by KGE model is able to measure the reliability of triple (e_i, r_k, e_j) in $O \cup \mathbf{V}_H^{T\,*}$. The bottom $\theta\%$ triples with the lowest prediction scores are denoted as Δ_-. It will be excluded from $O \cup \mathbf{V}_H^{T\,*}$ to alleviate the impact of noise.

Algorithm 1: Learning Procedure of UniKER

Input: Observed facts in knowledge bases O; threshold to eliminate noise $\theta\%$; threshold to include useful hidden triples Ψ; a set of definite Horn rules $\mathcal{F}$

Output: KG embeddings

1 **for** $t = 1 : MAX\_ITER$ **do**

2   // **Update KG via Logical Reasoning**

3   Derive $\mathbf{v}_H^{T\,t*}$ from O and update $O \leftarrow O \cup \mathbf{v}_H^{T\,t*}$

4   // **Update KG via Embedding-based Inference**

5   KG embedding learning based on O;

6   Compute Δ_- and update $O \leftarrow O - \Delta_-$;

7   Compute Δ_+ and update $O \leftarrow O \cup \Delta_+$;

8 **end**

3.5.1.3 Integrating Embedding and Logical Rule Reasoning in an Iterative Manner

Since logical rules and KGE can mutually enhance each other, UniKER proposes a unified framework to integrate KGE and definite Horn rules-based inference iteratively. The pseudo-code of UniKER can be found in Algorithm 1. MAX_ITER is the user specified max iterations to run the algorithm, which highly depends on the given KG. UniKER usually sets MAX_ITER as 2 to 4. For each iteration of UniKER, it is comprised of two steps. First, it conducts logical reasoning to update KG. Following forward chaining algorithm, by triggering all rules whose premises are satisfied, UniKER derives entailed triple set $\mathbf{v}_H^{T\,t*}$ at t-th iteration, which is a subset of $\mathbf{v}_H^{T\,*}$ ($\mathbf{v}_H^{T\,*} = \cup_{t=1}^{+\infty} \mathbf{v}_H^{T\,t*}$). Then, the newly inferred triples $\mathbf{v}_H^{T\,t*}$ are added to KG by updating $O = O \cup \mathbf{v}_H^{T\,t*}$. Second, UniKER focuses on embedding-based inference to update KG. KGE is learned based on the updated KG after the first step. With the learned embeddings, Δ_-, which is the bottom $\theta\%$ triples with lowest prediction scores, are eliminated from O. Meanwhile, Δ_+, which are potentially useful hidden triples, are added to O.

3.5.2   Connection to Existing Approaches

We categorize all existing methods according to two aspects: (1) whether they capture mutual interaction between KGE and logical inference; and (2) whether they conduct exact logical inference. The summary is given in Table 3.3. For the first aspect, both embedding-based variational inference to MLN methods and UniKER provide the interaction between

Table 3.3 Comparison of different neuro-symbolic methods for KG completion

Categories	Methods	Interactive	Exact logical inference
Embedding-based	pLogicNet [47]	✓	✕
Variational	ExpressGNN [50]	✓	✕
Inference to MLN	pGAT [51]	✓	✕
Fuzzy logic-based	KALE [54]	✕	✕
Regularization	RUGE [58]	✓	✕
	Rocktäschel et al. [52]	✕	✕
UniKER		✓	✓

embedding and logical inference while most fuzzy logic-based regularization approaches make only a one-time injection of logical rules to enhance embedding. For the second aspect, both embedding-based variational inference to MLN methods and fuzzy logic-based regularization methods follow the framework of fuzzy logic to combine logical rule and KGE, which can only approximate the optimal solution of MAX-SAT problem. UniKER is the first to use forward chaining to conduct exact inference, which provides an optimal solution to the original MAX-SAT problem. The detailed connection between UniKER and both categories of methods is discussed below.

Comparison to Embedding-based Variational Inference to MLN. The general objective of embedding-based variational inference for MLN can be written as:

$$\mathcal{L}_{\text{KGE}}(q_\theta) + \lambda \mathcal{L}_{\text{ELBO}}(q_\theta, p_w) \tag{3.35}$$

where the variational distribution q_θ is defined using a KGE model and p_w is the true posterior defined over MLN. $\mathcal{L}_{\text{KGE}}(q_\theta)$ denotes the loss of the base KGE model. By optimizing $\mathcal{L}_{\text{ELBO}}(q_\theta, p_w)$, the KL divergence between q_θ and p_w can be minimized. In this way, the knowledge contained in rules can be transferred into the embeddings. Due to the nature of the approximate solution provided by variational inference and the information loss caused by the sampling procedure, q_θ can only approximate the optimum of the MAX-SAT problem, and no guarantees are provided on the quality of the solutions obtained. Instead of guiding the learning of the embedding model via variational inference, UniKER directly solves the MAX-SAT problem and use the derived knowledge $\mathbf{v}_H^{T\,*}$ to train the embedding model, which leads to superior reasoning.

Comparison to Fuzzy Logic-based Regularization Approaches. The general objective of fuzzy logic-based regularization approaches can be written as:

$$\mathcal{L}_{\text{KGE}} + \lambda \mathcal{L}_{\text{Logic}} \tag{3.36}$$

where $\mathcal{L}_{\text{KGE}}$ denotes the loss of the base KGE model while $\mathcal{L}_{\text{Logic}}$ corresponds to the satisfaction loss of the sampled ground rules. When we follow Łukasiewicz logic to define

Table 3.4 Comparison of space and time complexity for model training

Method		Space Complexity	Time Complexity	
			Grounding	Embedding
KGE	TransE [17]	$O(n_e d + n_r d)$	–	$O(n_t d)$
	Dismult [23]	$O(n_e d + n_r d)$	–	$O(n_t d)$
Logical	KALE [54]	$O(n_e d + n_r d)$	$O(\theta n_l n_e^{l+1})$	$O(n_t d + \theta n_l n_e^{l+1} d)$
Rule-based	Rocktäschel et al. [52]	$O(n_e d + n_r d + n_e n_r)$	$O(n_l n_e a^l)$	$O(n_e n_r d + n_e d^2 + n_r d^2 + n_l n_e a^l d)$
Regularization	RUGE [58]	$O(n_e d + n_r d)$	$O(\theta n_l n_e^{l+1})$	$O(n_t d + \theta n_l n_e^{l+1} d)$
Our Model	UniKER	$O(n_e d + n_r d)$	$O(n_l n_e a^l)$	$O(n_t d + n_l n_e a^l d)$

the satisfaction loss and incorporate all ground rules into the calculation of $\mathcal{L}_{\text{Logic}}$, $\mathcal{L}_{\text{Logic}}$ becomes a convex program that reasons over a relaxed version of the MAX-SAT problem, as previously discussed in Sect. 3.2.3.2, which only approximates the exact logical inference. Instead, UniKER solves the MAX-SAT problem exactly using forward chaining, thanks to the definite Horn rules. The better exploitation of logical rules lead to better KG and thus more powerful KGE and thus logical reasoning itself. Moreover, $\mathcal{L}_{\text{Logic}}$ makes only a one-time injection of logical rules to enhance embedding, where logical reasoning will not be further enhanced even after the KGE gets improved. On the contrary, UniKER is able to capture the interactive nature between embedding and logical inference.

Theoretical Computational Complexity Analysis of UniKER. To theoretically demonstrate the superiority of our proposed UniKER in terms of efficiency, we compare the space and time complexity of UniKER and other methods that combine KG embedding and logical rules. More precisely, we focus solely on logical rule-based regularization approaches as the complexity of embedding-based variational inference for MLN can vary widely and is heavily dependent on the number of iterations needed to achieve convergence. Obviously, they have a much higher computational cost than UniKER does. As both logical rule-based regularization approaches and UniKER consists of two parts, grounding logical rules and embedding learning, we include the complexity of both parts in Table 3.4. Note that grounding only contributes to the time complexity without affecting space complexity. Let n_e denote the number of entities, n_r denote the number of relations, and n_t denote the number of observed triples; additionally, let l represent the length of the rule body, n_l denote the number of template rules, and θ represent the sampling ratio; finally, let a denote the average degree of entities and d represent the dimension of the embedding space. We can see that: (1) For space complexity, UniKER is the same as other logical rule-based regularization

Table 3.5 Data statistics

Dataset	Type	#Entity	#Relation	#Triple	#Rule
Family	Family network	3007	12	28356	41
FB15k-237	Freebase knowledge	14541	237	310116	300
WN18RR	Lexical network	40943	11	93003	11

approaches; (2) For time complexity, considering $a \ll n_e$, if the sampling ratio is not small enough, UniKER is much smaller than other logical rule-based regularization approaches.

3.5.3   Experiments

3.5.3.1 Experimental Setup

Datasets. UniKER conducts experiments on three real-world KGs (i.e., Family [61], FB15k-237 [17] and WN18RR [17]). The input logical rules are generated by AMIE+ [62] automatically. The detailed statistics of these KGs are provided in Table 3.5. FB15K237 and WN18RR are the most widely used large-scale benchmark datasets for KGE models, which do not suffer from test triple leakage in the training set. The Family dataset is selected due to better interpretability and high intuitiveness.

   Compared Methods. UniKER is evaluated against SOTA algorithms, including (1) basic KGE models (e.g., RESCAL [22], SimplE [25], HypER [63], TuckER [64], TransE [17], DistMult [23] and RotatE [21]), (2) traditional logical rule-based methods (e.g., MLN [7] and BLP [65]), (3) two classes of approaches combining embedding model with logical rules (two representative methods KALE [54] and RUGE [58] for PSL-based regularization approaches, and pLogicNet [47], ExpressGNN [50] and pGAT [51] for embedding-based variational inference of MLN), and (4) other approaches to combining embedding model with logical rules (e.g., BoxE [66]). To show that UniKER can be easily adapted to various KGE models, TransE [17], DistMult [23], and RotatE [21] are chosen as the base models for UniKER.

   Evaluation Metrics. To compare the reasoning ability of UniKER and the aforementioned baseline algorithms, UniKER masks the head or tail entity of each test triple, and requires each method to predict the masked entity. During the evaluation, UniKER uses the filtered setting [17][3] and three evaluation metrics, i.e., Hit@1, Hit@10, and MRR. Hit@k

---

[3] Although test triples and training triples have no overlap, it is still possible that a test triple and a training triple share head and relation (or relation and tail). It is possible that the model predicts the entity where the entire triple is seen in the training, which should be correct but unfortunately will

measures the proportion of test triples for which the correct head or tail entity is ranked among the top k predictions made by the model. For example, Hit@1 measures whether the correct answer is ranked at the very top of the list of predicted answers, while Hit@10 measures whether the correct answer is ranked within the top 10 predicted answers. MRR measures the average reciprocal rank of the correct entity among all the ranked entities for each test triple, where the reciprocal rank is 1/rank.

The dataset is partitioned randomly into a training set and a test set with a 8:2 ratio. In order to show the reasoning also benefit from KGE, any triples that can be directly inferred from the training set via logical rule reasoning are deliberately left out of the test set. To fairly compare all baseline methods, this same setting is consistently applied to all of them. We compare different algorithms on the KG inference task.

3.5.3.2 Results on KG Completion Task

To compare different algorithms on the KG completion task, we mask the head or tail entity of each test triple and require each method to predict the masked entity. The results of BLP, MLN, and pLogicNet are taken from the original papers that are summarized in [47]. As the results are only reported on the FB15k-237 and WN18RR datasets for these baselines, we compare UniKER with them on these two datasets.

Table 3.6 shows the comparison results, from which we find that: (1) UniKER outperforms KGE models in most cases with significant performance gain, which is due to the utilization of additional knowledge from logical rules; (2) UniKER also achieves better performance than existing two classes of approaches that combine the embedding model with logical rules as it provides an exact optimal solution to a satisfiable problem defined over all ground rules rather than employing sampling strategies to do approximation.

3.5.3.3 Efficiency Analysis

Besides the promising results on KG reasoning, our UniKER is superior in terms of efficiency. We have theoretically analyzed the computational complexity of UniKER in Sect. 3.5.2. Learning procedure for UniKER consists of two components, (1) finding the optimal truth assignment problem defined over all ground Horn rules using forward chaining algorithm and (2) optimize the embedding model according to the optimal truth assignment. The efficiency of forward chaining highly depends on KG datasets. Thus, we provide a further investigation of the scalability of forward chaining on real-world datasets in this section. Note that forward chaining learns the optimal truth assignment for the satisfiable problem iteratively, the number of iterations required to achieve the optimal solution may influence its scalability. To compare the scalability of forward chaining against a number of SOTA (State-Of-The-Art) inference algorithms for MLN, three small-scale datasets (e.g.,

---

be considered as false as it is not included in the test. In the filtered setting, any entity that appears in the training set is removed from the candidate entities to rank to avoid this issue.

Table 3.6 Effectiveness on KG completion task

Model	Family			FB15k-237			WN18RR		
	Hit@1	Hit@10	MRR	Hit@1	Hit@10	MRR	Hit@1	Hit@10	MRR
RESCAL	0.489	0.894	0.639	0.108	0.322	0.179	0.123	0.239	0.162
SimplE	0.335	0.888	0.528	0.150	0.443	0.249	0.290	0.351	0.311
HypER[†]	0.364	0.903	0.551	0.252	0.520	0.341	0.436	0.522	0.465
TuckER[†]	0.373	0.898	0.567	0.266	0.544	0.358	**0.443**	0.526	0.470
BLP[†]	–	–	–	0.062	0.150	0.092	0.187	0.358	0.254
MLN	0.655	0.732	0.694	0.067	0.160	0.098	0.191	0.361	0.259
Forward Chaining[‡]	**0.919**	0.919	0.919	**0.586**	0.586	**0.586**	0.323	0.323	0.323
KALE	0.433	0.869	0.598	0.131	0.424	0.230	0.032	0.353	0.172
RUGE	0.495	0.962	0.677	0.098	0.376	0.191	0.251	0.327	0.280
ExpressGNN	0.105	0.282	0.164	0.150	0.317	0.207	0.036	0.093	0.054
pLogicNet	0.683	0.874	0.768	0.261	0.567	0.364	0.301	0.410	0.340
pGAT[†]	–	–	–	0.377	0.609	0.457	0.395	0.578	0.459
BoxE[†]	–	–	–	–	0.538	0.337	–	0.541	0.451
TransE	0.221	0.874	0.453	0.231	0.527	0.330	0.007	0.406	0.165
UniKER-TransE	0.873	**0.971**	0.916	0.463	**0.630**	0.522	0.040	0.561	0.307
DistMult	0.360	0.885	0.543	0.220	0.486	0.308	0.304	0.409	0.338
UniKER-DistMult	0.770	0.945	0.823	0.507	0.587	0.533	0.432	0.538	0.485
RotatE	0.787	0.933	0.862	0.237	0.526	0.334	0.421	0.563	0.469
UniKER-RotatE	0.886	**0.971**	**0.924**	0.495	0.612	0.539	0.437	**0.580**	**0.492**

[†] Results on FB15k-237 and WN18RR are taken from the original papers
[‡] Forwarding chaining assigns either 1 or 0 to triples, thus ranking is degenerated to whether the entities with score 1 is correct

RC1000, sub-YAGO3-10, and sub-Family) are included in our experiments due to the high time complexity of the MLN inference algorithms. The RC1000 dataset is a commonly used benchmark dataset for inference in MLN, while sub-Family and sub-YAGO3-10 are subsets of the Family and YAGO3-10 datasets, respectively. We first conduct two experiments on the datasets. (1) As presented in Fig. 3.8, we record the proportion of inferred triples accumulated in every iteration over all inferred triples. The result shows that forward chaining can achieve the optimal solution within 12 iterations and infer over 70% correct triples within only 4 iterations. (2) We evaluate the scalability of forward chaining against a number of SOTA inference algorithms for MLN (e.g., MCMC [9], MC-SAT [67], BP [12], liftedBP [11] and Tuffy [68]). Forward chaining runs $100 - 100, 000$ times faster than them.

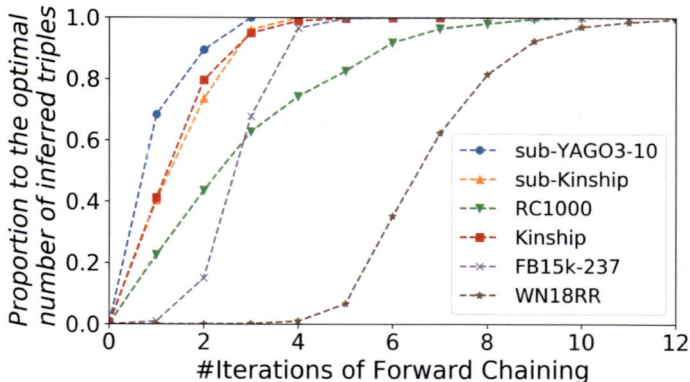

Fig. 3.8 Proportion to the optimal number of inferred triples w.r.t. #iterations for efficiency analysis of Forward Chaining

Table 3.7 Efficiency Analysis on Family Dataset

Model	Time per Epoch	#Epochs for Convergence
KALE	>1000 s	500
RUGE	>1000 s	800
ExpressGNN	168 s	200
pLogicNet	7.2 s	600
UniKER-TransE	6.5 s	400

Some widely used algorithms MCMC and MC-SAT cannot even handle RC1000 dataset, which indicates the scalability of UniKER.

Then, we compare the overall run time of our proposed UniKER with other methods. As shown in Table 3.7, UniKER, which is able to conduct exact logical inference, is still faster than other neuro-symbolic methods.

3.5.3.4 Mutual Enhancement Between KGE and Logical Inference

We have further investigated the potential benefits brought by the mutual interaction between KGE and logical inference.

- **Enhancement of Logical Inference via KGE**. On one hand, high-quality embedding learned by KGE models is useful to prepare more complete KGs via including useful hidden triples, which the performance of logical inference highly depends on. To show the benefit brought by KGE over logical inference, we evaluate UniKER-TransE against forward chaining on Family Dataset with the triple classification task, which aims to predict correct facts in the testing data. In order to create a testing set for classification, we

Table 3.8 UniKER-TransE versus Forward Chaining on Family dataset (whose test set only retains triples that can be inferred by logical rules) on triple *True/False* classification task

Model	Precision	Recall	F1
Forward Chaining	**1.000**	0.919	0.958
UniKER-TransE	0.991	**0.955**	**0.973**

Table 3.9 Results of reasoning of UniKER-TransE versus TransE on Family dataset (whose test set eliminates triples that can derive from logical rules)

Model	Hit@1	Hit@3	Hit@10	MRR
TransE	0.267	0.651	0.803	0.476
UniKER-TransE	**0.710**	**0.866**	**0.904**	**0.816**

randomly corrupt relations of correct testing triplets for negative triples construction. It results in a total of $2 \times$ #Test triplets with an equal number of positive and negative examples. During the evaluation, we adopt three evaluation metrics, i.e., precision, recall, and F1. As shown in Table 3.8, we can observe that although the precision slightly decreases, UniKER outperforms forward chaining with significant performance gain in terms of recall and F1, which validates the enhancement brought by the KGE model over logical inference.

- **Enhancement of KGE via Logical Inference**. On the other hand, logical rules are useful to gather more reliable triples for KGE by exploiting the symbolic compositionality of KG relations, which leads to the enhancement of the reasoning ability of the KGE model. To investigate the added value brought by logical rules over KGE, we evaluate UniKER-TransE against TransE on the Family dataset on the KG completion task. As some triples in the test dataset can be directly derived from logical rules, to ensure the improvement comes from the reasoning ability enhancement of the KGE model, we exclude the triples derived directly from rules from the test data. As presented in Table 3.9, we can observe that UniKER-TransE outperforms the TransE model with huge performance gain, especially in terms of Hit@1, which can be ascribed to the added value brought by logical rules over KGE.

3.6   Summary and Discussions

Knowledge graph (KG) completion refers to the task of predicting missing or incomplete information in a knowledge graph. Symbolic methods and neural methods are two broad categories of approaches used for KG completion.

Symbolic methods rely on logical reasoning and rule-based approaches to infer new facts based on existing ones. One of the main advantages of symbolic methods is that they can be easily interpreted and validated by human experts. However, symbolic methods have limited scalability and they struggle to capture complex patterns in the data, as logical rules may not be able to cover all possible cases.

On the other hand, neural methods use neural networks to learn representations of entities and relations in the KG and use these representations to predict missing links. Neural methods have the advantage of being able to learn complex and non-linear patterns in the data. However, they are also difficult to interpret and validate and may require large amounts of data and computational resources.

Neuro-symbolic methods aim to combine the strengths of symbolic and neural methods by integrating logical reasoning and representation learning. These methods typically use neural networks to learn representations of entities and relations and use logical rules or constraints to guide the learning process. This allows neuro-symbolic methods to leverage the interpretability of symbolic methods, while also benefiting from the learning capabilities of neural methods.

However, neuro-symbolic methods are still an early area of research, and their effectiveness for KG completion is still being explored. For example, although there have been attempts to integrate neural and symbolic methods using probabilistic programming frameworks, scalability issues have limited their effectiveness. To overcome these limitations, the UniKER algorithm has been introduced as a cutting-edge method that successfully combines symbolic reasoning and representation learning to tackle KG completion tasks.

We will only be able to cover the main approaches for KG completion due to space constraints. It is worth noting that there are other promising directions in this area, which are discussed below.

Path-based KG Completion
Path-based methods concentrate on discovering paths between entities in a KG and use the existence or absence of specific paths to predict missing links. The reasoning paths found by path-based KG completion methods inherently provide an interpretable basis for their predictions. Representative works in this domain can be broadly categorized into traditional *path ranking algorithm* and recent *reinforcement learning-based methods*.

- **Path Ranking Algorithm**: The Path Ranking Algorithm is an early approach that employs random walks to generate paths between entities. It then ranks these paths as features for a binary classifier to predict missing links in KG. Although the method is simple, it relies on random walks to generate paths between entities, which can be computationally intensive, particularly for large-scale KGs with millions of nodes and edges. Notable methods in this category include Path Ranking Algorithm (PRA) [69], and its extensions such as Path-RNN [70] and Chains of reasoning [71].
- **Reinforcement Learning Based Methods**: Since enumerating all possible relation paths is impractical, reinforcement learning-based methods have been proposed to avoid enu-

merating all possible relation paths in the KB by searching within a small neighborhood around the query entity. The most representative methods in this category include: Deep-Path [72], MINERVA [73], MWalk [74] and MultiHop [75].

References

1. K. Cheng, Z. Yang, M. Zhang, and Y. Sun. Uniker: A unified framework for combining embedding and definite horn rule reasoning for knowledge graph inference. In *Proceedings of the Conference on Empirical Methods in Natural Language Processing (EMNLP)*, 2021.
2. J. Graupmann, R. Schenkel, and G. Weikum. The SphereSearch engine for unified ranked retrieval of heterogeneous XML and web documents. In *Proceedings of the 31st VLDB*, pages 529–540. VLDB Endowment, 2005.
3. D. Lukovnikov, A. Fischer, J. Lehmann, and S. Auer. Neural network-based question answering over knowledge graphs on word and character level. In *Proceedings of the International World Wide Web Conference (WWW)*, pages 1211–1220. International World Wide Web Conferences Steering Committee, 2017.
4. C. Xiong, R. Power, and J. Callan. Explicit semantic ranking for academic search via knowledge graph embedding. In *Proceedings of the International World Wide Web Conference (WWW)*, pages 1271–1279. International World Wide Web Conferences Steering Committee, 2017.
5. S. W.-t. Yih, M.-W. Chang, X. He, and J. Gao. Semantic parsing via staged query graph generation: Question answering with knowledge base. In *Proceedings of the Joint Conference of the 53rd Annual Meeting of the ACL and the 7th International Joint Conference on Natural Language Processing of the AFNLP*, 2015.
6. C. H. Papadimitriou. Computational complexity. In *Encyclopedia of computer science*, pages 260–265. 2003.
7. M. Richardson and P. Domingos. Markov logic networks. *Machine learning*, 62(1-2):107–136, 2006.
8. M. J. Wainwright, M. I. Jordan, et al. Graphical models, exponential families, and variational inference. *Foundations and Trends® in Machine Learning*, 1(1–2):1–305, 2008.
9. C. M. Carlo. Markov chain monte carlo and gibbs sampling. *Lecture notes for EEB*, 581, 2004.
10. H. Poon, P. M. Domingos, and M. Sumner. A general method for reducing the complexity of relational inference and its application to mcmc. In *Proceedings of AAAI Conference on Artificial Intelligence (AAAI)*, volume 8, pages 1075–1080. Chicago, IL, 2008.
11. P. Singla and P. M. Domingos. Lifted first-order belief propagation. In *Proceedings of AAAI Conference on Artificial Intelligence (AAAI)*, volume 8, pages 1094–1099, 2008.
12. J. S. Yedidia, W. T. Freeman, and Y. Weiss. Generalized belief propagation. In *Advances in Neural Information Processing Systems (NeurIPS)*, pages 689–695, 2001.
13. J. Besag. Statistical analysis of non-lattice data. *Journal of the Royal Statistical Society Series D: The Statistician*, 24(3):179–195, 1975.
14. S. H. Bach, M. Broecheler, B. Huang, and L. Getoor. Hinge-loss markov random fields and probabilistic soft logic. *Journal of Machine Learning Research*, 2017.
15. P. Hájek. *Metamathematics of fuzzy logic*, volume 4. Springer Science & Business Media, 2013.
16. Q. Wang, Z. Mao, B. Wang, and L. Guo. Knowledge graph embedding: A survey of approaches and applications. *IEEE Transactions on Knowledge and Data Engineering*, 29(12):2724–2743, 2017.

17. A. Bordes, N. Usunier, A. Garcia-Duran, J. Weston, and O. Yakhnenko. Translating embeddings for modeling multi-relational data. In *Advances in Neural Information Processing Systems (NeurIPS)*, pages 2787–2795, 2013.

18. Z. Wang, J. Zhang, J. Feng, and Z. Chen. Knowledge graph embedding by translating on hyperplanes. In *Proceedings of AAAI Conference on Artificial Intelligence (AAAI)*, pages 1112–1119. AAAI Press, 2014.

19. Y. Lin, Z. Liu, M. Sun, Y. Liu, and X. Zhu. Learning entity and relation embeddings for knowledge graph completion. In *Proceedings of AAAI Conference on Artificial Intelligence (AAAI)*, 2015.

20. G. Ji, S. He, L. Xu, K. Liu, and J. Zhao. Knowledge graph embedding via dynamic mapping matrix. In *Proceedings of the Annual Meeting of Associations for Computational Linguistics (ACL)*, pages 687–696. The Association for Computer Linguistics, 2015.

21. Z. Sun, Z.-H. Deng, J.-Y. Nie, and J. Tang. Rotate: Knowledge graph embedding by relational rotation in complex space. In *International Conference on Learning Representations (ICLR)*, 2018.

22. M. Nickel, V. Tresp, and H.-P. Kriegel. A three-way model for collective learning on multi-relational data. In *International Conference on Machine Learning (ICML)*, pages 809–816. Omnipress, 2011.

23. B. Yang, W.-t. Yih, X. He, J. Gao, and L. Deng. Embedding entities and relations for learning and inference in knowledge bases. *arXiv preprint* arXiv:1412.6575, 2014.

24. T. Trouillon, J. Welbl, S. Riedel, É. Gaussier, and G. Bouchard. Complex embeddings for simple link prediction. In *International Conference on Machine Learning (ICML)*, pages 2071–2080, 2016.

25. S. M. Kazemi and D. Poole. Simple embedding for link prediction in knowledge graphs. In *Advances in Neural Information Processing Systems (NeurIPS)*, pages 4284–4295, 2018.

26. M. Nickel, L. Rosasco, T. A. Poggio, et al. Holographic embeddings of knowledge graphs. In *Proceedings of AAAI Conference on Artificial Intelligence (AAAI)*, pages 1955–1961. AAAI Press, 2016.

27. H. Liu, Y. Wu, and Y. Yang. Analogical inference for multi-relational embeddings. In *International Conference on Machine Learning (ICML)*, pages 2168–2178. PMLR, 2017.

28. Y. LeCun, Y. Bengio, et al. Convolutional networks for images, speech, and time series. *The handbook of brain theory and neural networks*, 3361(10):1995, 1995.

29. M. Schuster and K. K. Paliwal. Bidirectional recurrent neural networks. *IEEE transactions on Signal Processing*, 45(11):2673–2681, 1997.

30. A. Vaswani, N. Shazeer, N. Parmar, J. Uszkoreit, L. Jones, A. N. Gomez, Ł. Kaiser, and I. Polosukhin. Attention is all you need. *Advances in Neural Information Processing Systems (NeurIPS)*, 30, 2017.

31. T. N. Kipf and M. Welling. Semi-supervised classification with graph convolutional networks. *arXiv preprint* arXiv:1609.02907, 2016.

32. X. Dong, E. Gabrilovich, G. Heitz, W. Horn, N. Lao, K. Murphy, T. Strohmann, S. Sun, and W. Zhang. Knowledge vault: A web-scale approach to probabilistic knowledge fusion. In *Proceedings of the ACM SIGKDD International Conference on Knowledge Discovery and Data Mining (KDD)*, pages 601–610, 2014.

33. R. Socher, D. Chen, C. D. Manning, and A. Ng. Reasoning with neural tensor networks for knowledge base completion. In *Advances in Neural Information Processing Systems (NIPS)*, 2013.

34. T. Dettmers, P. Minervini, P. Stenetorp, and S. Riedel. Convolutional 2d knowledge graph embeddings. In *Proceedings of AAAI Conference on Artificial Intelligence (AAAI)*, 2018.

35. D. Q. Nguyen, T. D. Nguyen, D. Q. Nguyen, and D. Phung. A novel embedding model for knowledge base completion based on convolutional neural network. *arXiv preprint* arXiv:1712.02121, 2017.
36. X. Jiang, Q. Wang, and B. Wang. Adaptive convolution for multi-relational learning. In *Proceedings of the Conference of the North American Chapter of the Association for Computational Linguistics: Human Language Technologies (NAACL-HLT)*, pages 978–987, 2019.
37. S. Vashishth, S. Sanyal, V. Nitin, N. Agrawal, and P. Talukdar. Interacte: Improving convolution-based knowledge graph embeddings by increasing feature interactions. In *Proceedings of AAAI Conference on Artificial Intelligence (AAAI)*, volume 34, pages 3009–3016, 2020.
38. L. Guo, Z. Sun, and W. Hu. Learning to exploit long-term relational dependencies in knowledge graphs. In *International Conference on Machine Learning (ICML)*, pages 2505–2514. PMLR, 2019.
39. Q. Wang, P. Huang, H. Wang, S. Dai, W. Jiang, J. Liu, Y. Lyu, Y. Zhu, and H. Wu. Coke: Contextualized knowledge graph embedding. *arXiv preprint* arXiv:1911.02168, 2019.
40. J. Devlin, M.-W. Chang, K. Lee, and K. Toutanova. Bert: Pre-training of deep bidirectional transformers for language understanding. *arXiv preprint* arXiv:1810.04805, 2018.
41. Z. Wu, S. Pan, F. Chen, G. Long, C. Zhang, and S. Y. Philip. A comprehensive survey on graph neural networks. *IEEE Transactions on Neural Networks and Learning Systems*, 32(1):4–24, 2020.
42. M. Schlichtkrull, T. N. Kipf, P. Bloem, R. Van Den Berg, I. Titov, and M. Welling. Modeling relational data with graph convolutional networks. In *The Semantic Web: 15th International Conference*, pages 593–607. Springer, 2018.
43. C. Shang, Y. Tang, J. Huang, J. Bi, X. He, and B. Zhou. End-to-end structure-aware convolutional networks for knowledge base completion. In *Proceedings of AAAI Conference on Artificial Intelligence (AAAI)*, volume 33, pages 3060–3067, 2019.
44. I. Goodfellow, J. Pouget-Abadie, M. Mirza, B. Xu, D. Warde-Farley, S. Ozair, A. Courville, and Y. Bengio. Generative adversarial networks. *Communications of the ACM*, 63(11):139–144, 2020.
45. L. Cai and W. Y. Wang. Kbgan: Adversarial learning for knowledge graph embeddings. In *Proceedings of the 2018 Conference of the North American Chapter of the Association for Computational Linguistics: Human Language Technologies (NAACL-HLT)*, pages 1470–1480, 2018.
46. D. M. Blei, A. Kucukelbir, and J. D. McAuliffe. Variational inference: A review for statisticians. *Journal of the American statistical Association*, 112(518):859–877, 2017.
47. M. Qu and J. Tang. Probabilistic logic neural networks for reasoning. In *Advances in Neural Information Processing Systems (NeurIPS)*, pages 7710–7720, 2019.
48. R. M. Neal and G. E. Hinton. A view of the em algorithm that justifies incremental, sparse, and other variants. In *Learning in Graphical Models*, pages 355–368. Springer, 1998.
49. M. D. Hoffman, D. M. Blei, C. Wang, and J. Paisley. Stochastic variational inference. *Journal of Machine Learning Research*, 2013.
50. Y. Zhang, X. Chen, Y. Yang, A. Ramamurthy, B. Li, Y. Qi, and L. Song. Can graph neural networks help logic reasoning? *arXiv preprint* arXiv:1906.02111, 2019.
51. L. V. Harsha Vardhan, G. Jia, and S. Kok. Probabilistic logic graph attention networks for reasoning. In *Companion Proceedings of the Web Conference 2020*, pages 669–673, 2020.
52. T. Rocktäschel, S. Singh, and S. Riedel. Injecting logical background knowledge into embeddings for relation extraction. In *Proceedings of the Conference of the North American Chapter of the Association for Computational Linguistics: Human Language Technologies (NAACL-HLT)*, pages 1119–1129, 2015.

53. M. Collins, S. Dasgupta, and R. E. Schapire. A generalization of principal components analysis to the exponential family. In *Advances in Neural Information Processing Systems (NeurIPS)*, volume 13, page 23, 2001.

54. S. Guo, Q. Wang, L. Wang, B. Wang, and L. Guo. Jointly embedding knowledge graphs and logical rules. In *Proceedings of the Conference on Empirical Methods in Natural Language Processing (EMNLP)*, pages 192–202, 2016.

55. X. Chen, M. Chen, W. Shi, Y. Sun, and C. Zaniolo. Embedding uncertain knowledge graphs. In *Proceedings of AAAI Conference on Artificial Intelligence (AAAI)*, pages 3363–3370. AAAI Press, 2019.

56. T. Demeester, T. Rocktäschel, and S. Riedel. Lifted rule injection for relation embeddings. *arXiv preprint* arXiv:1606.08359, 2016.

57. S. Rendle, C. Freudenthaler, Z. Gantner, and L. Schmidt-Thieme. Bpr: Bayesian personalized ranking from implicit feedback. *arXiv preprint* arXiv:1205.2618, 2012.

58. S. Guo, Q. Wang, L. Wang, B. Wang, and L. Guo. Knowledge graph embedding with iterative guidance from soft rules. In *Proceedings of AAAI Conference on Artificial Intelligence (AAAI)*, volume 32, 2018.

59. A. Horn. On sentences which are true of direct unions of algebras1. *The Journal of Symbolic Logic*, 16(1):14–21, 1951.

60. E. Salvat and M.-L. Mugnier. Sound and complete forward and backward chainings of graph rules. In *International Conference on Conceptual Structures*, pages 248–262. Springer, 1996.

61. W. W. Denham. *The detection of patterns in Alyawara nonverbal behavior*. PhD thesis, University of Washington, Seattle., 1973.

62. L. Galárraga, C. Teflioudi, K. Hose, and F. M. Suchanek. Fast rule mining in ontological knowledge bases with amie+. *The VLDB Journal*, 24(6):707–730, 2015.

63. I. Balažević, C. Allen, and T. M. Hospedales. Hypernetwork knowledge graph embeddings. In *International Conference on Artificial Neural Networks*, pages 553–565. Springer, 2019.

64. I. Balažević, C. Allen, and T. M. Hospedales. Tucker: Tensor factorization for knowledge graph completion. *arXiv preprint* arXiv:1901.09590, 2019.

65. L. De Raedt and K. Kersting. Probabilistic inductive logic programming. In *Probabilistic Inductive Logic Programming*, pages 1–27. Springer, 2008.

66. R. Abboud, I. Ceylan, T. Lukasiewicz, and T. Salvatori. Boxe: A box embedding model for knowledge base completion. *Advances in Neural Information Processing Systems (NeurIPS)*, 33:9649–9661, 2020.

67. H. Poon and P. Domingos. Sound and efficient inference with probabilistic and deterministic dependencies. In *Proceedings of AAAI Conference on Artificial Intelligence (AAAI)*, volume 6, pages 458–463, 2006.

68. F. Niu, C. Ré, A. Doan, and J. Shavlik. Tuffy: Scaling up statistical inference in markov logic networks using an rdbms. *Proceedings of the VLDB Endowment*, 4(6):373–384, 2011.

69. N. Lao, T. Mitchell, and W. Cohen. Random walk inference and learning in a large scale knowledge base. In *Proceedings of the Conference on Empirical Methods in Natural Language Processing (EMNLP)*, pages 529–539, 2011.

70. A. Neelakantan, B. Roth, and A. McCallum. Compositional vector space models for knowledge base completion. *arXiv preprint* arXiv:1504.06662, 2015.

71. R. Das, A. Neelakantan, D. Belanger, and A. McCallum. Chains of reasoning over entities, relations, and text using recurrent neural networks. *arXiv preprint* arXiv:1607.01426, 2016.

72. W. Xiong, T. Hoang, and W. Y. Wang. Deeppath: A reinforcement learning method for knowledge graph reasoning. *arXiv preprint* arXiv:1707.06690, 2017.

73. R. Das, S. Dhuliawala, M. Zaheer, L. Vilnis, I. Durugkar, A. Krishnamurthy, A. Smola, and A. McCallum. Go for a walk and arrive at the answer: Reasoning over paths in knowledge bases

using reinforcement learning. In *International Conference on Learning Representations (ICLR)*, 2017.

74. Y. Shen, J. Chen, P.-S. Huang, Y. Guo, and J. Gao. M-walk: Learning to walk over graphs using monte carlo tree search. *Advances in Neural Information Processing Systems (NeurIPS)*, 31, 2018.

75. X. V. Lin, R. Socher, and C. Xiong. Multi-hop knowledge graph reasoning with reward shaping. *arXiv preprint* arXiv:1808.10568, 2018.

Complex Query Answering

4

"It is not the answer that enlightens, but the question." —*Eugene Ionesco*

4.1 Overview

In the preceding chapter, we provided a summary of the state-of-the-art approaches for KG completion, which primarily focus on answering one-hop queries. However, these methods cannot handle complex queries, which hinders their applicability in more sophisticated reasoning tasks. For instance, one-hop KG completion is insufficient for answering questions such as "Which universities did the Turing Award winners in the field of deep learning work at?" due to the involvement of multiple relations between entities.

First-Order Logic (FOL) offers a rich and expressive language for representing complex relations between entities in a KG. For instance, the above question "Which universities did the Turing Award winners in the field of deep learning work at?" can be expressed as the First-Order Logical (FOL) query, as shown below:

$$V_? : \exists V \ \text{Win}^{-1}(\text{Turing Award}, V) \ \wedge \ \text{Field}^{-1}(\text{Deep Learning}, V) \ \wedge \ \text{University}(V, V_?) \tag{4.1}$$

In general, FOL queries contain *target variables*, denoted as $V_?$, and several *bound variables*, denoted as $V_1, \ldots, V_k$, which are all entities in KG. In the above example, $V_?$ is the single target variable and V is the only bound variable bounded by the existential quantifier. The goal of the query is to find a set of entities such that when grounding the target variable with these entities, the FOL defined in the query can be satisfied. Formally, a frequently used FOL query can be defined below.

K. Cheng and Y. Sun, *Knowledge Graph Reasoning*, Synthesis Lectures on Data, Semantics, and Knowledge, https://doi.org/10.1007/978-3-031-72008-6_4

Definition 4.1 (*First-order Logic Queries*) FOL queries are expressed with existential quantifier ($\exists$), logical connectors including conjunction ($\wedge$), disjunction ($\vee$), and negation ($\neg$). Under the disjuctive normal form (DNF) representation, an FOL query q can be defined in the form:

$$q[V_?] := V_? : \exists V_1, \ldots, V_k \; c_1 \vee c_2 \vee \ldots \vee c_n$$

where $c_i (1 \leq i \leq n)$ denotes ith conjunctive clause. Each literal in these conjunctive clauses has the form of $r(e, V)$, $\neg r(e, V)$, $r(V, V')$ or $\neg r(V, V')$, where $r \in \mathcal{R}$ denote a relation in KG, $e \in \mathcal{E}$ is an entity, and V and V' denote either target variable or bound variables.

There are several types of more restrictive and thus simpler FOL queries, which are briefly defined below.

Definition 4.2 (*Conjunctive Queries*) Conjunctive queries are a special case of FOL queries that involve only existential quantifier ($\exists$) and conjunction ($\wedge$):

$$q[V_?] := V_? : \exists V_1, \ldots, V_k \; P_1 \wedge P_2 \wedge \ldots \wedge P_n$$

where $P_i (1 \leq i \leq n)$ denotes the ith atomic formula (a.k.a. a positive literal). Each atomic formula is in the form of $r(e, V)$ or $r(V, V')$, where $r \in \mathcal{R}$ denotes a relation in KG, $e \in \mathcal{E}$ is an entity, and V and V' denote either target variable or bound variables.

The query of Eq. 4.1 is an example of conjuctive query.

Definition 4.3 (*Existential Positive First-Order (EPFO) Queries*) EPFO queries extends conjuctive queries by including disjuction operator $\vee$, which is another special case of FOL queries:

$$q[V_?] := V_? : \exists V_1, \ldots, V_k \; c_1 \vee c_2 \vee \ldots \vee c_n$$

where $c_i (1 \leq i \leq n)$ denotes ith conjunctive clause with only positive literals. In other words, each literal in these conjunctive clauses has the form of $r(e, V)$ or $r(V, V')$, where $r \in \mathcal{R}$ denote a relation in KG, $e \in \mathcal{E}$ is an entity, and V and V' denote either target variable or bound variables.

The utilization of First-Order Logic (FOL) in query formulation offers significant flexibility. It allows for more expressive and richer queries, involving multiple predicates, variables, and nested subqueries, thereby enabling users to define a broader range of queries in different use cases. As a result, the development of advanced techniques to effectively handle complex queries formulated in FOL becomes crucial.

Two popular approaches for complex query answering in KG are (1) *traditional* subgraph matching-based methods, and (2) *recent* logical query-embedding methods.

- **Subgraph matching-based methods**: They rely on search algorithms to find a subgraph within a KG that corresponds to a specified query.
- **Logical query-embedding methods**: They turn a FOL query into a vector in an embedding space and search entities in the KG with a similar embedding.

In the following sections, we will introduce the most representative methods in each category and discuss their pros and cons.

4.2   Subgraph Matching-Based Query Answering

Subgraph matching-based methods are the most traditional approaches to answering complex queries, especially conjunctive queries. They aim to identify subgraphs within the KG that match a given query pattern. For example, the question "Which Universities did the Turing Award winners in the field of deep learning work at?" can be expressed as a query graph in Fig. 4.1. To answer this question, we can use subgraph matching methods to find subgraphs in a KG that match the query graph in Fig. 4.1, where the query graph specifies the entities and desired relations between entities.

4.2.1   Overview of Subgraph Matching-Based Methods

Subgraph matching-based methods are used to answer queries in a knowledge graph by finding a subgraph that matches the structure of the query. Here is a general step-by-step process:

- **Query Formulation**: The initial step involves constructing a **query graph** Q to the query. This involves identifying the nodes (entities) and edges (relationships) from the query. For conjunctive queries, each atomic formula ($r(e, V)$ or $r(V, V')$) corresponds to an edge in KG and the entire query corresponds to a collection of edges and thus forms a

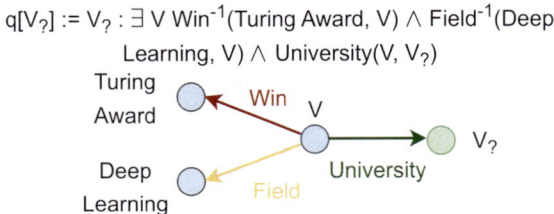

Fig. 4.1 The graph representation of the query "Which Universities did the Turing Award winners in the field of deep learning work at?", which can be expressed as the conjunctive query $V_? : \exists V \text{ Win}^{-1}(\text{Turing Award}, V) \land \text{Field}^{-1}(\text{Deep Learning}, V) \land \text{University}(V, V_?)$

graph. For instance, Eq. 4.1 is a conjunctive query with *three* atomic formulas, which corresponds to a graph in Fig. 4.1 with four nodes and *three* edges.

- **Subgraph Matching**: After formulating the query, the subsequent step is to identify all subgraphs within the **target graph** $G = \{\mathcal{E}, \mathcal{R}, O\}$ that align with the structure of the query graph Q. The process of subgraph matching involves finding all sets of nodes and edges in the KG that are isomorphic to the query graph Q.
- **Result Extraction**: After the matching subgraphs are found, the next step is to extract the relevant information from these subgraphs to answer the query. This might involve returning the nodes and edges of the matched subgraphs or extracting specific information from the nodes and edges (such as the names of the universities in the example above).

4.2.2   Representative Methods of Subgraph Matching-Based Methods

Subgraph matching focuses on finding subgraphs in the KG (G) that match a given query graph (Q) exactly. This approach is often used when the query graph is small and well-defined, such as for conjuctive queries, and the user expects the results to be precise and unambiguous.

One of the most representative approaches for subgraph matching is the algorithm proposed by *Ullmann* [2]. The basic approach is to enumerate all possible mappings of vertices in Q to those in G using a depth-first tree-search algorithm. Each node at level l of the search-tree maps node v_i in Q to a different vertex in G. Each path from the root to the leaf in the search tree represents a complete mapping of the vertices in Q to those in G. Any such mapping that preserves node adjacency in Q and G represents a matching from Q to a subgraph of G. If no such mapping preserves node adjacency, then no matching exists. To illustrate the Ullmann algorithm, let us consider a simple toy example as described below.

Example 4.2.1 Consider two graphs Q (query graph) and G (target graph) in Fig. 4.2, to find the map between two graphs, we utilize a depth-first search and backtracking approach. Beginning with the first vertex v_1 of the query graph Q, we attempt to map it to a compatible

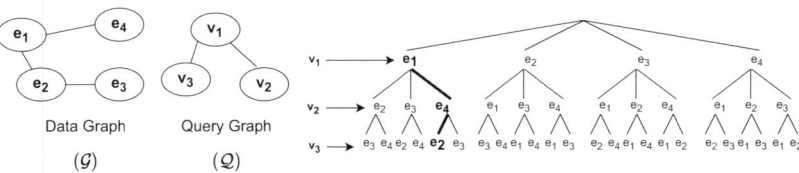

Fig. 4.2 Illustration of the Ullmann's algorithm. **Left:** an example of a data graph G and a query graph Q. **Right:** The search tree for Ullmann's algorithm, mapping vertices from query graph Q to target graph G. The path highlighted in red represents a match for Q in G

vertex in the target graph $\mathcal{G}$. All possible mappings are presented as a path from the root to the leaf in the search tree, as shown in Fig. 4.2. Among the possible mappings, one valid solution is $v_1 \rightarrow e_1, v_2 \rightarrow e_4, v_3 \rightarrow e_2$ because it maps each node in the query graph to a unique node in the target graph, such that the edges between the nodes in the query graph are also present in the target graph. It is essential to note that there may be more than one valid solution. For instance, $v_1 \rightarrow e_1, v_2 \rightarrow e_2, v_3 \rightarrow e_4$ is another valid solution.

This toy example demonstrates how the Ullmann algorithm works to find the set of subgraphs of the target graph $\mathcal{G}$ that match the query graph Q. Since the search space increases exponentially with the size of the target graphs, subgraph matching is NP-complete. It is impractical to solve subgraph matching in large graphs.

4.2.3   A Query Language for Subgraph Matching Algorithms—SPARQL

Subgraph matching algorithms can be used to efficiently search KGs for relevant information, and they can be customized to different query languages, such as SPARQL [3]. SPARQL [3] has been proposed as the standard query language and protocol for graph databases. SPARQL models the data as a directed graph, consisting of triples in the form of (head entity, relation, tail entity). Just like SQL allows users to retrieve and modify data in a relational database, SPARQL provides the same functionality for NoSQL graph databases, by specifying queries that describe the relations between entities in the KG.

For example, a typical SPARQL query consists of a SELECT clause, which specifies the variables to be returned in the result set, and a WHERE clause, which specifies the patterns of relations between entities to be matched. The WHERE clause in a SPARQL query is comprised of triple patterns that specify the relations between entities in the KG. Each triple pattern consists of three elements, which can be *variables* or *specific entities*, and describe *the connections between them*. Let's use the example "Which universities did the Turing Award winners in the field of deep learning work at?" in Fig. 4.1 to demonstrate how SPARQL can be used to answer complex queries from a KG.

Example 4.2.2 Let's assume we have a KG that contains information about Turing Award winners, their affiliations, and their research interests. To answer the example question, we can write a SPARQL query that retrieves the universities where the Turing Award winners in the field of deep learning work at. Here is an example SPARQL query:

```
SELECT ?university
WHERE {
  ?person win Turing_Award .
  ?person field Deep_learning .
  ?person workAt ?university .
}
```

In general, SPARQL is a powerful and expressive query language that can retrieve complex patterns of relations between entities in a KG. However, SPARQL queries can be computationally expensive to execute, especially when querying large and complex KGs with many entities and relations.

4.2.4   Summary

Subgraph matching has long been an effective technique for querying KGs and extracting intricate relations between entities. In contrast to machine learning approaches, subgraph matching methods do not require KG training, making them applicable to any graph without a training phase. Additionally, the results derived from subgraph matching methods are often easily interpretable, as they directly correspond to the original graph structure and properties. This approach can be customized to cater to specific requirements and query patterns and can be combined with other techniques to improve result accuracy and efficiency. For instance, SPARQL is a widely used language that facilitates subgraph matching.

Despite the strong interpretability and generalizability of subgraph matching methods for answering complex queries in KGs, they exhibit some disadvantages:

- **Difficulty handling real-world KGs**: Knowledge graphs (KGs) often contain noise and significant incompleteness, which can adversely affect the performance of subgraph-matching-based methods, especially when answering complex queries with many variables. Incomplete KGs may yield empty query results, while noisy triples can result in incorrect answers.
- **Scalability**: Subgraph-matching-based methods suffer from scalability issues when applied to large KGs, as their complexity typically increases exponentially with KG size.
- **Limited expressiveness**: Subgraph-matching-based methods might struggle to capture certain complex semantic relationships between entities in the KG due to their inherent limited expressiveness. For example, consider the query "Find a person who has not visited any European country?" This query includes negation (i.e., "not visited") and universal quantification (i.e., "any"). Subgraph-matching-based methods would struggle to handle this query, as they are not designed to handle negation or universal quantification.

4.3   Logical Query Embedding-Based Query Answering

Inspired by the effectiveness of embedding-based methods in handling large-scale real-world KGs, logical query embedding methods have been proposed to map complex queries in the First-Order Logic (FOL) form into continuous vectors. In comparison to subgraph matching methods, logical query embedding methods can handle incomplete and noisy knowledge graphs, are much more scalable, and can accommodate a broader range of FOL queries.

4.3.1 Overview of Logical Query Embedding Methods

Take the same question "Which Universities did the Turing Award winners in the field of deep learning work at?" as an example, it can be expressed as the FOL query q in Eq. 4.1, which is:

$$V_? : \exists V \; \text{Win}^{-1}(\text{Turing Award}, V) \; \wedge \; \text{Field}^{-1}(\text{Deep Learning}, V) \; \wedge \; \text{University}(V, V_?)$$

where $V_?$ is the target variable. The objective of query answering is to identify a set of specific entities, called *answer set*, which can be substituted for the variable $V_?$ in Eq. 4.1 to satisfy the logical formula.

The fundamental idea behind logical query embedding methods is to encode both the logical query and entities into a lower-dimensional vector space, where the entities that fulfill the query are close to the query in the embedding space. Specifically, we represent the set of entities that satisfy a given query q as S_q, which is the query embedding. Based on this concept, a typical logical query embedding method comprises three main components: (1) design an embedding space for both entities and queries; (2) design functions that model various operations such as relation projections and logical operations in the embedding space; and (3) a score function that assesses the compatibility between an entity and the query.

Using the query example of Eq. 4.1, we will introduce the major components of logical embedding-based approach below, which are illustrated in Fig. 4.3.

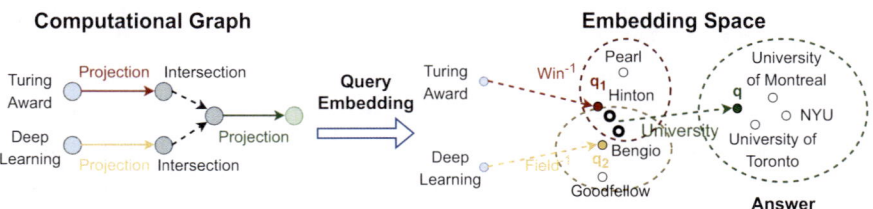

Fig. 4.3 Overview of a general logical query embedding framework using the FOL query in Eq. (4.1) as an example. It typically involves three steps to answer a given FOL query: (1) Transform the query into its DAG graph representation; (2) Generate an embedding of the query based on this DAG. This process begins with the embeddings of the query's anchor nodes (e.g., the entity *"Turing Award"* and *"Deep Learning"*) and applies logical operations such as projection **P** and conjunction **C** iteratively to produce an embedding **q** that corresponds to the query; (3) Utilize the generated query embedding to rank the entities based on a score function

4.3.1.1 The Modeling

There are several key concepts in the representation learning-based query answering solution.

First, the answer to a query is a set of entities, thus representing a query means to *represent a set*. This requires a careful design on the embedding space of entities and sets of entities.

Second, an FOL query is defined over logical operations of atomic formulas (e.g., Win^{-1}(Turing Award, V)). We need to (1) define the embedding of atomic formulas, which is also a set corresponding to a subquery, and (2) define the query embedding recursively based on subqueries' embeddings. The entire process needs to be differentiable, which requires us handling relation projection and logical operations as differentiable functions of embeddings.

Third, we need to provide a score function to measure the possibility of an entity belonging to a set, based on their embeddings.

Design the Embedding Space

For all the entities e in the KG $\mathcal{G}$ and any FOL query q, we need to design their embedding space, which could be vectors, boxes, and distributions, as introduced in future sections.

Embedding-based Operation Modeling

Each FOL query is recursively defined over subqueries, and the most basic ones are atomic formulas (atomic queries) that correspond to predicates in the KG. For example, query Eq. 4.1 contains atomic queries such as Win^{-1}(Turing Award, V), $Field^{-1}$(Deep Learning, V) and University(V, $V_?$).

If an atomic query contains an entity (e.g., Win^{-1}(Turing Award, V)), the entity will be treated as an *anchor node* as illustrated in Fig. 4.3 (e.g., "Turing Award"), and the relation projects the entity into a set of potential entities, denoted as a variable node. If an atomic query contains variables only (e.g., University(V, $V_?$)), the relation projects a set to another set. Therefore, each atomic query is a set itself.

To get an order on which these subqueries to be evaluated, a computational graph will be constructed, where the nodes are entities or variables and the edges are projections and logical operators. A computational graph is a directed acyclic graph (DAG), where the starting nodes or anchor nodes are entities. The computation flow starts from anchor nodes and gradually goes to the nodes that are one hop away, two hops away, until it reaches the target variable node.

In order to make the whole pipeline differentiable, it is necessary to approximate the fundamental operations such as relation projection and logical operators using embedding-based functions.

- **Projection** ($\mathcal{P}$): Given an embedding that represents an entity or a set of entities and a relation r_k, the projection operation $\mathcal{P}$ outputs a new embedding that represents the set of entities that are projected by r_k via the input entity or entity set. For example, Win^{-1} project entity "Turing Award" into a set of Turing award winners, which needs to be represented as an embedding.

- **Logical Operations**: Some commonly used logical operations are conjunction (C), disjunction (D), and negation (N). As each atomic query is corresponding to a set, the logical operations now correspond to set operations.

  - **Conjunction** (C): Conjunction ($\wedge$) corresponds to the set operation *intersection* ($\cap$). Given a set of query embeddings $\{\mathbf{q}_1, \ldots, \mathbf{q}_n\}$, the conjunction operation C outputs a new query embedding $\mathbf{q}$ which represents the intersection of n entity sets $\cap_{i=1}^{n} S_{q_i}$, where S_{q_i} is the entity set corresponding to query q_i.

  - **Disjunction** (D): Disjunction ($\vee$) corresponds to the set operation *union* ($\cup$). Given a set of query embeddings $\{\mathbf{q}_1, \ldots, \mathbf{q}_n\}$, the disjunction operation D outputs a new query embedding $\mathbf{q}$ which represents the union of n entity sets, i.e., $\cup_{i=1}^{n} S_{q_i}$, where S_{q_i} is the entity set corresponding to query q_i.

  - **Negation** (N): Negation ($\neg$) corresponds to the set operation *complement*. Given a set of entities $S \subseteq \mathcal{E}$, the negation operation outputs its complement $\overline{S} \equiv \mathcal{E} \setminus S$.

The Score Function

Each logical query answering method designs a score function $\phi(q, e)$ to evaluate the compatibility between the entity embedding $\mathbf{e}$ and the query embedding $\mathbf{q}$. A higher score indicates a greater possibility that the entity satisfies the query, and thus, a higher degree of confidence in the answer. The score function has to be consistent with the embedding space design for entities and queries.

4.3.1.2 The Training Process

As shown in Fig. 4.3, the forward computation of logical query embedding usually consists of three steps:

- Convert the given FOL query into an expression of basic logical operations. For instance, given an input query in Eq. (4.1), the query embedding framework first transforms it to its DAG graph as a computational graph.
- Generate the embedding of the query by executing the logical expression in order. For example, to generate an embedding of the query in Eq. (4.1), the query embedding framework starts with the embeddings of the query's anchor nodes (i.e., the embeddings of the entity *"Turing Award"* and *"Deep Learning"*) and iteratively applies logical operations such as projection P and conjunction C to generate an embedding $\mathbf{q}$ that corresponds to the query.
- Compute the score function between the query embedding and entity embeddings.

Table 4.1 Summary of Notations

e	Entity
q	FOL query
S_q	The answer to query q (a set of entities)
$\mathbf{e}$	The embedding vectors corresponding to e
$\mathbf{q}$	The embedding vectors corresponding to q
$\phi(q, e)$	Score function between q and e

Loss functions used in KG completion tasks, such as cross-entropy loss and ranking-based loss, can be defined based on labeled query and answer pairs. The goal is to learn the best parameters in the model to minimize the loss function.

Before we introduce the most representative logical query embedding methods, we first summarize notations in Table 4.1.

4.3.2   Representative Methods of Logical Query Embedding

Having provided an overview of the general logical query embedding framework, we will now provide a detailed introduction to the most prominent logical query embedding methods including GQE [4], Query2Box [5], and BetaE [6], along with a discussion of their pros and cons. The main differences between these models lie in their assumptions on how to represent entities, queries, and logical operations.

4.3.2.1 GQE
Graph Query Embeddings (GQE) [4] makes the first attempt to perform logical operations within a low-dimensional embedding space. It considers only *conjunctive logical queries*. As introduced in Sect. 4.1, the conjunctive queries are a special case of first-order logic queries that are constructed from atomic formulas using conjunction operation ($\wedge$) and existential quantification ($\exists$), but not using disjunction ($\vee$), negation ($\neg$), or universal quantification ($\forall$). Therefore, only two differentiable operators, projection $\mathcal{P}$ and conjunction $\mathcal{C}$, are needed. In GQE, both entities and queries are associated with a d-dimensional vector, i.e., $\mathbf{e}, \mathbf{q} \in \mathbb{R}^d$.

- **Projection** ($\mathcal{P}$). In particular, GQE models projection as a linear transformation. Given an embedding $\mathbf{q}$ (which may be either an entity or a subquery embedding) and a relation r_k, the projection operator outputs a new embedding:

$$\mathcal{P}_{r_k}(\mathbf{q}) = \mathbf{R}_k \mathbf{q} \tag{4.2}$$

where $\mathbf{R}_k \in \mathbb{R}^{d \times d}$ is a trainable parameter matrix for relation r_k.

- **Conjunction** (C). Given a set of query embeddings $\mathbf{q}_1, \ldots, \mathbf{q}_n$ with the same entity type t (e.g., proteins, drugs), the conjunction operation ($\wedge$) performs deep set intersection in the embedding space as follows:

$$C(\{\mathbf{q}_1, \ldots, \mathbf{q}_n\}) = \mathbf{W}_t \Psi(\mathrm{NN}(\mathbf{q}_i), \forall i = 1, \ldots, n) \tag{4.3}$$

where NN denotes a neural network, while Ψ represents a permutation invariant function (such as an elementwise mean or min of a set of vectors),[1] and $\mathbf{W}_t$ is a transformation matrix that is specific to the entity type t.

To perform query inference, GQE takes the corresponding computational query graph as input, and then projects the anchor nodes' embeddings according to their outgoing relations. When a node includes multiple incoming edges in the query DAG, an intersection operation is employed to aggregate the incoming information. The process continues until we reach the target variable of the query. We denote the final query embedding as $\mathbf{q}$.

Score Function

Let $\mathbf{e}$ denote the embedding of entity e. The score of entity e to be the answer of the query q can be calculated by the cosine similarity between the query embedding and the entity embedding:

$$\phi(q, e) = \frac{\mathbf{q} \cdot \mathbf{e}}{\|\mathbf{q}\| \, \|\mathbf{e}\|} \tag{4.4}$$

Training Objective

Once the logical query embedding model has been constructed, the model parameters can be learned following standard machine learning training. A common margin-based pairwise ranking loss is employed to define the objective function.

$$\mathcal{L}(q, e) = \max(0, \gamma - \phi(q, e) + \phi(q, e')) \tag{4.5}$$

In the case of GQE, the value of γ is set to 1 because the score function $\phi(q, e)$ produces a value in the range of $[0, 1]$. Setting $\gamma = 1$ ensures that the score function is normalized to the same range as the cosine similarity. To calculate this loss for a training query q, GQE uniformly samples a positive example node $e \in S_q$ and a negative example node $e' \notin S_q$ from the training data.

4.3.2.2 Query2Box

We can see that GQE focuses only on a conjunctive logical query without considering other logical operation such as disjunction operation. In addition, GQE models a query as a single

---

[1] The conjunction operation is permutation invariantto the input, and thus the function Ψ must also be permutation invariant to ensure that the conjunction operation behaves properly.

point in d-dimensional space, so it is challenging to properly represent a set. To address the limitations of GQE, Query2Box [5] addresses the more general Existential Positive First-order (EPFO) logical queries that involve $\vee$ in addition to $\exists$ and $\wedge$. In particular, Query2Box models a query answer set as a box and the entity embedding to be a point. Formally, a query is represented as a box embedding, which can be determined by its center vector and offset vector: $\mathbf{q} = (\text{Cen}(\mathbf{q}), \text{Off}(\mathbf{q}))$. Its corresponding box can be defined as:

$$\text{Box}_{\mathbf{q}} = \{x \in \mathbb{R}^d : \text{Cen}(\mathbf{q}) - \text{Off}(\mathbf{q}) \le x \le \text{Cen}(\mathbf{q}) + \text{Off}(\mathbf{q})\} \tag{4.6}$$

where $\text{Cen}(\mathbf{q}) \in \mathbb{R}^d$ is the center of the box, and $\text{Off}(\mathbf{q}) \in \mathbb{R}^d_{\ge 0}$ is the offset of the box.

Based on the box embedding, Query2Box supports the projection operation, conjunction operation and disjunction operation as follows.

- **Projection** ($\mathcal{P}$). To model the projection operation, Query2Box defines relation embedding as another box embedding $\mathbf{r_k} = (\text{Cen}(\mathbf{r_k}), \text{Off}(\mathbf{r_k}))$. Given a query embedding $\mathbf{q}$, it models the projection corresponding to relation r_k as $\mathcal{P}_{r_k}(\mathbf{q}) = \mathbf{q} + \mathbf{r_k}$, which gives a new box with the translated center and larger offset.
- **Conjunction** (C). Since Query2Box models a query answer set as a box, the basic idea of the conjunction operation is to generate a smaller box that lies inside a set of boxes (i.e., queries). Given a set of query embeddings $\{\mathbf{q}_1, \ldots, \mathbf{q}_n\}$, their intersection can be calculated by performing attention over the box centers and shrinking the box offset using the sigmoid function:

$$\text{Cen}(\mathbf{q}) = \sum_i \mathbf{a}_i \odot \text{Cen}(\mathbf{q}_i), \mathbf{a}_i = \frac{\exp(\text{MLP}(\mathbf{q}_i))}{\sum_k \exp(\text{MLP}(\mathbf{q}_k))}$$

$$\text{Off}(\mathbf{q}) = \text{Min}(\text{Off}(\mathbf{q}_1), \ldots, \text{Off}(\mathbf{q}_n)) \odot \sigma(\text{DeepSets}(\{\mathbf{q}_1, \ldots, \mathbf{q}_n\}))$$

where $\odot$ is the dimension-wise product, σ is the sigmoid function and DeepSets is the permutation-invariant deep architecture. Specifically, the DeepSets used in Query2Box is defined as:

$$\text{DeepSets}(\{\mathbf{q}_1, \ldots, \mathbf{q}_n\}) = \text{MLP}((1/n) \cdot \sum_{i=1}^{n} \text{MLP}(\mathbf{q}_i)) \tag{4.7}$$

- **Disjunction** ($\mathcal{D}$). As we mentioned before, Query2Box aims to answer Existential Positive First-order (EPFO) queries, which also involve disjunction ($\vee$) operation. Since the box embedding can be located anywhere in the vector space, the result of the disjunction (or union) operation is not a simple box. To solve this problem, Query2Box converts an EPFO query to a Disjunctive Normal Form (DNF), i.e., the disjunction of conjunctive queries such that the disjunction operation is moved to the last step of the computation. In this way, Query2Box represents an EPFO query as *a set of individual boxes*, where each box is obtained for each conjunctive query in the DNF. The query embedding for an EPFO query q can be written as $\mathbf{q} = \mathbf{q}_1 \vee \cdots \vee \mathbf{q}_n$. Then, Query2Box answers the EPFO query by aggregating the nearest neighbor entities to any of the boxes. The distance between entity embedding $\mathbf{e}$ and $\mathbf{q}$ is defined as the smallest distance between the entity and any of the boxes:

$$\text{dist}_{\text{agg}}(\mathbf{e}; \mathbf{q}) = \min(\{\text{dist}_{\text{box}}(\mathbf{e}, \mathbf{q}_1), \ldots, \text{dist}_{\text{box}}(\mathbf{e}, \mathbf{q}_n)\}) \tag{4.8}$$

where the distance function is defined next in detail.

Score Function

To decide whether an entity e is the answer to the query, Query2Box defines the distance between a query embedding $\mathbf{q}$ and an entity embedding $\mathbf{e}$ as follows:

$$\text{dist}_{\text{box}}(\mathbf{e}, \mathbf{q}) = \text{dist}_{\text{outside}}(\mathbf{e}; \mathbf{q}) + \alpha \cdot \text{dist}_{\text{inside}}(\mathbf{e}; \mathbf{q}) \tag{4.9}$$

where $\text{dist}_{\text{outside}}(\mathbf{e}; \mathbf{q})$ denotes the distance between the entity and the closest corner or side of the box (0 if the entity is inside the box), and $\text{dist}_{\text{inside}}(\mathbf{e}; \mathbf{q})$ denotes the distance between that closest point and the center of the box. The two distances are defined as:

$$\text{dist}_{\text{outside}}(\mathbf{e}; \mathbf{q}) = \|\text{Max}(\mathbf{e} - \mathbf{q}_{\text{max}}, 0) + \text{Max}(\mathbf{q}_{\text{min}} - \mathbf{e}, 0)\|_1$$
$$\text{dist}_{\text{inside}}(\mathbf{e}; \mathbf{q}) = \|\text{Cen}(\mathbf{q}) - \text{Min}(\mathbf{q}_{\text{max}}, \text{Max}(\mathbf{e}, \mathbf{q}_{\text{min}}))\|_1$$

where $\mathbf{q}_{\text{max}} = \text{Cen}(\mathbf{q}) + \text{Off}(\mathbf{q})$ and $\mathbf{q}_{\text{min}} = \text{Cen}(\mathbf{q}) - \text{Off}(\mathbf{q})$. The score function $\phi(q, e)$ can be considered as negative of the distance function.

Training Objective

Margin-based cross-entropy loss is used in Query2Box training.

$$\mathcal{L}(q, e) = -\log \sigma(\gamma - \text{dist}_{\text{box}}(\mathbf{e}, \mathbf{q})) - \sum_{i=1}^{k} \frac{1}{k} \log \sigma(\text{dist}_{\text{box}}(\mathbf{e}', \mathbf{q}) - \gamma) \tag{4.10}$$

where γ denotes the margin and $\mathbf{e}'$ denotes the embedding of the negative answers.

Query2Box supports three types of logical operations, including projection ($\mathcal{P}$), conjunction (C), and disjunction ($\mathcal{D}$). To improve the expressiveness of the model, NewLook [7] extends Query2Box to support negation via difference operator.

4.3.2.3 BetaE

It has been shown in Query2Box that representing sets as boxes is superior to representing them as points, as boxes have volumes and intersection operation can be naturally defined. However, it is challenging for box embedding to handle disjunction and negation, due to these operations lead to geometric shapes that are no longer boxes.

To further support negation operation and model uncertainty, BetaE [6] models both the entities and queries as d independent Beta distributions. The Beta distribution is denoted as Beta(α, β), which has two shape parameters $\alpha > 0$ and $\beta > 0$. Its probability density function is defined as:

$$p(x) = \frac{x^{\alpha-1}(1-x)^{\beta-1}}{B(\alpha, \beta)} \tag{4.11}$$

where $x \in [0, 1]$ and $B(\alpha, \beta)$ denotes the beta function serving the purpose of normalization. Each entity is considered as as a special case of set, and a set is represented as $\mathbf{q} = [(\alpha_1, \beta_1), \ldots, (\alpha_d, \beta_d)]$. Without of loss of generality, we now explain all the definitions when $d = 1$.

- **Projection** ($\mathcal{P}$). A transformation neural network is learned for each relation r_k to project from one Beta embedding $\mathbf{q}$ to another Beta embedding $\mathbf{q}'$:

$$\mathbf{q}' = \mathcal{P}_{r_k}(\mathbf{q}) = \text{MLP}_{r_k}(\mathbf{q}) \tag{4.12}$$

  where $\text{MLP}_{r_k}(\cdot)$ is a multi-layer perceptron with parameter specific to relation r_k.
- **Conjunction** ($\mathcal{C}$). The conjunction is modeled as a weighted interpolation of Beta distributions. Given a set of query embeddings $\{\mathbf{q}_1, \ldots, \mathbf{q}_n\}$, the distribution representing their intersection can be calculated by taking the weighted product of the PDFs of the input Beta embeddings:

$$p_{C(\{\mathbf{q}_1,\ldots,\mathbf{q}_n\})}(x) = \frac{1}{Z} p_{\mathbf{q}_1}^{w_1}(x) p_{\mathbf{q}_2}^{w_2}(x) \ldots p_{\mathbf{q}_n}^{w_n}(x) \tag{4.13}$$

  where Z is a normalization constant and w_i is the attention weight for query $\mathbf{q}_i$, which can be calculated as:

$$w_i = \frac{\exp(\text{MLP}(\mathbf{q}_i))}{\sum_{i'} \exp(\text{MLP}(\mathbf{q}_{i'}))} \tag{4.14}$$

  We can see that the form of the distribution for the intersection $p_{C(\{\mathbf{q}_1,\ldots,\mathbf{q}_n\})}$ is another beta distribution, with parameters $\sum w_i \alpha_i$ and $\sum w_i \beta_i$, where α_i, β_i are parameters for the i-th beta distribution (Proof is ommitted here. A trick is to use the fact $\sum_i (w_i \alpha_i - w_i) = \sum_i w_i \alpha_i - 1$, due to the attention weights sum up to 1, i.e., $\sum_i w_i = 1$).
- **Negation** ($\mathcal{N}$). Since the negation operation aims to output an embedding to represent the complement of the input, its density function should be the inversion of the density function of the input, which can be defined as:

$$\mathcal{N}([\alpha, \beta]) = [(\frac{1}{\alpha}, \frac{1}{\beta})] \tag{4.15}$$

We can check that $\mathcal{N}(\mathcal{N}([\alpha, \beta])) = [\alpha, \beta]$, which preserves the property that negation's negation is the set itself.

- **Disjunction** ($\mathcal{D}$). It is more challenging for BetaE to model disjunction directly. Instead, following De Morgan's law, which we previously introduced in Sect. 2.2.3, disjunction is computed using the logical operation conjunction and negation.

Because BetaE provides full support for first-order logic (FOL) queries, it can learn the query embedding for any FOL query.

Score Function
We denote the final query embedding as $\mathbf{q}$. The distance between entity embedding $\mathbf{e} = [(\alpha_1^e, \beta_1^e), \ldots, (\alpha_d^e, \beta_d^e)]$ and $\mathbf{q} = [(\alpha_1^q, \beta_1^q), \ldots, (\alpha_d^q, \beta_d^q)]$ is defined as the sum of KL divergence between the two Beta embeddings along each dimension, which can be considered as negative to the score function $\phi(q, e)$:

$$\text{dist}(\mathbf{e}; \mathbf{q}) = \sum_{k=1}^{d} \text{KL}(p_{e,k}; p_{q,k}) \tag{4.16}$$

where $p_{e,k}$ (or $p_{q,k}$) represents the k-th Beta distribution with parameters α_k^e and β_k^e (or α_k^q and β_k^q).

Training Objective
BetaE utilizes the same margin-based cross-entropy loss as is used by Query2Box, as presented in Eq. 4.10.

4.3.3   Summary

Logical query embedding methods translate complex queries into a continuous embeddings, enabling the retrieval of query answers based on similarity measures. These methods leverage representation learning techniques, which are particularly effective in handling incomplete and noisy Knowledge Graphs (KGs).

A significant challenge for logical query embedding methods is the representation of sets. The way sets are represented plays a critical role as it can impact the effectiveness and efficiency of the embedding method. Various approaches have been proposed for rep-

Table 4.2 Summary of logical query embedding models

Method	Query modeling	Supported operators
GQE [4]	A single point in a d-dimensional space	$\exists, \wedge$
Query2Box [5]	Box in a d-dimensional space	$\exists, \wedge, \vee$
NewLook [7]	Box in a d-dimensional space	$\exists, \wedge, \vee, \neg^*$
BetaE [6]	Beta distribution	$\exists, \wedge, \vee, \neg$

*Negation is supported via difference operator

resenting sets. For instance, GQE represents a set as a single point in a low-dimensional space, which is limited in capturing set characteristics. Query2Box addresses this limitation by utilizing box embeddings to model queries. However, they may encounter difficulties when representing negation operations. In contrast, BetaE represents sets as beta distributions over embeddings, enabling effective modeling of uncertainty and diversity. Table 4.2 summarizes the logical operators supported by various logical query embedding models. It is worth noting that only NewLook and BetaE [6] offer complete support for first-order logic (FOL) queries.

Although logical query embedding has shown excellent performance in answering complex queries, these methods necessitate training on the KG, which heavily relies on labeled query and answer pairs. Inherent approximation errors caused by ad-hoc assumptions in continuous vector representations may also impact the quality of query answers. This requires an algorithm that can provide theoretical guarantees to ensure embedding-based functions do preserve the logical axioms and less relied on additional training signals.

4.4   FuzzQE: Introducing Fuzzy Logic for First-Order-Logic (FOL) Query Answering

From the last section, we can see that embedding-based logical query answering is more efficient and effective compared to traditional subgraph matching-based approaches. However, there are still limitations in existing embedding-based approaches. First, in terms of how to design an embedding space for sets, we need to make sure it is closed under all logical operations, which is only partially true for existing approaches. Second, The general idea of logical query embedding models is to recursively define the embedding of a query (e.g., $q_1 \wedge q_2$) based on logical operations on its sub-queries' embeddings (e.g., q_1 and q_2). These logical operations have to satisfy logical laws, which serve as additional constraints to learning-based query embedding models. Unfortunately, most existing query embedding models have (partially) neglected these laws, which results in inferior performance. Third, a large number of labeled question-answer pairs are needed for the current training, and we need to propose methods that can be trained in a self-supervised manner.

To address these issues, the FuzzQE [1] algorithm has been introduced as a state-of-the-art approach to logical query embedding. By modeling queries as fuzzy sets and utilizing fuzzy logic to define logical operators within the embedding space, FuzzQE ensures that logical laws are satisfied, leading to improved performance. In addition, FuzzQE can be trained based on simple knowledge graph completion task, making it trainable in a self-supervised manner.

4.4.1   Logical Laws and Model Properties

Logical laws or laws of logic, are fundamental principles that form the basis for logical reasoning in various logical systems. These laws guarantee the soundness of a logical system, which means that every conclusion derived from the system is true if the given premises are true. By satisfying logical laws, logical query embedding methods ensure that the underlying logical system is consistent. In this section, we examine the logical principles that Boolean logic and fuzzy logic share [8], and derive a set of fundamental characteristics that logical operators ought to exhibit.

Axiomatic Systems of Logic

Let $\mathcal{L}$ be the set of all the valid logic formulas under a logic system, and $\psi_1, \psi_2, \psi_3 \in \mathcal{L}$ represent logical formulae. $I(\cdot)$ denotes the truth value of a logical formula. The semantics of Boolean Logic is defined by (i) the interpretation $I : \mathcal{L} \to \{0, 1\}$, (ii) the Modus Ponen inference rule "from ψ_1 and $\psi_1 \to \psi_2$ infer ψ_2", which characterizes logic implication ($\to$) as follows:

$$\psi_1 \to \psi_2 \quad \text{holds if and only if} \quad I(\psi_2) \geq I(\psi_1)$$

and (iii) a set of axioms written in Hilbert-style deductive systems [9]. Those axioms define other logic connectives via logic implication ($\to$). For example, the following three axioms characterize the conjunction ($\wedge$) of Boolean logic [10]:

$$\psi_1 \wedge \psi_2 \to \psi_1$$
$$\psi_1 \wedge \psi_2 \to \psi_2$$
$$(\psi_3 \to \psi_1) \to ((\psi_3 \to \psi_2) \to (\psi_3 \to \psi_1 \wedge \psi_2))$$

The first two axioms guarantee that the truth value of $\psi_1 \wedge \psi_2$ never exceeds the truth values of ψ_1 and ψ_2, and the last one enforces that $I(\psi_1 \wedge \psi_2) = 1$ if $I(\psi_1) = I(\psi_2) = 1$. The three axioms also imply commutativity and associativity of logical conjunction $\wedge$.

Model Properties

Let $\phi(q, e)$ be the embedding-based score function indicating the probability that the entity e can answer the query q. This means that $\phi(q, e)$ estimates the truth value $I(q[e])$, where $q[e]$ is a logical formula that uses e to fill q, denoted as ψ. For example, given the query $q = V_? : Compose(John\ Lennon, V_?)$ and the entity $e =$ "$Let\ it\ Be$", $\phi(q, e)$ estimates the truth value of the logical formula $Compose(John\ Lennon, Let\ it\ Be)$. We can thus use logical laws to deduce reasonable properties that a query embedding model should possess. For instance, let $\psi_1 = q_1(e)$ and $\psi_2 = q_2(e)$, $\psi_1 \wedge \psi_2 \to \psi_1$ is an axiom that characterizes logic conjunction ($\wedge$), which enforces that $I(\psi_1 \wedge \psi_2) \leq I(\psi_1)$. Accordingly, we expect the embedding model to satisfy $\phi(q_1 \wedge q_2, e) \leq \phi(q_1, e)$, i.e., an entity e is less likely to satisfy $q_1 \wedge q_2$ than q_1.

Table 4.3 Here we list eight logical laws (I–VIII) from classical logic [8] and give the corresponding properties that a query embedding model should possess. ψ_1, ψ_2, ψ_3 represent logical formulae. ϕ denotes the scoring function that estimates the probability that the entity e can answer the query q. $\phi(q, e) \uparrow \Rightarrow \phi(\neg q, e) \downarrow$ means $\phi(\neg q, e)$ is monotonically decreasing with regard to $\phi(q, e)$

		Logical law	Model property
$\wedge$	I	Conjunction Elimination	
		$\psi_1 \wedge \psi_2 \rightarrow \psi_1$	$\phi(q_1 \wedge q_2, e) \leq \phi(q_1, e)$
		$\psi_1 \wedge \psi_2 \rightarrow \psi_2$	$\phi(q_1 \wedge q_2, e) \leq \phi(q_2, e)$
	II	Commutativity	
		$\psi_1 \wedge \psi_2 \leftrightarrow \psi_2 \wedge \psi_1$	$\phi((q_1 \wedge q_2), e) = \phi((q_2 \wedge q_1), e)$
	III	Associativity	
		$(\psi_1 \wedge \psi_2) \wedge \psi_3 \leftrightarrow$ $\psi_1 \wedge (\psi_2 \wedge \psi_3)$	$\phi((q_1 \wedge q_2) \wedge q_3, e) = \phi(q_1 \wedge (q_2 \wedge q_3), e)$
$\vee$	IV	Disjunction Amplification	
		$\psi_1 \rightarrow \psi_1 \vee \psi_2$	$\phi(q_1, e) \leq \phi(q_1 \vee q_2, e)$
		$\psi_2 \rightarrow \psi_1 \vee \psi_2$	$\phi(q_2, e) \leq \phi(q_1 \vee q_2, e)$
	V	Commutativity	
		$\psi_1 \vee \psi_2 \leftrightarrow \psi_2 \vee \psi_1$	$\phi((q_1 \vee q_2), e) = \phi((q_2 \vee q_1), e)$
	VI	Associativity	
		$(\psi_1 \vee \psi_2) \vee \psi_3 \leftrightarrow$ $\psi_1 \vee (\psi_2 \vee \psi_3)$	$\phi((q_1 \vee q_2) \vee q_3, e) = \phi(q_1 \vee (q_2 \vee q_3), e)$
$\neg$	VII	Involution	
		$\neg\neg\psi_1 \leftrightarrow \psi_1$	$\phi(q, e) = \phi(\neg\neg q, e)$
	VIII	Non-contradiction	
		$\psi_1 \wedge \neg\psi_1 \rightarrow \overline{0}$	$\phi(q, e) \uparrow \Rightarrow \phi(\neg q, e) \downarrow$

Based on the axioms and deduced logical laws of classical logic [11], we summarize a series of model properties that a logical query embedding model should possess in Table 4.3. The list is not exhaustive but indicative.

4.4.2   Framework of FuzzQE

To satisfy logical laws, in this section, we introduce a novel framework—FuzzQE, which draws from fuzzy logic and uses the fuzzy conjunction, disjunction, and negation operations to define the logical operators in the vector space.

4.4.2.1 Queries and Entities in Fuzzy Space

Predicting whether an entity can answer a query means predicting the probability that the entity belongs to the answer set of this query. FuzzQE embeds queries and entities to the *fuzzy space* $[0, 1]^d$, a subspace of $\mathbb{R}^d$ [12].

- **Query Embedding.** Consider a query q and its fuzzy answer set S_q, its embedding $\mathbf{S}_q$ is defined as a fuzzy vector $\mathbf{S}_q \in [0, 1]^d$ [12]. Intuitively, let Ω denote the universe of all the elements, and let $\{U_i\}_{i=1}^d$ denote a partition over Ω, i.e., $\Omega = \cup_{i=1}^d U_i$ and $U_i \cap U_j = \emptyset$ for $i \neq j$. Each dimension i of $\mathbf{S}_q$ denotes the probability whether the corresponding subset U_i is part of the answer set S_q, i.e., $\mathbf{S}_q(i) = \Pr(U_i \subseteq S_q)$. Note for the query embedding in FuzzQE, the all-one vector $\mathbf{1}$ represents the universe set (i.e., Ω), and the all-zero vector $\mathbf{0}$ represents an empty set $\emptyset$.
- **Entity Embedding.** For an entity e, FuzzQE considers its embedding $\mathbf{p}_e$ from the same fuzzy space, i.e., $\mathbf{p}_e \in [0, 1]^d$. To model its uncertainty, FuzzQE models it as a categorical distribution to fall into each subset U_i, namely, $\mathbf{p}_e(i) = \Pr(e \in U_i)$, and $\sum_{i=1}^d \mathbf{p}_e(i) = 1$.
- **Score Function.** Accordingly, the score function $\phi(q, e)$ is defined as the expected probability that e belongs to the fuzzy set S_q:

$$\phi(q, e) = \Pr(e \in S_q)$$
$$= \sum_{i=1}^d \Pr(e \in U_i) \Pr(U_i \subseteq S_q)$$
$$= \mathbf{S}_q{}^\top \mathbf{p}_e$$

The above representation and scoring provide the following benefits: (i) The representation is endowed with a probabilistic interpretation, and (ii) each dimension of the embedding vector is between $[0, 1]$, which satisfies the domain and range requirements of fuzzy logic and allows the model to execute *element-wise* fuzzy conjunction/disjunction/negation.

4.4.2.2 Relation Projection

Atomic queries like $q = V_? : Compose(John\ Lennon, V_?)$ serve as building blocks of complex queries. To embed atomic queries, FuzzQE associates each relation $r \in \mathcal{R}$ with a projection operator $\mathcal{P}_r$, which is modeled by a neural network with a weight matrix $\mathbf{W}_r \in \mathbb{R}^{d \times d}$ and a bias vector $\mathbf{b}_r \in \mathbb{R}^d$, and transforms an anchor entity embedding $\mathbf{p}_e$ into a query embedding:

$$\mathbf{S}_q = \mathcal{P}_r(\mathbf{p}_e) = \mathbf{g}(\mathrm{LN}(\mathbf{W}_r \mathbf{p}_e + \mathbf{b}_r))$$

where LN is Layer Normalization [13], and $\mathbf{g} : \mathbb{R}^d \mapsto [0, 1]^d$ is a mapping function that constrains $\mathbf{S}_q \in [0, 1]^d$. Particularly, FuzzQE considers two different choices for $\mathbf{g}$:

$$\text{Logistic function} : \mathbf{g}(x) = \frac{1}{1 + e^{-(x)}}$$

$$\text{Bounded rectifier} : \mathbf{g}(x) = \min(\max(x, 0), 1)$$

To reduce model size, FuzzQE follows RGCN [14] and adopts *basis-decomposition* to define $\mathbf{W}_r$ and $\mathbf{b}_r$:

$$\mathbf{W}_r = \sum_{j=1}^{K} \alpha_{rj} \mathbf{M}_j; \quad \mathbf{b}_r = \sum_{j=1}^{K} \alpha_{rj} \mathbf{v}_j$$

Namely, $\mathbf{W}_r$ as a linear combination of K basis transformations $\mathbf{M}_j \in \mathbb{R}^{d \times d}$ with coefficients α_{rj} that depend on r. Similarly, $\mathbf{b}_r$ is a linear combination of K basis vectors $\mathbf{v}_j \in \mathbb{R}^d$ with coefficients α_{rj}. This form prevents the rapid growth in the number of parameters with the number of relations and alleviates overfitting on rare relations. It can be seen as a form of effective weight sharing among different relation types [14].

Relation projection from one set (a sub-query) to its answer can be modeled similarly, where we only need to replace $\mathbf{p}_e$ with the embedding of sub-query $\mathbf{S}_q$.

In principle, any sufficiently expressive neural network or translation-based KG embedding model [15, 16] could be employed as the relation projection operator in our framework.

4.4.2.3 Fuzzy Logic Based Logical Operators

Fuzzy logic is mathematically equivalent to fuzzy set theory [9], with fuzzy conjunction equivalent to the fuzzy set intersection, fuzzy disjunction equivalent to the fuzzy set union, and fuzzy negation equivalent to the fuzzy set complement. Fuzzy logic could thus be used to define operations over fuzzy vectors. As discussed in Sect. 2.2.4, the three most prominent t-norm based logic systems are product logic, Gödel logic, and Łukasiewicz logic [17]. With reference to product logic, FuzzQE computes the embeddings of $q_1 \wedge q_2$, $q_1 \vee q_2$, and $\neg q$ as follows:

$$q_1 \wedge q_2 : \quad C(\mathbf{S}_{q_1}, \mathbf{S}_{q_2}) = \mathbf{S}_{q_1} \circ \mathbf{S}_{q_2}$$
$$q_1 \vee q_2 : \quad \mathcal{D}(\mathbf{S}_{q_1}, \mathbf{S}_{q_2}) = \mathbf{S}_{q_1} + \mathbf{S}_{q_2} - \mathbf{S}_{q_1} \circ \mathbf{S}_{q_2}$$
$$\neg q : \quad \mathcal{N}(\mathbf{S}_q) = \mathbf{1} - \mathbf{S}_q$$

where $\circ$ denotes element-wise multiplication (fuzzy conjunction), $\mathbf{1}$ is the all-one vector, and $C, \mathcal{D}, \mathcal{N}$ denote the embedding based logical operators respectively.

Alternatively, the conjunction and disjunction operators can be designed based on Gödel logic as follows:

$$q_1 \wedge q_2 : \quad C(\mathbf{S}_{q_1}, \mathbf{S}_{q_2}) = \min(\mathbf{S}_{q_1}, \mathbf{S}_{q_2})$$
$$q_1 \vee q_2 : \quad \mathcal{D}(\mathbf{S}_{q_1}, \mathbf{S}_{q_2}) = \max(\mathbf{S}_{q_1}, \mathbf{S}_{q_2})$$

where min, max denotes element-wise minimum and maximum operations respectively. One good property of Gödel logic is that conjunction and disjunction operators are idempotent, meaning $C(\mathbf{S}_q, \mathbf{S}_q) = \mathbf{S}_q$ and $\mathcal{D}(\mathbf{S}_q, \mathbf{S}_q) = \mathbf{S}_q$.

We omit Łukasiewicz logic here since its output domain is heavily concentrated in $\{0, 1\}$, which causes a query embedding learning problem.

4.4.2.4 Model Learning and Inference

Given a query q, FuzzQE optimizes the following objective:

$$L = -\log \sigma \left(\frac{1}{Z_q} \phi(q, e) - \gamma \right) - \frac{1}{k} \sum_{i=1}^{k} \log \sigma \left(\gamma - \frac{1}{Z_q} \phi(q, e') \right)$$

where $e \in S_q$ is an answer to the query, $e' \notin S_q$ represents a random negative sample, and γ denotes the margin. Z_q is an L_2 norm-based scaling factor, which is introduced as a means to balance margin sensitivity between queries during training.

In the loss function, FuzzQE uses k random negative samples and optimizes the average. FuzzQE seeks to maximize $\phi(q, e)$ for $e \in S_q$ and minimize $\phi(q, e')$ for $e' \in S_q$.

Note that, different from previous models, logical operators in FuzzQE do not contain parameters. The only parameters are entity embeddings and the relation projection related parameters. This makes training much simpler, and can be trained using KG completion tasks in a self-supervised manner.

For the model inference, given a query q, FuzzQE embeds it as $\mathbf{S}_q$ and ranks all the entities by $\phi(q, \cdot)$.

4.4.2.5 Theoretical Analysis

In this subsection, our aim is to demonstrate that FuzzQE satisfies all the logical laws listed in Table 4.3. We provide several propositions along with their proofs below. These propositions are proven using product logic, and the same can be established for Gödel logic as well.

Proposition 4.1 *Our conjunction operator C is (1) commutative, (2) associative, and satisfies (3) conjunction elimination.*

(1) Commutativity: $\phi(q_1 \wedge q_2, e) = \phi(q_2 \wedge q_1, e)$.

Proof We have $C(\mathbf{S}_{q1}, \mathbf{S}_{q2}) = q_1 \circ q_2 = q_2 \circ q_1 = C(\mathbf{S}_{q2}, \mathbf{S}_{q1})$ where $\circ$ denotes element-wise multiplication.
Therefore, $\phi(q_1 \wedge q_2, e) = \mathbf{p}_e^\mathsf{T} C(\mathbf{S}_{q1}, \mathbf{S}_{q2}) = \mathbf{p}_e^\mathsf{T} C(\mathbf{S}_{q2}, \mathbf{S}_{q1}) = \phi(q_2 \wedge q_1, e)$. □

(2) Associativity: $\phi((q_1 \wedge q_2) \wedge q_3, e) = \phi(q_1 \wedge (q_2 \wedge q_3), e)$.

Proof Since $C(C(\mathbf{S}_{q_1}, \mathbf{S}_{q_2})), \mathbf{S}_{q_3}) = q_1 \circ q_2 \circ q_3 = C(\mathbf{S}_{q_1}, C(\mathbf{S}_{q_2}, \mathbf{S}_{q_3}))$, we have

$$\phi((q_1 \wedge q_2) \wedge q_3, e)$$
$$= \mathbf{p}_e{}^\top C(C(\mathbf{S}_{q_1}, \mathbf{S}_{q_2})), \mathbf{S}_{q_3})$$
$$= \mathbf{p}_e{}^\top C(\mathbf{S}_{q_1}, C(\mathbf{S}_{q_2}, \mathbf{S}_{q_3}))$$
$$= \phi(q_1 \wedge (q_2 \wedge q_3), e)$$

$\square$

(3) Conjunction elimination: $\phi(q_1 \wedge q_2, e) \leq \phi(q_1, e), \phi(q_1 \wedge q_2, e) \leq \phi(q_2, e)$.

Proof $\phi(q_1 \wedge q_2, e) \leq \phi(q_1, e)$ can be proved by

$$\phi(q_1 \wedge q_2, e)$$
$$= \mathbf{p}_e{}^\top C(\mathbf{S}_{q_1}, \mathbf{S}_{q_2})$$
$$= \mathbf{p}_e{}^\top (\mathbf{S}_{q_1} \circ \mathbf{S}_{q_2})$$
$$= \sum_{i=1}^{d} \mathbf{p}_{ei} \mathbf{S}_{q_{1i}} \mathbf{S}_{q_{2i}}$$
$$\leq \sum_{i=1}^{d} \mathbf{p}_{ei} \mathbf{S}_{q_{1i}}$$
$$= \phi(q_1, e)$$

$\phi(q_1 \wedge q_2, e) \leq \phi(q_2, e)$ can be proved similarly. $\square$

Proposition 4.2 *Our disjunction operator $\mathcal{D}$ is (1) commutative, (2) associative, and satisfies (3) disjunction amplification.*

(1) Commutativity: $\phi(q_1 \vee q_2, e) = \phi(q_2 \vee q_1, e)$.

Proof We have $\mathcal{D}(\mathbf{S}_{q_1}, \mathbf{S}_{q_2}) = \mathbf{S}_{q_1} + \mathbf{S}_{q_2} - \mathbf{S}_{q_1} \circ \mathbf{S}_{q_2} = \mathbf{S}_{q_2} + \mathbf{S}_{q_1} - \mathbf{S}_{q_2} \circ \mathbf{S}_{q_1} = \mathcal{D}(\mathbf{S}_{q_2}, \mathbf{S}_{q_1})$. Therefore, $\phi(q_1 \vee q_2, e) = \mathbf{p}_e{}^\top \mathcal{D}(\mathbf{S}_{q_1}, \mathbf{S}_{q_2}) = \mathbf{p}_e{}^\top \mathcal{D}(\mathbf{S}_{q_2}, \mathbf{S}_{q_1}) = \phi(q_2 \vee q_1, e)$. $\square$

(2) Associativity: $\phi((q_1 \vee q_2) \vee q_3, e) = \phi(q_1 \vee (q_2 \vee q_3), e)$.

Proof

$$\mathcal{D}(\mathcal{D}(\mathbf{S}_{q1}, \mathbf{S}_{q2})), \mathbf{S}_{q3})$$
$$= \mathcal{D}(\mathbf{S}_{q1} + \mathbf{S}_{q2} - \mathbf{S}_{q1} \circ \mathbf{S}_{q2}, \mathbf{S}_{q3})$$
$$= (\mathbf{S}_{q1} + \mathbf{S}_{q2} - \mathbf{S}_{q1} \circ \mathbf{S}_{q2}) + \mathbf{S}_{q3} - (\mathbf{S}_{q1} + \mathbf{S}_{q2} - \mathbf{S}_{q1} \circ \mathbf{S}_{q2}) \circ \mathbf{S}_{q3}$$
$$= \mathbf{S}_{q1} + \mathbf{S}_{q2} + \mathbf{S}_{q3} - \mathbf{S}_{q1} \circ \mathbf{S}_{q2} - \mathbf{S}_{q1} \circ \mathbf{S}_{q3} - \mathbf{S}_{q2} \circ \mathbf{S}_{q3} + \mathbf{S}_{q1} \circ \mathbf{S}_{q2} \circ \mathbf{S}_{q3}$$
$$= \mathcal{D}(\mathbf{S}_{q1}, \mathcal{D}(\mathbf{S}_{q2} \cdot \mathbf{S}_{q3}))$$

Therefore

$$\phi((q_1 \vee q_2) \vee q_3, e)$$
$$= \mathbf{p}_e{}^\mathsf{T} \mathcal{D}(\mathcal{D}(\mathbf{S}_{q1}, \mathbf{S}_{q2})), \mathbf{S}_{q3})$$
$$= \mathbf{p}_e{}^\mathsf{T} \mathcal{D}(\mathbf{S}_{q1}, \mathcal{D}(\mathbf{S}_{q2}, \mathbf{S}_{q3}))$$
$$= \phi(q_1 \vee (q_2 \vee q_3), e)$$

$\square$

(3) Disjunction amplification: $\phi(q_1 \vee q_2, e) \geq \phi(q_1, e)$, $\phi(q_1 \vee q_2, e) \geq \phi(q_2, e)$.

Proof $\phi(q_1 \vee q_2, e) \geq \phi(q_1, e)$ can be proved by

$$\phi(q_1 \vee q_2, e)$$
$$= \mathbf{p}_e{}^\mathsf{T} \mathcal{D}(\mathbf{S}_{q1}, \mathbf{S}_{q2})$$
$$= \mathbf{p}_e{}^\mathsf{T} (\mathbf{S}_{q1} + \mathbf{S}_{q2} - \mathbf{S}_{q1} \circ \mathbf{S}_{q2})$$
$$= \sum_{i=1}^{d} \mathbf{p}_{ei} (\mathbf{S}_{q1_i} + \mathbf{S}_{q2_i} - \mathbf{S}_{q1_i} \mathbf{S}_{q2_i})$$
$$= \sum_{i=1}^{d} \mathbf{p}_{ei} \mathbf{S}_{q1_i} + \mathbf{p}_{ei} \mathbf{S}_{q2_i} (1 - \mathbf{S}_{q1_i})$$
$$\geq \sum_{i=1}^{d} \mathbf{p}_{ei} \mathbf{S}_{q1_i}$$
$$= \phi(q_1, e)$$

$\phi(q_1 \vee q_2, e) \geq \phi(q_2, e)$ can be proved similarly. $\square$

Proposition 4.3 *Our   negation   operator N is   (1)   involutory   and   satisfies (2) non-contradiction.*

(1) Involution $\phi(q, e) = \phi(\neg\neg q, e)$

Proof

$$\mathcal{N}(\mathcal{N}(q)) = \mathbf{1} - (\mathbf{1} - \mathbf{S}_q) = \mathbf{S}_q$$

Therefore $\phi(\neg\neg q, e) = \mathbf{p}_e{}^\top \mathcal{N}(\mathcal{N}(\mathbf{S}_q)) = \phi(q, e)$. □

(2) Non-contradiction $\phi(q, e) \uparrow \Rightarrow \phi(\neg q, e) \downarrow$

Proof $\phi(\neg q, e) = \mathcal{N}(q) \circ \mathbf{p}_e = (\mathbf{1} - \mathbf{S}_q) \circ \mathbf{p}_e = 1 - \mathbf{S}_q \circ \mathbf{p}_e$. The last equation holds as $\mathbf{p}_e$ is a stochastic vector and its elements sum up to 1. Therefore, $\phi(\neg q, e) = 1 - \phi(q, e)$, and thus $\phi(\neg q, e)$ is monotonically decreasing with regard to $\phi(q, e)$. □

4.4.3 Connection to Existing Approaches

Despite the strong capability of representation learning-based logical query answering methods in handling missing edges, most logical operators designed in existing studies do not satisfy the axiomatic system of classical logic, limiting their performance. This section examines the three representative logical query embedding models introduced in Sect. 4.3, namely GQE [4], Query2Box [5], and BetaE [6], regarding their capability of satisfying the properties in Table 4.3. We summarize our findings in Table 4.4.

Analysis of Prior Models on Model Properties

GQE, Query2Box, BetaE represent queries as vectors, boxes (axis-aligned hyper-rectangles), and Beta distributions, respectively. The embedding-based logical operators transform embeddings of sub-queries into embeddings of the outcome query. A brief summary of the logical operators of these models is given below.

Conjunction ($\wedge$). Figure 4.4 illustrates embedding-based conjunction operators of the three models, which take embeddings of queries q_1, q_2 as input and produce an embedding for $q_1 \wedge q_2$. GQE, Query2Box, and BetaE are purposely constructed to be permutation invariant [4–6], and their conjunction operators all satisfy *commutativity* (Law II). The conjunction operators of GQE and BetaE do not satisfy *associativity* (III) since they rely on the operation of averaging, which is not associative. GQE does not satisfy *conjunction elimination* (I); for example, supposing that $\mathbf{p}_e = \frac{1}{2}(\mathbf{S}_{q_1} + \mathbf{S}_{q_2})$, $\mathbf{S}_{q_1} \neq \mathbf{S}_{q_2}$, we have $\phi(q_1 \wedge q_2, e) = \cos(\mathbf{p}_e, \frac{1}{2}(\mathbf{S}_{q_1} + \mathbf{S}_{q_2})) > \cos(\mathbf{p}_e, \mathbf{S}_{q_1}) = \phi(q_1, e)$ (assuming $\mathbf{S}_{q_1}$ has a smaller angle to $\mathbf{p}_e$ compared to $\mathbf{S}_{q_2}$). BetaE does not satisfy *conjunction elimination* (I) for similar reasons.

Disjunction ($\vee$). Previous works handle disjunction in two ways: the *Disjunctive Normal Form (DNF) rewriting* approach proposed by Query2Box [5], and the *De Morgan's law*

Table 4.4 Comparisons of different models regarding the properties of logical operations. *Expressivity* indicates whether the model can handle such logical operations, and *closed* indicates whether the embedding is in a closed form. *Commu., Asso., Elim., Ampli., Inv.* and *Non-contra.* stand for commutativity, associativity, conjunction elimination, disjunction amplification, involution, and non-contradiction respectively

	∧				∨				¬		
	Expressivity (Closed)	Com.	Asso.	Elim.	Expressivity (Closed)	Com.	Asso.	Ampli.	Expressivity (Closed)	Inv.	Non-contra.
GQE	✓ (✓)	✓	✗	✗	✓ (✗)	✓	✓	✓	✗	N/A	N/A
Query2Box	✓ (✓)	✓	✓	✓	✓ (✗)	✓	✓	✓	✗	N/A	N/A
BetaE	✓ (✓)	✓	✗	✗	(i) DNF ✓ (✗) (ii) DM ✓ (✓)	✓	✓	✓ ✗	✓ (✓)	✓	✗
FuzzQE	✓ (✓)	✓	✓	✓	✓ (✓)	✓	✓	✓	✓ (✓)	✓	✓

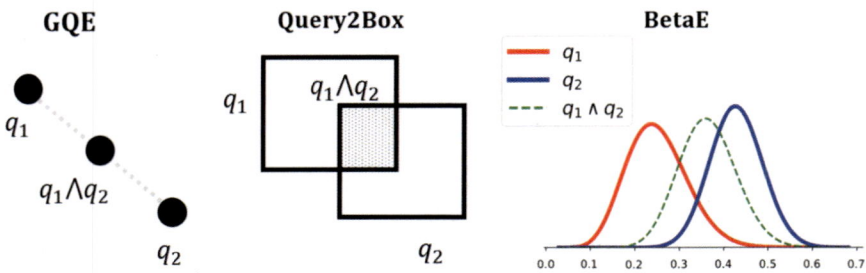

Fig. 4.4 Illustration of query embeddings and embeddings of conjunctive queries in GQE, Query2Box, and BetaE. The conjunction operators take embeddings of queries q_1, q_2 as input and produce an embedding for $q_1 \wedge q_2$

(DM) approach proposed by BetaE [6]. The DNF rewriting method involves rewriting each query as a DNF to ensure that disjunction only appears in the last step, which enables the model to simply retain all input embeddings. The model correspondingly cannot represent the disjunction result as a closed form; for example, the disjunction of two boxes remains two separate boxes instead of one [5]. The DM approach uses De Morgan's law $\psi_1 \vee \psi_2 \equiv \neg(\neg\psi_1 \wedge \neg\psi_2)$ to compute the disjunctive query embedding, which requires the model to have a conjunction operator and a negation operator. This approach advantageously produces representation in a closed form, allowing disjunction to be performed at any step of the computation. The disadvantage is that if the negation operator does not work well, the error will be amplified and affect disjunction. The DM variant of BetaE, namely BetaE$_{\text{DM}}$, does not satisfy *disjunction amplification* (IV) since its negation operator violates *non-contradiction* (VIII).

Negation ($\neg$). The negation operator $\mathcal{N}_\alpha$, $\mathcal{N}_\beta$ of BetaE are defined as follows:

$$\mathcal{N}_\alpha(\mathbf{S}_q)(i) = 1/\mathbf{S}_{q_\alpha}(i), \quad i = 1, ..., d$$
$$\mathcal{N}_\beta(\mathbf{S}_q)(i) = 1/\mathbf{S}_{q_\beta}(i), \quad i = 1, ..., d$$

BetaE has proved that its negation operator is *involutory* (VII) [6]. However, this operator lacks the *non-contradiction* property (VIII), as BetaE $\phi(\neg q, e)$ is not monotonically decreasing with regard to $\phi(q, e)$. Figure 4.5 shows a one-dimensional case where the negation operator of BetaE does not satisfy non-contradiction, as $\phi(\neg q, e)$ is not monotonically decreasing with regard to $\phi(q, e)$.

4.4.4 Experiments

In this section, we evaluate the ability of FuzzQE to answer complex FOL queries over incomplete KGs.

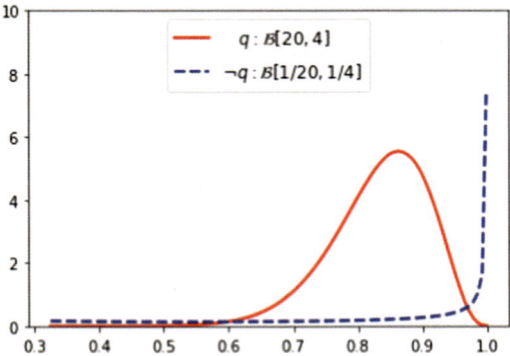

Fig. 4.5 Illustration of a one-dimensional example where the negation operator of BetaE does not satisfy non-contradiction, i.e. $\phi(\neg q, e)$ is not monotonically decreasing with regard to $\phi(q, e)$. The y-axis indicates the score, and the x-axis indicates the value of e

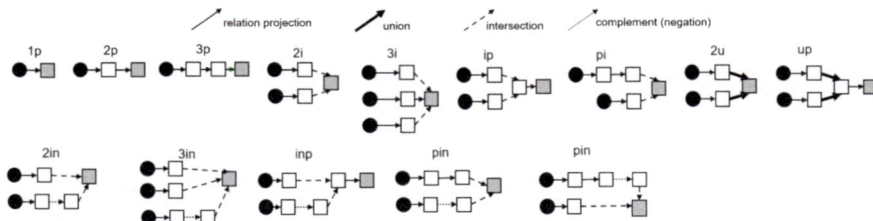

Fig. 4.6 Query structure types in the datasets provided by BetaE [6]. Naming convention: p for relation projection, i for conjunction (intersection), n for negation (complement), u for disjunction (union). 10 query structures are used for both training and evaluation: *1p, 2p, 3p, 2i, 3i, 2in, 3in, inp, pni, pin*. In order to test the generalization capability of the model, 4 query structures (*ip, pi, 2u, up*) are not present in training and only included for evaluation

4.4.4.1 Evaluation Setup

Datasets. We evaluate our model on two benchmark datasets provided by [6], which contain 14 types of logical queries on FB15k-237 [18] and NELL995 [19] respectively. The 14 types of query structures in the datasets are shown in Fig. 4.6. Note that these datasets provided by BetaE [6] are an improved and expanded version of the datasets provided by Query2Box [5]. Compared to the earlier version, the new datasets [6] contain 5 new types of queries that involve negation. The validation/test set of the original 9 query types is regenerated to ensure that the number of answers per query is not excessive, making this task more challenging. In the new datasets, 10 query structures are used for both training and evaluation: $1p, 2p, 3p, 2i, 3i, 2in, 3in, inp, pni, pin$. 4 query structures ($ip, pi, 2u, up$) are not used for training but only included in evaluation in order to evaluate the model's generalization ability of answering queries with logical structures that the model has never seen during training. We exclude FB15k [15] since this dataset suffers from major test leakage [18].

Table 4.5 Knowledge graph dataset statistics as well as training, validation, and test edge splits

Dataset	Entities	Relations	Training edges	Validation edges	Test edges	Total edges
FB15k-237	14505	237	272115	17526	20438	310079
NELL	63361	200	114213	143234	14267	142804

Table 4.6 Number of training, validation, and test queries for different query structures. For columns that list multiple query structures, the number in the table represents the number of each query structure

	Training		Validation		Test	
Dataset	1p/2p/3p/2i/3i	2in/3in/inp/pin/pni	1p	Others	1p	Others
FB15k-237	149,689	149,68	20,101	5,000	2,812	5,000
NELL995	107,982	10,798	16,927	4,000	17,034	4,000

The KG statistics are summarized in Table 4.5 and the numbers of training/validation/test queries are list in Table 4.6.

Evaluation Protocol. We follow the evaluation protocol in [6]. To evaluate the model's generalization capability over incomplete KGs, the datasets are masked out so that each validation/test query answer pair involves imputing at least one missing edge. For each answer to a test query, we use the Mean Reciprocal Rank (MRR) as the major evaluation metric. We use the *filtered* setting [15] and filter out other correct answers from ranking before calculating the MRR.

Baselines and Model Configurations. We consider three logical query embedding baselines for answering complex logical queries on KGs: GQE [4], Query2Box [5], and BetaE [6]. We also compare with one recent state-of-the-art query optimization model CQD [20]. For GQE, Query2Box, and BetaE we use implementation provided by [6].[2] For BetaE and CQD, we compare with the model variant that generally provides better performance, namely BetaE$_{DNF}$ and CQD-BEAM. CQD cannot process complex logical queries during training and is thus trained with KG edges. In these baselines, BetaE is the only available baseline that can handle negation. Therefore, for GQE, Query2Box, and CQD, we compare with them only on EPFO queries (queries with $\exists$, $\wedge$, $\vee$ and without negation).

For FuzzQE, we report results using the logic system that provides the best average MRR on the validation set. we use AdamW [21] as the optimizer. Training terminates with early stopping based on the average MRR on the validation set with a patience of 15k steps. We repeat each experiment three times with different random seeds and report the average results.

---

[2] https://github.com/snap-stanford/KGReasoning.

4.4.4.2 Main Results: Trained with FOL Queries

We first test the ability of FuzzQE to model arbitrary FOL queries when complex logical queries are available for training. Results are reported in Table 4.7.

Comparison with Query Embedding As shown in Table 4.7, FuzzQE consistently outperforms all the logical query embedding baselines. For EPFO queries, FuzzQE improves the average MRR of best baseline BetaE [6] by 3.3% (a 15% relative improvement) on FB15k-237 and 4.7% (a 19% relative improvement) on NELL995. For queries with negation, FuzzQE significantly outperforms the only available baseline BetaE. On average, FuzzQE improves the MRR by 3.0% (54% relatively) on FB15k-237 and 2.1% (36% relatively) on NELL995 for queries containing negation. We hypothesize that this significant enhancement comes from the principled design of our negation operator that satisfies the axioms, while BetaE fails to satisfy the non-contradiction property.

Comparison with Query Optimization: CQD We next compare FuzzQE with a recent query optimization baseline, CQD [20] on EPFO queries. On average, FuzzQE provides 2.5% and 0.9% absolute improvement in MRR on FB15k-237 and NELL995 respectively. It is worth noting that FuzzQE outperforms CQD on most complex query structures on NELL995 even with slightly worse $1p$ query answering performance. We hypothesize that the $1p$ query answering performance difference on NELL995 comes from the differenct abilities of different relation projection/link prediction models to encode sparse knowledge graphs.

A major motivation for learning logical query embedding is its high inference efficiency. We compare with CQD with regard to the time for answering a query. On a NVIDIA® GP102 TITAN Xp (12GB), the average time for CQD to answer a FOL query on FB15k-237 is 13.9 ms (milliseconds), while FuzzQE takes only 0.3 ms. On NELL995, where the number of entities is 4 times the number in FB15k-237, the average time for CQD is 68.1 ms, whereas FuzzQE needs only 0.4 ms. CQD takes 170 times longer than FuzzQE. The reason is that CQD is required to score all the entities for each subquery to obtain the top-k candidates for beam search.

4.4.4.3 Trained with only Link Prediction

This experiment tests the ability of the model to generalize to arbitrary complex logical queries when it is trained with only the link prediction task. To evaluate it, we train FuzzQE and other logical query embedding models using only KG edges (i.e., $1p$ queries). For baseline models GQE, Query2Box, and BetaE, we adapt them following the experiment settings of the Q2B-AVG-1P model discussed in [5]. Specifically, we set all the sub-query weights to 1.0 for this experiment.

As shown in Table 4.8, FuzzQE is able to generalize to complex logical queries of new query structures even if it is trained on link prediction and provides significantly better performance than baseline models. Compared to the best baseline, FuzzQE improves the average MRR by 3.6% (20% relatively) for EPFO queries on FB15k-237 and 5.4% (26%

Table 4.7 MRR results (%) on answering FOL queries. We report MRR results (%) on test FOL queries. Avg_{EPFO} and Avg_{Neg} denote the average MRR on EPFO queries (queries with $\exists$, $\wedge$, $\vee$ and without negation) and queries containing negation respectively. Results of GQE, Query2Box, and BetaE are taken from [6]

Type of model	Model	Avg_{EPFO}	Avg_{Neg}	1p	2p	3p	2i	3i	pi	ip	2u	up	2in	3in	inp	pin	pni
FB15k-237																	
Query embedding	GQE	16.3	N/A	35.0	7.2	5.3	23.3	34.6	16.5	10.7	8.2	5.7	N/A	N/A	N/A	N/A	N/A
	Query2Box	20.1	N/A	40.6	9.4	6.8	29.5	42.3	21.2	12.6	11.3	7.6	N/A	N/A	N/A	N/A	N/A
	BetaE	20.9	5.5	39.0	10.9	10.0	28.8	42.5	22.4	12.6	12.4	9.7	5.1	7.9	7.4	3.5	3.4
	FuzzQE	**24.2**	**8.5**	42.2	**13.3**	**10.2**	**33.0**	**47.3**	**26.2**	**18.9**	**15.6**	**10.8**	**9.7**	**12.6**	**7.8**	**5.8**	**6.6**
Query optimization	CQD	21.7	N/A	**46.3**	9.9	5.9	31.7	41.3	21.8	15.8	14.2	8.6	N/A	N/A	N/A		N/A
NELL995																	
Query embedding	GQE	18.6	N/A	32.8	11.9	9.6	27.5	35.2	18.4	14.4	8.5	8.8	N/A	N/A	N/A	N/A	N/A
	Query2Box	22.9	N/A	42.2	14.0	11.2	33.3	44.5	22.4	16.8	11.3	10.3	N/A	N/A	N/A	N/A	N/A
	BetaE	24.6	5.9	53.0	13.0	11.4	37.6	47.5	24.1	14.3	12.2	8.5	5.1	7.8	10.0	3.1	3.5
	FuzzQE	**29.3**	**8.0**	58.1	**19.3**	**15.7**	39.8	**50.3**	**28.1**	**21.8**	**17.3**	**13.7**	**8.3**	**10.2**	**11.5**	**4.6**	**5.4**
Query optimization	CQD	28.4	N/A	**60.0**	16.5	10.4	**40.4**	49.6	27.6	20.8	16.8	12.6	N/A	N/A	N/A	N/A	N/A

Table 4.8 MRR results (%) of logical query embedding models that are trained with only link prediction. This task tests the ability of the model to generalize to arbitrary complex logical queries, when no complex logical query data is available for training. Avg_{EPFO} and Avg_{Neg} denote the average MRR on EPFO ($\exists$, $\land$, $\lor$) queries and queries containing negation respectively

Model	Avg_{EPFO}	Avg_{Neg}	1p	2p	3p	2i	3i	pi	ip	2u	up	2in	3in	inp	pin	pni
FB15k-237																
GQE	17.7	N/A	41.6	7.9	5.4	25.0	33.6	16.3	10.9	11.9	6.2	N/A	N/A	N/A	N/A	N/A
Query2Box	18.2	N/A	42.6	6.9	4.7	27.3	36.8	17.5	11.1	11.7	5.5	N/A	N/A	N/A	N/A	N/A
BetaE	15.8	0.5	37.7	5.6	4.4	23.3	34.5	15.1	7.8	9.5	4.5	0.1	1.1	0.8	0.1	0.2
FuzzQE	**21.8**	**6.6**	**44.0**	**10.8**	**8.6**	**32.3**	**41.4**	**22.7**	**15.1**	**13.5**	**8.7**	**7.7**	**9.5**	**7.0**	**4.1**	**4.7**
NELL995																
GQE	21.7	N/A	47.2	12.7	9.3	30.6	37.0	20.6	16.1	12.6	9.6	N/A	N/A	N/A	N/A	N/A
Query2Box	21.6	N/A	47.6	12.5	8.7	30.7	36.5	20.5	16.0	12.7	9.6	N/A	N/A	N/A	N/A	N/A
BetaE	19.0	0.4	53.1	6.0	3.9	32.0	37.7	15.8	8.5	10.1	3.5	0.1	1.4	0.1	0.1	0.1
FuzzQE	**27.1**	**7.3**	**57.6**	**17.2**	**13.3**	**38.2**	**41.5**	**27.0**	**19.4**	**16.9**	**12.7**	**9.1**	**8.3**	**8.9**	**4.4**	**5.6**

relatively) on NELL995. Regarding queries with negation, our model drastically outperforms the only available baseline BetaE across datasets. In addition, compared with the ones trained with complex FOL queries (in Table 4.7), It is worth noting that FuzzQE trained with only link prediction can outperform BetaE models that are trained with extra complex logical queries in terms of average MRR (in Table 4.7). This demonstrates the superiority of the logical operators in FuzzQE, which are designed in a principled and learning-free manner. Meanwhile, FuzzQE can still take advantage of additional complex queries as training samples to enhance entity embeddings.

4.5   Summary and Discussions

Complex query answering in KGs refers to the process of retrieving answers to queries in the form of First-Order Logical (FOL). Complex queries in KGs can be challenging to answer because they may involve multiple steps or relations between entities. For example, a query such as "Which University did the Turing Award winner work on deep learning work at?" involves reasoning about multiple relations between researchers and affiliations, researchers and research areas, as well as researchers and awards. To answer complex queries in KGs, various approaches can be used, including traditional subgraph matching methods and more recent logical query embedding methods.

Subgraph matching is a well-studied problem in graph theory. It involves searching for a pattern or subgraph within a larger graph that corresponds to a specified query. Since the results obtained from subgraph matching methods are typically easy to interpret, they ensure the correctness and interpretability of answers to complex queries. However, the computational complexity of subgraph matching can make it prohibitively expensive when working with large and complex KGs containing numerous entities and relations. Furthermore, sub-graph matching may be susceptible to noise and errors in the data, potentially leading to inaccuracy in the results.

Logical query embedding is a more recent approach that employs neural-symbolic techniques to answer complex queries. The core idea is to embed the logical query graph and entities into a low-dimensional vector space, bringing entities that answer the query graph closer to the query in the embedding space. Since logical query embedding utilizes representation learning techniques for answering logical queries, it can efficiently handle incomplete and noisy KGs. Moreover, this approach enables users to directly express queries using first-order logic, thereby accommodating a wider range of query types. However, logical query embedding methods require KG training, which can be both time-consuming and computationally demanding. Additionally, these methods may exhibit lower interpretability and be prone to approximation errors.

Despite ongoing advancements in logical query embedding, the field is still in its early stages. One issue is that many existing logical query embedding models do not ensure that the logical operations they use satisfy logical laws, leading to inferior performance. In response to this limitation, the FuzzQE model has been introduced as a cutting-edge approach to logical query embedding that defines logical operators using fuzzy logic in the vector space, ensuring that logic laws are satisfied and improving performance.

Owing to space constraints, our discussion will primarily focus on the main approaches to complex query answering. Nonetheless, it's crucial to recognize that there are other promising avenues in this field, which we will touch upon below.

Improve interpretability of Logical Query Embedding Methods
While FuzzQE employs fuzzy logic in the vector space to define logical operators, ensuring the satisfaction of logic laws and enabling the differentiation of logic operations, it can be challenging to interpret the set of entities encoded by an intermediate embedding. This leaves the reasoning process opaque to users.

To improve interpretability, GNN-QE [22], follows symbolic methods that yield a set of assignments for each intermediate variable. Specifically, it breaks down a complex First-Order Logic (FOL) query into an expression over fuzzy sets, thereby achieving interpretability for intermediate variables. Each basic operation in the expression is either a relation projection or a logical operation (such as conjunction, disjunction, and negation). The design of the relation projection is such that it is a Graph Neural Network (GNN) predicting the fuzzy set of tail entities given a fuzzy set of head entities and a relation.

Combine with Large Language Model for KG Question Answering
All the methods outlined in this section necessitate a formal logical query as input. In practical terms, defining such a query may demand substantial effort from a human expert. In recent years, Large Language Models (LLMs), such as OpenAI's GPT-4, have demonstrated exceptional capabilities in parsing and understanding natural language queries. Integrating LLMs with KGs for question answering allows users to pose questions in natural language and retrieve answers from KGs, fostering more user-friendly interactions.

Recent studies which employed LLMs to bridge the gap between natural language questions and structured KGs fall into two main categories:

- **Entity/Relation Extraction**: In this category, LLMs are used to identify entities and relations mentioned in natural language questions. Subsequently, the extracted entity-relation pairs are utilized to query knowledge graphs for answers [23–26].
- **Answer Reasoning**: When LLMs are employed as answer reasoners, they combine retrieved facts from the KGs with natural language questions and candidate answers. This concatenated information is then input into LLMs to predict answer scores [27–29].

Utilizing KGs can offer a source of reliable information, invaluable for mitigating issues related to hallucination. By integrating LLMs to facilitate the connection between natural language queries and structured KGs, we can establish AI systems that are contextually aware and transparent. This approach extends the advantageous reasoning capabilities of KGs to the realm of generation-based question-answering, leading to more trustworthy responses.

References

1. X. Chen, Z. Hu, and Y. Sun. Fuzzy logic based logical query answering on knowledge graphs. In *Proceedings of AAAI Conference on Artificial Intelligence (AAAI)*, volume 36, pages 3939–3948, 2022.
2. J. R. Ullmann. An algorithm for subgraph isomorphism. *Journal of the ACM (JACM)*, 23(1):31–42, 1976.
3. J. Pérez, M. Arenas, and C. Gutierrez. Semantics and complexity of sparql. *ACM Transactions on Database Systems (TODS)*, 34(3):1–45, 2009.
4. W. Hamilton, P. Bajaj, M. Zitnik, D. Jurafsky, and J. Leskovec. Embedding logical queries on knowledge graphs. *Advances in Neural Information Processing Systems (NeurIPS)*, 31, 2018.
5. H. Ren, W. Hu, and J. Leskovec. Query2box: Reasoning over knowledge graphs in vector space using box embeddings. *arXiv preprint* arXiv:2002.05969, 2020.
6. H. Ren and J. Leskovec. Beta embeddings for multi-hop logical reasoning in knowledge graphs. *Advances in Neural Information Processing Systems (NeurIPS)*, 33:19716–19726, 2020.
7. L. Liu, B. Du, H. Ji, C. Zhai, and H. Tong. Neural-answering logical queries on knowledge graphs. In *Proceedings of the ACM SIGKDD International Conference on Knowledge Discovery and Data Mining (KDD)*, pages 1087–1097, 2021.
8. H.-J. Zimmermann. *Fuzzy set theory-and its applications*. Springer Science & Business Media, 2011.
9. G. Klir and B. Yuan. *Fuzzy sets and fuzzy logic*, volume 4. Prentice hall New Jersey, 1995.
10. K. Chvalovskỳ. On the independence of axioms in bl and mtl. *Fuzzy Sets and Systems*, 197:123–129, 2012.
11. J. C. Fodor and M. Roubens. *Fuzzy preference modelling and multicriteria decision support*, volume 14. Springer Science & Business Media, 2013.
12. A. Katsaras and D. B. Liu. Fuzzy vector spaces and fuzzy topological vector spaces. *Journal of Mathematical Analysis and Applications*, 58(1):135–146, 1977.
13. J. L. Ba, J. R. Kiros, and G. E. Hinton. Layer normalization. *stat*, 1050:21, 2016.

14. M. Schlichtkrull, T. N. Kipf, P. Bloem, R. Van Den Berg, I. Titov, and M. Welling. Modeling relational data with graph convolutional networks. In *The Semantic Web: 15th International Conference*, pages 593–607. Springer, 2018.

15. A. Bordes, N. Usunier, A. Garcia-Duran, J. Weston, and O. Yakhnenko. Translating embeddings for modeling multi-relational data. In *Advances in Neural Information Processing Systems (NeurIPS)*, pages 2787–2795, 2013.

16. G. Ji, S. He, L. Xu, K. Liu, and J. Zhao. Knowledge graph embedding via dynamic mapping matrix. In *Proceedings of the Annual Meeting of Associations for Computational Linguistics (ACL)*, pages 687–696. The Association for Computer Linguistics, 2015.

17. E. P. Klement, R. Mesiar, and E. Pap. *Triangular norms*, volume 8. Springer Science & Business Media, 2013.

18. K. Toutanova and D. Chen. Observed versus latent features for knowledge base and text inference. In *Proceedings of the 3rd Workshop on Continuous Vector Space Models and Their Compositionality*, pages 57–66, 2015.

19. W. Xiong, T. Hoang, and W. Y. Wang. Deeppath: A reinforcement learning method for knowledge graph reasoning. *arXiv preprint* arXiv:1707.06690, 2017.

20. E. Arakelyan, D. Daza, P. Minervini, and M. Cochez. Complex query answering with neural link predictors. *arXiv preprint* arXiv:2011.03459, 2020.

21. I. Loshchilov and F. Hutter. Decoupled weight decay regularization. *arXiv preprint* arXiv:1711.05101, 2017.

22. Z. Zhu, M. Galkin, Z. Zhang, and J. Tang. Neural-symbolic models for logical queries on knowledge graphs. *arXiv preprint* arXiv:2205.10128, 2022.

23. D. Lukovnikov, A. Fischer, and J. Lehmann. Pretrained transformers for simple question answering over knowledge graphs. In *Proceedings of the International Semantic Web Conference (ISWC)*, pages 470–486. Springer, 2019.

24. N. Hu, Y. Wu, G. Qi, D. Min, J. Chen, J. Z. Pan, and Z. Ali. An empirical study of pre-trained language models in simple knowledge graph question answering. In *Proceedings of the International World Wide Web Conference (WWW)*, pages 1–32. Springer, 2023.

25. M. Yasunaga, H. Ren, A. Bosselut, P. Liang, and J. Leskovec. Qa-gnn: Reasoning with language models and knowledge graphs for question answering. *arXiv preprint* arXiv:2104.06378, 2021.

26. D. Luo, J. Su, and S. Yu. A bert-based approach with relation-aware attention for knowledge base question answering. In *2020 International Joint Conference on Neural Networks (IJCNN)*, pages 1–8. IEEE, 2020.

27. Y. Xu, C. Zhu, R. Xu, Y. Liu, M. Zeng, and X. Huang. Fusing context into knowledge graph for commonsense question answering. *arXiv preprint* arXiv:2012.04808, 2020.

28. M. Zhang, R. Dai, M. Dong, and T. He. Drlk: dynamic hierarchical reasoning with language model and knowledge graph for question answering. In *Proceedings of the 2022 Conference on Empirical Methods in Natural Language Processing (EMNLP)*, pages 5123–5133, 2022.

29. Y. Yan, R. Li, S. Wang, H. Zhang, Z. Daoguang, F. Zhang, W. Wu, and W. Xu. Large-scale relation learning for question answering over knowledge bases with pre-trained language models. In *Proceedings of the 2021 Conference on Empirical Methods in Natural Language Processing (EMNLP)*, pages 3653–3660, 2021.

Logical Rule Learning

5

"To attain knowledge, add things everyday. To attain wisdom, remove things every day."—Lao Tse

5.1 Overview

Logical rules are widely used to represent domain knowledge and hypothesis, which is fundamental to symbolic reasoning-based human intelligence and belongs to the regime of *inductive* reasoning (i.e., going from specific to general). Very recently, it has been demonstrated that integrating logical rules into regular learning tasks can further enhance learning performance in a label-efficient manner, such as KG completion tasks discussed in Chap. 3. Despite the promising reasoning ability of symbolic methods, they require the set of logical rules to be specified by hand, which are usually *labor-intensive*. To reduce the demand on human efforts, *automatically* learning logical rules from examples in KGs becomes critical. Logical rules can facilitate the *generalization* of knowledge from specific examples or scenarios, enabling AI systems to apply learned knowledge to novel situations. This ability to generalize is crucial for transfer learning, which enables AI systems to adapt and reuse knowledge from one domain to another. Additionally, learning logical rules allows for knowledge representation in a format that is easily understandable by humans. Logical rules are often presented as "if-then" statements, which are easy to comprehend, interpret, and justify. This interpretability is valuable for decision-making processes and fosters trust in AI systems.

Formally, logical rule learning aims to learn logical rules in the following form:

$$r_h(x_h, y_h) \leftarrow r_{b_1}(x_{b_1}, y_{b_1}) \wedge \cdots \wedge r_{b_n}(x_{b_n}, y_{b_n}) \tag{5.1}$$

where the predicate $r_h(x_h, y_h)$ is called *rule head* (or *conclusion*), and $r_{b_1}(x_{b_1}, y_{b_1}) \wedge \cdots \wedge r_{b_n}(x_{b_n}, y_{b_n})$ is called *rule body* (or *premise*). Combining rule head and rule body, we denote

© The Author(s), under exclusive license to Springer Nature Switzerland AG 2025   107
K. Cheng and Y. Sun, *Knowledge Graph Reasoning*, Synthesis Lectures on Data, Semantics, and Knowledge, https://doi.org/10.1007/978-3-031-72008-6_5

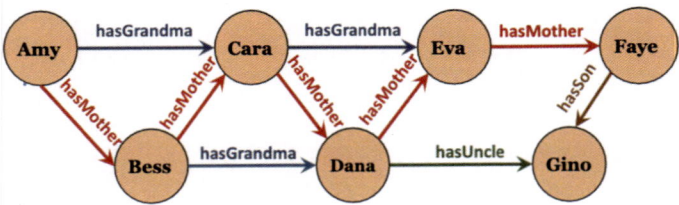

Fig. 5.1 An instance of a kinship knowledge graph is depicted, where various relationships are denoted by arrows of distinct colors

a logical rule as (*Head*, *Body*). The length of a rule is denoted as n, which is the number of predicates appearing in its body. For a more comprehensive overview of logical rules, please refer to Sect. 2.3. An example of rule learning is shown in Fig. 5.1, where two rules can be extracted from the observed KG:

$$\delta_1 := \text{hasGrandma}(x, y) \leftarrow \text{hasMother}(x, z) \wedge \text{hasMother}(z, y)$$
$$\delta_2 := \text{hasUncle}(x, y) \leftarrow \text{hasMother}(x, z_1) \wedge \text{hasMother}(z_1, z_2) \wedge \text{hasSon}(z_2, y) \quad (5.2)$$

The fundamental idea of the logical rule learning methods is to assign a plausibility score $s(\text{Head}, \text{Body})$ to each rule candidate (*Head*, *Body*) within a designated *rule space*. This score function, denoted as $s(\cdot)$, is used to evaluate the likelihood of each rule candidate. Further explanation regarding the rule space will be provided in Sect. 5.2.

There are two primary categories of logical rule learning: (1) *traditional* search-based methods and (2) *recent* neuro-symbolic integration approaches.

- **Search-Based Methods**: These methods are a traditional approach to logical rule learning. They involve searching through the rule space to identify the optimal set of logical rules that explain the data. Typically, these methods rely on heuristics and pruning techniques to improve the efficiency of the search process. They may struggle with larger or more complex datasets.
- **Neuro-symbolic Integration**: neuro-symbolic integration is a modern approach to logical rule learning that combines the strengths of rule-based symbolic reasoning and connectionist neural networks. Neural networks are used to learn representations of the data, while symbolic logic is used to derive high-level rules from the learned representations. This approach is more promising as it can learn patterns that are difficult to be expressed using symbolic logic alone.

In the following subsections, we will provide a detailed explanation of these two categories of methods, including a comparison of their strengths and weaknesses.

5.2   Search-Based Logical Rule Learning

Search-based methods are traditional approaches to rule learning. These methods treat logical rules as discrete structures within KGs, such as closed paths, and model rule learning as a discrete optimization problem. The goal is to search over a discrete rule space to find the best set of rules that can effectively explain a given set of evidences.

Formally, we can define a *rule space* for rule learning in a KG as follows: Given a knowledge graph $G = \{\mathcal{E}, \mathcal{R}, \mathcal{O}\}$, let Δ be the set of possible Horn rules that can be learned from G, where each rule is represented as a pair (*Head, Body*), denoting a Horn rule in the form *Head* $\leftarrow$ *Body*. *Head* $= r_h(x_h, y_h)$ is a single atom (a.k.a., atomic formula) representing the head of the rule (i.e., the conclusion) and *Body* $= r_{b_1}(x_{b_1}, y_{b_1}) \wedge \cdots \wedge r_{b_n}(x_{b_n}, y_{b_n})$ is a conjunction of atoms representing the body of the rule (i.e., the premise). A formal definition of Horn rules can be found in Sect. 2.3.

The rule space for logical rules with a length of n can be formally defined as a structured space that encompasses all possible ways of constructing $r_{b_1}(x_{b_1}, y_{b_1}), \ldots, r_{b_n}(x_{b_n}, y_{b_n})$. For instance, in a KG with four relations {*hasMother, hasGrandma, hasUncle, hasSon*}, the search space for chain-like Horn rules with a length of 2 and a head relation *hasGrandma* can be visualized as a tree shown in Fig. 5.2. Here, a chain-like Horn rule is a special form of Horn rule where the rule body has a chain-like structure, which corresponds to a path in the KG. An example of a chain-like horn rule is given below:

$$r_h(x, y) \leftarrow r_{b_1}(x, z_1) \wedge r_{b_2}(z_1, z_2) \wedge \cdots \wedge r_{b_n}(z_{n-1}, y) \tag{5.3}$$

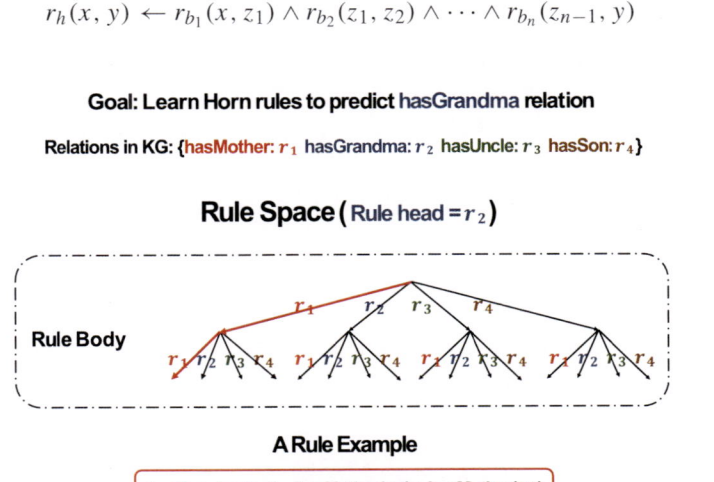

Goal: Learn Horn rules to predict hasGrandma relation

Relations in KG: {hasMother: r_1 hasGrandma: r_2 hasUncle: r_3 hasSon: r_4}

Rule Space (Rule head $= r_2$)

A Rule Example

hasGrandma(x,y) ← hasMother(x,z) ∧ hasMother(z,y)

Fig. 5.2 The search space for rules with head relation r_2 and body length 2. A path from the root to the leaf corresponds to a possible rule body. Together with the head relation, it forms a candidate rule. The figure highlights an example of a candidate rule that corresponds to the path in red

For a more comprehensive overview of chain-like Horn rules, please refer to Sect. 5.2. Each path in Fig. 5.2 from the root to the leaf corresponds to a candidate rule body, which, when combined with the head relation, forms a candidate rule. The highlighted path in red shows an example of a candidate rule in rule space.

$$\text{hasGrandma}(x, y) \leftarrow \text{hasMother}(x, z) \wedge \text{hasMother}(z, y) \qquad (5.4)$$

The rule space size of a chain-like Horn rule is $|\mathcal{R}|^n$, where $|\mathcal{R}|$ denotes the number of relations in the KG and n denotes the rule length. For instance, considering Horn rules with a length of 2 and a head relation *hasGrandma* in Fig. 5.2, the rule space comprises 4^2 potential rules. It is clear that the search space for rule learning methods can be vast, especially as rule length increases. Due to the potentially large rule space, the primary focus of search-based methods is to efficiently navigate the rule space to find the rules that meet the criterion.

Existing search-based methods for rule learning can be largely divided into two categories: (1) *Inductive Logic Programming (ILP)* and (2) *Association Rule Mining*. ILP is a subfield of logic programming, which aims at learning from examples to induce a set of rules or hypotheses that can be used to make predictions or classify new examples. Association rule mining is proposed by the data mining community, which is widely used to identify correlations in the data. In the following section, we will explore the most representative methods in each category.

5.2.1   Inductive Logic Programming (ILP)

Inductive Logic Programming (ILP) [2, 3] is a subfield of Artificial Intelligence (AI) that was first proposed in the late 1980s by Stephen Muggleton. The main objective of ILP is to induce logical rules or hypotheses from a given set of examples or data, typically represented in the form of predicates (e.g., triples in KG). The formal definition of the ILP problem is provided as follows:

Given a knowledge base (KB) B,[1] a set of positive examples denoted as E^+, and a set of negative examples denoted as E^-, ILP aims to learn a set of Horn rules, denoted as Δ, which are able to entail all the positive examples while excluding any of the negative examples:

$$\forall P \in E^+ : B \wedge \Delta \models P$$
$$\forall P \in E^- : B \wedge \Delta \not\models P$$

where P denotes the examples (i.e., ground predicates), $\models$ denotes logical entailment, and the symbol $\not\models$ is used to indicate that a specific model does not entail a given formula. For

---

[1] Knowledge base (KB) is a more general concept than knowledge graph, which contains (1) facts that are beyond binary predicates and (2) rules.

instance, the expression $\forall P \in E^- : B \wedge \Delta \not\models P$ means that within the model $B \wedge \Delta$, any negative example $P \in E^-$ cannot be logically entailed.

ILP algorithms typically involve a search strategy in the rule space and a scoring function $s(\cdot)$ to evaluate the quality of each rule. ILP has been successfully applied to a variety of domains, such as bioinformatics and natural language processing. We now use an example to illustrate how ILP works.

Example 5.2.1 A KB denoted as B on kinship consists of the following facts:

$$\{male(Antony), female(Bess), female(Charlotte), female(Diana), male(Ed),$$
$$parent(Antony, Bess), parent(Antony, Charlotte), parent(Diana, Bess),$$
$$parent(Diana, Charlotte), parent(Ed, Diana), father(Antony, Bess),$$
$$father(Antony, Charlotte), mother(Diana, Bess)\}$$

Two positive examples $E^+ = \{father(Antony, Bess), father(Antony, Charlotte)\}$ are given, and ten negative examples E^- are listed below:

$$\{father(Antony, Diana), \quad father(Bess, Antony), \quad father(Bess, Charlotte),$$
$$father(Bess, Diana), \quad father(Charlotte, Antony), father(Charlotte, Bess),$$
$$father(Charlotte, Diana), \quad father(Diana, Antony), \quad father(Diana, Bess),$$
$$father(Diana, Charlotte)\}$$

In this case, the goal is to learn rules to infer the target relation (i.e, rule head): father(x, y). In order to learn rules, the general ILP approach begins with the target relation father(x, y) and an empty rule body. To construct the rule body, ILP adds a literal that provides maximal coverage of the positive examples E^+ and minimal coverage of the negative examples E^-. The possible candidate literals to be added to the body are given as follows, which are predicates in B (excluding the target predicate) filled with variables x, y, z:

$$\{male(x), \quad male(y), \quad female(x), \quad female(y), \quad parent(x, y),$$
$$parent(x, z), parent(y, x), parent(y, z), parent(z, x), parent(z, y)\}$$

To simplify this process, we will only focus on literals that have at least one variable in common with the target relation *father*(x, y).

In order to choose the most useful literal from the candidate set, Quinlan proposed a *gain heuristic* as the score function in his FOIL algorithm [4] to evaluate the contribution of a literal l to the target relation, which is defined as:

$$\text{Gain}(l) = H * (\log_2(|E^+_{\text{post}}|/(|E^+_{\text{post}}| + |E^-_{\text{post}}|)) - \log_2(|E^+_{\text{pre}}|/(|E^+_{\text{pre}}| + |E^-_{\text{pre}}|)))$$

$$(5.5)$$

where $E^+_{\text{post}} \subseteq E^+$ ($E^-_{\text{post}} \subseteq E^-$) refer to the positive examples (negative examples) that can be entailed by the rule *after* adding the literal; $E^+_{\text{pre}} \subseteq E^+$ ($E^-_{\text{pre}} \subseteq E^-$) refer to the positive example (negative examples) that can be entailed by the rule *before* adding the literal; and

H is the number of positive examples that satisfy the rule before adding the new literal and are still covered after adding the literal.

According to the definition of the gain, we compute the gain value for all the literals. As an example, let us compute the gain value for the literal male(x), given the starting rule with rule head father(x, y) and an empty body. Before adding the literal male(x), the rule covers 2 positive examples and 10 negative examples, i.e., $|E_{\text{pre}}^{+}| = 2$ and $|E_{\text{pre}}^{-}| = 10$, respectively. After adding the literal, the rule father(x, y) ← male(x) covers 2 positive examples and 1 negative examples, denoted as $|E_{\text{post}}^{+}| = 2$ and $|E_{\text{post}}^{-}| = 1$, respectively. Since the number of positive examples that satisfy the rule remains constant before and after the literal is added, we have $H = 2$. Using the gain heuristic formula, we can compute the gain value for the literal male(x) as:

$$\text{Gain(male}(x)) = 2 * (\log_2(2/3) - \log_2(2/12)) = 4.0 \qquad (5.6)$$

Similarly, the gain values for all the other literals can be computed in the same way as follows:

$$\{male(x) : 4.0 \qquad male(y) : 0.0 \qquad female(x) : 0.0 \qquad female(y) : 0.83$$
$$parent(x, y) : 3.17 \; parent(x, z) : 2.0 \quad parent(y, x) : 0.0 \quad parent(y, z) : 0.0$$
$$parent(z, x) : 0.0 \; parent(z, y) : 0.83\}$$

We observe that the literal male(x) has the highest gain value. We add male(x) to the rule body and get father(x, y) ← male(x). As this rule still entails one negative example (father(Antony, Diana)), we keep looking for additional literals. The gain value for all the literals is given as:

$$\{male(x) : 0.0 \qquad male(y) : 0.0 \qquad female(x) : 0.0 \qquad female(y) : 0.0$$
$$parent(x, y) : 1.17 \; parent(x, z) : 0.0 \; parent(y, x) : 0.0 \; parent(y, z) : 0.0$$
$$parent(z, x) : 0.0 \; parent(z, y) : 0.0\}$$

As the literal $parent(x, y)$ has the highest gain and the resulting rule is satisfied by all the positive and negative examples. Hence, we have successfully learned the rule:

$$\delta_1 := \text{father}(x, y) \leftarrow \text{male}(x) \wedge \text{parent}(x, y)$$

Algorithm 1 presents a general algorithm for the ILP approach. The algorithm takes as input a set of positive and negative examples (denoted as E^{+} and E^{-}, respectively), a background knowledge base B (which may contain previously learned rules or logical axioms), and a specific target relation (i.e., rule head). The algorithm initializes the rule body as empty and iteratively adds a literal to the rule body until the logical rule entails all positive examples and none of the negative examples. In each iteration, the algorithm selects the literal that maximally covers the positive examples and minimally covers the negative examples (Algorithm 1). Upon completion of the iterations, the algorithm outputs the learned rules. Note the specific implementation of this algorithm may vary depending on the ILP system and the type of data being learned.

Algorithm 1: General Algorithm of ILP Approach

Input: Background knowledge base B, positive examples E^+, negative examples E^-, target relation $r_h(x, y)$

Output: A set of Horn rules Δ

1   $\Delta := \emptyset$
2   **while** $E^+ \neq \emptyset$ **do**
3 | $(r_h(x, y), Body) :=$ Learn New Rule(B, E^+, E^-, r_h)
4 | $E^+ := E^+ -$ positive examples satisfied by $r_h(x, y) \leftarrow Body$
5 | $\Delta := \Delta \cup (r_h(x, y), Body)$
6   **end**
7   return Δ

Algorithm 2: Learn New Rule

Input: Background knowledge base B, positive examples E^+, negative examples E^-, target relation $r_h(x, y)$

Output: An Horn rule $r_h(x, y) \leftarrow Body$

1   $Body := \emptyset$
2   **while** $E^- \neq \emptyset$ **do**
3 | literal := choose_literal$(B, E^+, E^-, Body)$
4 | $Body :=$ literal $\wedge Body$
5 | $E^- := E^- -$ negative examples satisfied by $r_h(x, y) \leftarrow Body$
6   **end**
7   return $r_h(x, y) \leftarrow Body$

Summary

Inductive Logic Programming (ILP) is a specialized area within Artificial Intelligence (AI) that concentrates on deriving logical rules from given examples. ILP can incorporate domain-specific knowledge or constraints (i.e., represented as the background knowledge base in the input) and produces comprehensible rule sets that can be easily interpreted and understood by humans. It is ideal for applications where interpretability is essential, such as medical systems and judicial systems. Nevertheless, ILP techniques for rule learning utilize greedy search strategies, which might fall in locally optimal decisions.

5.2.2 Association Rule Mining-Based Approaches

ILP shares common ground with data mining techniques, as both aim to uncover general patterns from data. The association rule mining-based approach, inspired by association rule mining in the data mining field, offers an alternative to ILP methods. This approach measures

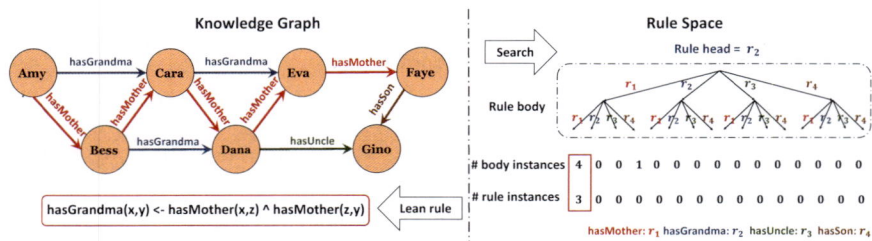

Fig. 5.3 Left: An example KG and a detected rule with length 2. Right: A search tree for rules with length 2 with head relation r_2. A path from the root to the leaf corresponds to a rule body. Together with the head relation, it forms a candidate rule

the plausibility of Horn rules via support and confidence based on the facts observed in KGs, which does not require a separate evaluation set of positive examples and negative examples (i.e., E^+ and E^-).

However, calculating support and confidence requires the counting of ground rules (or path instances) for all potential rules in the rule space as shown in Fig. 5.3, which has two main challenges. First, it requires the evaluation of all the potential rules in the rule space, which is exponential to the length of the rules, as discussed in Sect. 5.2. Second, it requires the enumeration of all the ground rules for each candidate rule to calculate its score. For example, in Fig. 5.3, given the candidate rule:

$$\text{hasGrandma}(x, y) \leftarrow \text{hasMother}(x, z) \wedge \text{hasMother}(z, y) \tag{5.7}$$

we observe three ground rules (rule instances) following the rule:

hasGrandma(Amy, Cara) ← hasMother(Amy, Bess) ∧ hasMother(Bess, Cara)

hasGrandma(Bess, Dana) ← hasMother(Bess, Cara) ∧ hasMother(Cara, Dana)   (5.8)

hasGrandma(Cara, Eva) ← hasMother(Cara, Dana) ∧ hasMother(Dana, Eva)

The computational complexity of grounding a chain-like Horn rule is $|\mathcal{E}|^{(n+1)}$, which depends on the total number of entities in the KG, denoted by $|\mathcal{E}|$, and the rule length, denoted by n. To alleviate the immense computational complexity, most research in this area incrementally prunes the search space while learning logical rules.

The most representative approach in this category is *AMIE* [5, 6], which contains two main steps. The first step is called *rule extending*, which involves generating candidate rules by iteratively extending existing rules using three types of mining operators.

- *Add dangling atom*, where a dangling atom includes one new variable and one shared variable with another atom of the rule. It can be considered as extending a body path with another relation.

- *Add instantiated atom*, where an atomic predicate instantiates one variable with an entity and shares the other variable with the rule. It can be considered as constraining a variable with a certain property, e.g., gender(x, female).
- *Add closing atom*, where both variables of a closing atom are shared with other predicates in the rule. This can be considered as the body path is closed with the shared two variables.

The second step in the AMIE approach is called *rule pruning*, which involves applying metrics such as *head coverage* and *confidence*, to evaluate the rules generated by the first step and output only plausible rules. The head coverage and confidence are defined as follows:

- *Head Coverage*: Head coverage of a rule is measured by the proportion of the head relation being covered by the predictions of the rule. Taking the rule in Eq. 5.3 as an example, its head coverage can be calculated as:

$$\text{hc}(r_h(x, y) \leftarrow Body) = \frac{\text{supp}(r_h(x, y) \leftarrow Body)}{|\{(x', y') : r_h(x', y')\}|} \quad (5.9)$$

where $Body := r_{b_1}(x, z_1) \wedge \cdots \wedge r_{b_n}(z_{n-1}, y)$, and $r_h(x', y')$ represents the collection of observed triples that belong to the relation r_h. The support of the rule dentoed as $\text{supp}(r_h(x, y) \leftarrow Body)$ is defined as the number of (x, y) pairs with relation r_h that can be covered by the rule:

$$\text{supp}(r_h(x, y) \leftarrow Body) = |\{(x, y) : \exists z_1, \ldots, z_{n-1}(r_h(x, y) \leftarrow Body)\}| \quad (5.10)$$

where $z_1, \ldots, z_{n-1}$ are the variables of the rule body $r_{b_1}(x, z_1) \wedge \cdots \wedge r_{b_n}(z_{n-1}, y)$ besides x and y.

- *Confidence*: Standard confidence is a metric that measures the strength of a rule by quantifying the proportion of times the rule is closed by relation r_h among all the instances where the premise occurs. Using the same example as in Eq. 5.3, its standard confidence can be calculated as:

$$\text{conf}(r_h(x, y) \leftarrow Body) = \frac{\text{supp}(r_h(x, y) \leftarrow Body)}{|\{(x, y)|\exists z_1, \ldots, z_{n-1} : Body\}|} \quad (5.11)$$

where $|\{(x, y)|\exists z_1, \ldots, z_{n-1} : Body\}|$ denotes the number of the body instances observed in the KG.

These metrics evaluate the plausibility of logical rules, they can be considered as the score function $s(\cdot)$ in AMIE. By utilizing these metrics, AMIE prunes the rules that fail to meet predefined thresholds for head coverage and confidence. The rules that remain are output as the final set of learned logical rules. Meanwhile, AMIE leverages the monotonicity of the two metrics with respect to the rule length, similar to the pruning in frequent pattern mining, and prune the longer rule candidates if the shorter ones already violate the threshold.

Overall, the rule-pruning step in AMIE plays a critical role in improving the efficiency and accuracy of the rule-learning process by filtering out unpromising or unreliable rules.

Putting together, AMIE utilizes a bottom-up approach to generate candidate rules from a KG. It starts by initializing a queue containing only the empty rule. Then, the algorithm dequeues a rule from the queue and checks whether the rule is closed or not. If the dequeued rule is closed, it is output as a candidate rule; otherwise, the algorithm applies all available operators to the rule. The available operators include "Add dangling atom", "Add instantiated atom", and "Add closing atom" that we discussed earlier. These operators are used to add atoms to the rule, and the resulting rules are added to the queue unless they are pruned out. The algorithm iteratively applies these steps to generate a set of candidate association rules. The top-k rules are selected from this set and presented to the user.

Summary

The association rule mining-based approach is particularly effective at generating simpler rules that highlight co-occurrence or correlation within the data. When compared to ILP, the association rule mining-based approach tends to exhibit greater resilience to noise in the data, as it measures a rule with metrics such as coverage or confidence. Also, it does not need negative examples for the learning process. Nevertheless, determining suitable thresholds for those metrics can be a complex task, as these thresholds significantly influence the quantity of discovered rules and the balance between their generality and specificity.

5.3   Neuro-Symbolic Integration for Logical Rule Learning

Despite being the most studied approach to rule learning since the earliest days of AI, searching-based methods suffer from several limitations, including:

- **Lack of Scalability**: Searching-based methods are not well-suited for large datasets or complex rules as fundamentally they are addressing the combinatorial discrete optimization problem, which is computationally expensive. Most searching-based methods for rule learning employ greedy search strategies that lead to local optimal yet still hard to scale [2].
- **Sensitivity to Incompleteness and Noises in KG**: Searching-based methods for rule learning can be sensitive to incompleteness and noise in the data, which can lead to missing important rules or the production of logical rules that fit the noise. This is particularly true for inductive logic programming (ILP) methods, where the objective is to learn rules that infer all positive examples and exclude all negative examples.

Neuro-symbolic integration offers an alternative method to learning logical rules by combining symbolic logical rule learning with neural network models, leveraging the strengths of both approaches to handle the challenges of learning from real-world KGs.

On one hand, neural networks can handle large-scale data by enabling end-to-end optimization through gradient-based methods. By exploiting the differentiability of neural networks, it is possible to apply continuous optimization techniques to the task of learning logical rules. This transition from a discrete to a continuous problem allows for a more effective exploration of the space of rules, which in turn enables handling the difficulties associated with managing large datasets.

On the other hand, representation learning-based neural network methods can largely alleviate the incompleteness and noise issues by capturing the correlation between entities and relations, as evidenced by knowledge graph completion (Chap. 3). This enables neuro-symbolic integration to learn complex patterns that may be difficult to express using symbolic logic alone.

Existing neuro-symbolic integration approaches can be roughly divided into two categories: (1) *differentiable searching-based methods*, which directly extend traditional searching-based methods by transforming the logical rule learning problem from a discrete optimization problem to a continuous one using a differentiable loss function; (2) *learning-based methods*, which combine various learning paradigms to learn rules from data, where the rules are represented in a symbolic form.

5.3.1 Differentiable Searching-Based Methods

Differentiable search-based methods combine traditional search-based logical rule learning with modern neural network models, transforming the rule learning problem from a discrete optimization problem to a continuous optimization problem. The differentiability of neural networks is exploited to enable this transformation. By formulating the rule learning problem as an end-to-end continuous optimization problem, these methods make the searching process differentiable, enabling the use of gradient-based optimization techniques such as stochastic gradient descent (SGD). Gradient-based optimization makes the learning process more efficient compared to combinatorial search techniques used in traditional searching-based rule learning methods, enabling better scalability for large-scale KGs. Furthermore, with the integration of deep learning architectures, these methods can effectively take advantage of representation learning capabilities. As a result, they are capable of learning complex patterns and exhibit greater robustness to noise and incompleteness in the data compared to traditional searching-based rule learning methods.

Differentiable searching-based methods can be further divided into two categories: (1) *Differentiable ILP*, which combines Inductive Logic Programming (ILP) with deep learning principles to learn logical rules; (2) *Matrix-based reasoning*, which integrates association rule mining-based approaches with deep gradient-based learning systems to learn logical rules.

5.3.1.1 Differentiable ILP

Differentiable Inductive Logic Programming (DILP) is a type of machine learning algorithm that combines the principles of Inductive Logic Programming (ILP) and deep learning to learn logic rules. In particular, DILP methods use differentiable logic programs that can be trained using gradient-based optimization techniques. Differentiable logic programs are similar to traditional logic programs but include additional operations, such as differentiable logic gates, that can be used to construct neural network-like structures. The most representative method in this category is Neural Theorem Provers (NTPs).

Neural Theorem Provers (NTPs)

Neural Theorem Provers (NTPs) [7] extends the traditional backward chaining algorithm to learn logic rules. The backward chaining algorithm, as previously discussed in Sect. 3.2.2.2, is a top-down reasoning approach used in logic programming and theorem proving. It begins with the goal (or conclusion) and works backward, recursively breaking the goal into sub-goals and searching for rules that can satisfy those subgoals.

The traditional backward chaining algorithm faces limitations when dealing with incomplete or noisy KGs. NTPs enhance the backward chaining algorithm by using continuous vector space embeddings to represent entities, relations, and rules, which makes it possible to capture similarities between different entities and relations. NTPs model logical rules in a continuous vector space, transforming the backward chaining procedure into a sequence of differentiable operations, which allows for end-to-end learning using gradient-based optimization methods. Following the principle of Inductive Logic Programming (ILP), these embeddings are learned end-to-end by maximizing the scores of ground predicates in the knowledge graph (KG), while minimizing the score of the ones not in the KG.

To illustrate how NTPs extend the backward chaining algorithm, we provide an example to compare the backward chaining algorithm and NTPs:

Example 5.3.1 (*Backward Chaining Algorithm*) Consider a simple KG with the following two facts and one rule:

$$Father(Anthony,\ Bob)$$

$$Father(Bob,\ Christian)$$

$$GrandFather(x,\ y) \leftarrow Father(x,\ z) \wedge Father(z,\ y)$$

Our goal is to prove the query "*GrandFather(Anthony, Christian)*." Backward chaining would proceed as follows: The query *GrandFather(Anthony, Christian)* can be verified by mapping it with the rule head *GrandFather(x, y)*. After replacing x with "*Anthony*" and y with "*Christian*" in the rule body, the task of proving the goal *GrandFather(Anthony, Christian)* is transformed into proving two subgoals: *Father(Anthony, z)* and *Father(z, Christian)*. By substituting z with "*Bob*", the subgoals *Father(Anthony, Bob)* and *Father(Bob, Christian)* can be recursively demonstrated as true. Thus, the backward chaining algorithm can successfully confirm the query *GrandFather(Anthony, Christian)*. □

Using the same example, we now show how NTPs extend the backward chaining algorithm for rule learning.

Example 5.3.2 (*Neural Theorem Provers (NTPs)*) Let us continue with the previous backward chaining example. In addition to entities *"Anthony"*, *"Bob"*, and *"Christian"*, assume we also have other two entities *"Tony"* and *"Chris"*, relations *"GrandFather* and *"Grandpa"*, and other related facts in the KG, where *"Tony"* is a nickname for *"Anthony"* and *"Chris"* is a nickname for *"Christian"*. Our goal now has changed slightly. Instead of proving the query *"GrandFather(Anthony, Christian)"*, we aim to prove the query *"GrandPa(Tony, Chris)"* by learning a new rule. Using the backward chaining algorithm, we cannot prove *"GrandPa(Tony, Chris)"* because there is no proof path that leads to the conclusion *"GrandPa(Tony, Chris)"*, where a *proof path* refers to the sequence of literals (i.e., ground predicates) that are used to derive a specific ground instance of a rule from the background knowledge. For instance, *GrandFather(Anthony, Christian) ← Father(Anthony, Bob) ∧ Father(Bob, Christian)* is a proof path leading to the conclusion *"GrandFather(Anthony, Christian)"*.

We now demonstrate how NTPs prove *"GrandPa(Tony, Chris)"* through the learning of new rules. Different from the backward chaining algorithm, NTPs learns embeddings for all relations and entities using a bilinear KG embedding model—ComplEx, which has been introduced previously in Sect. 3.3.3. For example, embeddings for relations $\mathbf{r}_{\text{GrandFather}}$ and $\mathbf{r}_{\text{GrandPa}}$, as well as for entities $\mathbf{e}_{\text{Anthony}}$ and $\mathbf{e}_{\text{Tony}}$, are represented in $\mathbb{C}^d$. With these embeddings, NTPs can compare symbols using a similarity measure between their respective embeddings, denoted as $f : \mathbb{C}^d \times \mathbb{C}^d \rightarrow [0, 1]$. For example, $\mathbf{e}_{\text{Anthony}}$ might be similar to $\mathbf{e}_{\text{Tony}}$ because they share similar neighboring nodes in the KG.

To prove the query *"GrandPa(Tony, Chris)"*, NTPs first compute its score via embedding-based score function. If the query cannot be directly inferred from the KG embedding model, NTPs performs backward chaining, which involves using human-predefined logical rules such as the rule *GrandFather(x, y) ← Father(x, z) ∧ Father(z, y)* in the background knowledge, or using a *parameterized rule* to represent an unknown rule to be learned. Parameterized rule is termed as parameterized, due to the fact that the predicates involved are unknown, and their representations are learned from the data. In our situation, since none of the rules in the background knowledge can directly deduce the query *"GrandPa(Tony, Chris)"*, our only option is to utilize parameterized rules to incorporate a new rule.

We define a parameterized rule using rule templates. To simplify the illustration, we adopt the following rule template to prove the query *"GrandPa(Tony, Chris)"*:

$$r_h(x, y) \leftarrow r_{b_1}(x, z) \land r_{b_2}(z, y) \tag{5.12}$$

where r_h, r_{b_1}, and r_{b_2} are unknown predicates represented as vectors $\mathbf{r_h}, \mathbf{r_{b_1}}, \mathbf{r_{b_2}} \in \mathbb{C}^d$, and we want to learn their embeddings from the training data. During training, the representations of parameterized rules are optimized along with all other symbolic representations (i.e., $\mathbf{r}_{\text{GrandFather}}$). This optimization ensures that the model can adapt parameterized rules in a manner that proofs for known facts succeed while proofs for sampled negative atoms fail, thereby inducing new rules. In our example, we want to prove the query "*GrandPa(Tony, Chris)*", and the facts "*Father(Tony, Bob)*" and "*Father(Bob, Chris)*" serve to instantiate the body of the parameterized rule $r_{b_1}(x, z) \wedge r_{b_2}(z, y)$. After training, when decoding the parameterized rule, we search the closest representations of the known predicates. We observe that $\mathbf{r_h}$ is akin to $\mathbf{r}_{GrandPa}$, $\mathbf{r_{b_1}}$ resembles $\mathbf{r}_{Father}$, and $\mathbf{r_{b_2}}$ shares similarities with $\mathbf{r}_{Father}$. Therefore, we are able to decode the parameterized rule in Eq. 5.12 as: $GrandPa(x, y) \leftarrow Father(x, z) \wedge Father(z, y)$

In this way, NTPs can be used for Inductive Logic Programming (ILP) by leveraging gradient descent, rather than conducting a combinatorial search over the space of rules. The advantage of using NTPs for rule learning is that they learn continuous embeddings for entities and relations, which can handle noisy, incomplete, or inconsistent KGs. Moreover, NTPs can identify equivalent entities and relations using similarity measures between embeddings, making them more flexible in handling queries that involve synonyms or aliases. However, a drawback of NTPs is that the continuous embeddings learned may not be easily interpretable by humans. The decoding process from parameterized rules to interpretable rules can make it difficult to understand the underlying reasoning process.

Connect differentiable ILP to traditional ILP

Differentiable ILP (DILP) methods extend ILP by incorporating deep learning ideas, offering a differentiable framework for joint learning of embeddings of symbols and interpretable rules. DILP methods can place similar symbols in close proximity in a vector space, enhancing logical rule learning by leveraging a single rule for many proofs of queries with symbols that have a similar representation. DILP methods have several advantages over traditional ILP methods. First, they can learn more complex logic programs than traditional ILP methods, which are often limited by the expressiveness of the logic language used. Second, DILP methods can learn from continuous and noisy data, whereas traditional ILP methods are typically designed for discrete and noise-free data. However, as DILP is an extension of ILP approaches, it still requires all possible proof paths to answer a given query, leading to computational inefficiency, even for a small KG. Although efforts have been made to reduce the proof paths, this remains a central drawback of DILP.

5.3.1.2 Matrix-Based Reasoning

Matrix-based reasoning is another differentiable searching-based method that builds upon association rule learning-based approaches. By using sparse matrix multiplication for logical inference, matrix-based reasoning turns the discrete searching problem into a differentiable problem, allowing logical rules to be learned from data using gradient-based optimization methods. Neural-LP is one of the most representative methods in this category. It is inspired by a recently developed differentiable logic called TensorLog [8]. We will begin by introducing TensorLog.

TensorLog

As discussed in Sect. 5.2.2, traditional association rule mining-based approaches require identifying all ground rules conforming to a candidate rule template to evaluate the plausibility of a single candidate rule. This process, known as logical inference following the candidate rule, involves discrete counting and can be computationally expensive when dealing with large datasets or complex rules, limiting its scalability to real-world applications. To address this challenge and perform logical inference more efficiently, TensorLog [8] was introduced. TensorLog makes the first attempt to establish a connection between logical inference and sparse matrix multiplication. As discussed in Sect. 2.3.2, the body of a chain-like Horn rule is essentially a path in the KG. The number of instances of such a path can be computed using matrix multiplication.

TensorLog defines an operator $\mathbf{M}^{(k)}$ for each relation r_k and a one-hot vector $\mathbf{e}_i$ for each entity e_i, where $\mathbf{M}^{(k)}$ is a matrix in $\{0, 1\}^{|\mathcal{E}| \times |\mathcal{E}|}$ such that its (i, j) entry is 1 if and only if the triple (e_i, r_k, e_j) is in the KG and $\mathbf{e}_i$ is a one-hot encoded vector $\{0, 1\}^{|\mathcal{E}|}$ such that only the i-th entry is 1. The scalar $\mathbf{e}_i^\mathsf{T} \mathbf{M}^{(b_1)} \mathbf{M}^{(b_2)} \dots \mathbf{M}^{(b_n)} \mathbf{e}_j$ is then equal to the number of paths connecting entity e_i to e_j through the chain-like rule body $r_{b_1}(x, z_1) \wedge r_{b_2}(z_1, z_2) \wedge \dots \wedge r_{b_n}(z_{n-1}, y)$. During inference, given a set of logical rules with r_h as the head relation, TensorLog can answer the query $(?, r_h, e_j)$ via a score function $f_{r_h}(e_i, e_j)$. The score of each head entity for the specific relation r_h and the tail entity e_j is defined as entries in the vector $\mathbf{v}$:

$$\mathbf{v} = \sum_{\mathbf{r}_b \in Body(r_h)} s(r_h, \mathbf{r}_b) \prod_{r_{b_i} \in \mathbf{r}_b} \mathbf{M}^{(r_{b_i})} \mathbf{e}_j \,, \tag{5.13}$$

where $Body(r_h)$ is the set of potential rule bodies whose rule head is r_h, $\mathbf{r}_b = [r_{b_1}, \dots, r_{b_n}]$ is a chain-like rule body and r_{b_i} is a relation in the body, $s(r_h, \mathbf{r}_b)$ denotes the learnable confidence score associated with the rule $r_h \leftarrow \mathbf{r}_b$, $\mathbf{e}_i$ and $\mathbf{e}_j$ are the one-hot encoded vectors for entities e_i and e_j, respectively. The score function is then computed as: $f_{r_h}(e_i, e_j) = \mathbf{e}_i^\mathsf{T} \mathbf{v}$.

Although TensorLog improves the efficiency of logical inference on large datasets using sparse matrix multiplication, it is limited as it can only learn the confidence score $s(r_h, \mathbf{r}_b)$, not rules. It is still a challenging task to extend TensorLog for differentiable logical rule learning. A straightforward approach is to reformulate Eq. (5.13) to learn $s(r_h, \mathbf{r}_b)$ in such a way that the score $f_{r_h}(e_i, e_j)$ for observed triples in KG is maximized. However, since each confidence score $s(r_h, \mathbf{r}_b)$ is associated with a specific rule $(r_h, \mathbf{r}_b)$, and the process of rule enumeration is intrinsically a discrete task, such a learning process is not suitable for gradient-based optimization.

To overcome this challenge, Neural-LP [9] turns the discrete searching problem into a differentiable problem, allowing logical rules to be learned from data using gradient-based optimization methods. In the following section, we will explain the technical details of Neural-LP.

Neural-LP

To allow the rule searching process to be differentiable, Neural-LP [9] extends TensorLog by exchanging the order of the summation and product in Eq. (5.13) to reduce the number of the parameter from $|\mathcal{R}|^N$ to $|\mathcal{R}|N$:

$$\prod_{n=1}^{N} \sum_{k=1}^{|R|} a_n^k \mathbf{M}^{(r_k)} \tag{5.14}$$

where N is the max length of rules, $|\mathcal{R}|$ is the number of relations in the KG, and a_n^k denote the weight assoicated with relation r_k when they are the n_{th} relation in the body. Note that Eqs. (5.13) and (5.14) differ in their parameterization, with the latter associating each relation in the rule with a weight, enabling rule enumeration and confidence score learning simultaneously within a differentiable framework. This innovation enables the use of gradient-based optimization methods for learning the confidence score $s(r_h, \mathbf{r}_b)$, which would otherwise be infeasible due to the discrete nature of the rule-searching process.

However, the parameterization in Eq. (5.14) has limited expressiveness since it assumes that all rules are of the same length. To address this limitation, Neural-LP proposes a recurrent formulation. In the recurrent formulation, Neural-LP employs auxiliary memory vectors $\mathbf{u}_n$ for each length n, which are initially set to the one-hot encoded vectors of entity e_j, i.e., to $\mathbf{e}_j$, to summarize an "average" score vector from every entity to entity j. To sequentially compose the differentiable tensor multiplication, Neural-LP designs a neural controller system based on an attention mechanism. To include all previous partial inferences, the Neural-LP model computes a weighted average of previous memory vectors using the memory attention vector $\mathbf{b}_n$ and softly applies the TensorLog operators using the operator attention vector $\mathbf{a}_n$ at each step. The final inference result is given by the last vector in memory, $\mathbf{u}_{N+1}$. The recursive formulas to compute the memory vectors are summarized below:

$$\mathbf{u}_0 = \mathbf{e}_j$$

$$\mathbf{u}_n = \sum_{k=1}^{|\mathcal{R}|} a_n^k \mathbf{M}^{(r_k)} \left(\sum_{\tau=0}^{n-1} b_n^\tau \mathbf{u}_\tau \right) \text{ for } 1 \leq n \leq N \tag{5.15}$$

$$\mathbf{u}_{N+1} = \sum_{\tau=0}^{N} b_{N+1}^\tau \mathbf{u}_\tau$$

The objective of Neural-LP is to learn rules that can best predict the facts in the KG, which is formulated as maximizing the log score function for a positive triple (e_i, r_h, e_j):

$$\log \mathbf{e}_i^\top \mathbf{u}_{N+1} \tag{5.16}$$

To recover logical rules from the neural controller system, Neural-LP expresses rules and their confidence score $s(r_h, \mathbf{r}_b)$ in terms of the attention vectors $\mathbf{a}_n, \mathbf{b}_n$.

Connect matrix-based reasoning to traditional association rule learning
Similar to association rule learning-based approaches, neural logic programming computes
the confidence score of every candidate rule in the rule space to select Horn rules with the
highest confidence score. However, to make the framework differentiable, neural logic programming replaces the discrete counting of ground rules with sparse matrix multiplication.
This transformation enables logical inference to be compiled into sequences of differentiable
tensor multiplication, allowing for the use of neural networks to learn logical rules. Despite
the benefits of this approach, neural logic programming can be computationally inefficient
due to its reliance on large matrix multiplication, and it makes fewer efforts in reducing the
large search space of logical rules. As a result, while it can be applied to some real-world
KGs such as WN18 [10] and FB15K [11], it is still not efficient enough to handle larger
KGs, such as YAGO3-10 [12]. The detailed statistics of these datasets are summarized in
Table 5.2. Additionally, unlike Neural Theorem Provers (NTPs), matrix-based reasoning
methods are unable to learn embeddings of entities and relations, which are essential for
identifying equivalent entities and relations. This limitation restricts their ability to handle
queries that involve synonyms or aliases.

5.3.2   Learning-Based Methods

While differentiable searching-based methods offer an elegant approach to combining symbolic logical rule search with learning by searching for rules that optimize a differentiable
loss function using gradient-based optimization algorithms, they also present several limitations:

- **Limited expressiveness**: Differentiable searching-based methods suffer from limited
  expressiveness compared to traditional rule-based systems. This is because they can only
  learn rules that are expressible in the search space of differentiable functions that the
  optimization algorithm can handle. For instance, Neural-LP is only capable of learning
  chain-like Horn rules since the body of these rules can be effectively modeled using
  matrix multiplication. In contrast, AMIE can learn Horn rules in a more general form.
- **Difficulty with complex rules**: Although differentiable searching-based methods often
  scale better than traditional searching-based methods, they still struggle to learn complex rules involving multiple variables and intricate interactions between them. This is
  because, when dealing with complex rule sets, the search space can be extensive. For
  instance, in order to learn long rules, NTPs have to involve deep proof paths, leading
  to computational inefficiency. Generally, the larger the search space, the more computationally expensive the optimization process becomes.
- **Limited interpretability of neural network components**: While the rules learned
  by differentiable searching methods are interpretable, the neural network components
  employed in the optimization may not be easily understandable. This can make it chal-

Table 5.1 Capabilities of neural-symbolic methods: differentiable searching-based methods versus learning-based methods

Capabilities	Differentiable searching-based methods	Learning-based methods
End-to-end	Yes	May vary
Differentiable	Yes	Yes
Complexity	High	May vary
Flexibility in learning paradigms	Limited	High

lenging to comprehend how the rules were learned, limiting the method's usefulness in certain applications. For example, the continuous embeddings learned by NTPs may not be easily interpretable by humans, making it difficult to understand the underlying reasoning process.

Learning-based methods offer an alternative approach to combining symbolic logical rule learning with neural network models. Rather than simply extending and improving traditional searching-based methods, learning-based methods can be integrated with a broader range of learning paradigms, which increases their versatility for learning different types of rules. For instance, learning-based methods can be combined with sequential generative models, which are useful for generating *chain-like Horn rules* in KGs, or with reinforcement learning models, which are particularly effective for modeling *compositional rules*. We have summarized and compared the capabilities of differentiable searching-based methods and learning-based methods in Table 5.1. We can observe that while differentiable searching-based methods offer some advantages, such as end-to-end learning and continuous search spaces, learning-based methods can excel in flexibility by supporting various learning paradigms, making them suitable for a diverse range of tasks.

RNNLogic [13] and R5 [14] are two recent learning-based methods for logical rule learning. Each method adopts a unique learning paradigm, offering different advantages in the rule learning process. RNNLogic separates rule generation and rule weight learning by introducing a rule generator and a reasoning predictor. The rule generator uses a Recurrent Neural Network (RNN) to generate rules, while the reasoning predictor learns the rule weights. RNNLogic can effectively learn logical rules from data while maintaining interpretability. On the other hand, R5 formulates rule learning as a sequential decision-making process and employs deep reinforcement learning to learn the logical rules. By treating rule discovery as a series of decisions made over steps, R5 can explore the search space more efficiently, potentially leading to better rule discovery and improved performance. In the following sections, we will provide a more detailed introduction to these two learning-based methods.

RNNLogic

RNNLogic [13] is the most representative learning-based method for logical rule learning. The inefficiency of existing rule learning methods usually comes from searching in a large search space. To reduce search space and learn better rules, RNNLogic is thus proposed to separate rule generation and rule weight learning by introducing a *rule generator* and a *reasoning predictor* respectively. Before delving into the technical details of the rule generator and reasoning predictor, we will formally define the rule learning problem in a probabilistic way.

In RNNLogic, a set of logical rules is considered as a latent variable denoted by $\mathbf{z} \subseteq \mathcal{R}^2 \cup \mathcal{R}^3 \cup \cdots \cup \mathcal{R}^N$, where $\mathcal{R}$ denotes the relation set and N is the maximum length of rules. Let $\mathbf{q} = (h, r, ?)$ denote the query with $h \in \mathcal{E}$ as head entity and $r \in \mathcal{R}$ as the query relation, and let a denote the answer to the query. The *rule generator*, denoted by $p_\theta(\mathbf{z}|\mathbf{q})$ with parameter θ, defines a prior distribution over a set of latent rules $\mathbf{z}$ conditioned on a query $\mathbf{q}$. On the other hand, the *reasoning predictor*, denoted by $p_w(a|\mathcal{G}, \mathbf{q}, \mathbf{z})$ with parameter w, provides the likelihood of the answer $a \in \mathcal{E}$ given the latent rules $\mathbf{z}$, the query $\mathbf{q}$, and the KG $\mathcal{G}$. By utilizing a rule generator and a reasoning predictor, a KG reasoning task can be formulated as predicting the correct answer a for a given query $\mathbf{q}$ and KG $\mathcal{G}$. This can be represented formally as the probability distribution $p(a|\mathcal{G}, \mathbf{q})$, which can be computed as follows:

$$p(a|\mathcal{G}, \mathbf{q}) = \sum_{\mathbf{z}} p_w(a|\mathcal{G}, \mathbf{q}, \mathbf{z}) p_\theta(\mathbf{z}|\mathbf{q}) = \mathbb{E}_{p_\theta(\mathbf{z}|\mathbf{q})}[p_w(a|\mathcal{G}, \mathbf{q}, \mathbf{z})] \tag{5.17}$$

To achieve the best performance for KG reasoning, RNNLogic aims to learn logic rules by jointly training the rule generator and reasoning predictor to maximize the likelihood of the training data. This is formally defined as follows:

$$\max_{\theta, w} O(\theta, w) = \mathbb{E}_{(\mathcal{G}, \mathbf{q}, a) \sim p_{\text{data}}}[\log p_{w,\theta}(a|\mathcal{G}, \mathbf{q})]$$
$$= \mathbb{E}_{(\mathcal{G}, \mathbf{q}, a) \sim p_{\text{data}}}[\log \mathbb{E}_{p_\theta(\mathbf{z}|\mathbf{q})}[p_w(a|\mathcal{G}, \mathbf{q}, \mathbf{z})]] \tag{5.18}$$

After formally defining the problem, we now proceed to present the technical specifications of the rule generator and the reasoning predictor.

Rule Generator. The rule generator is responsible for defining the distribution $p_\theta(\mathbf{z}|\mathbf{q})$. Given a query $\mathbf{q} = (e_i, r_n, ?)$, the rule generator aims at generating a set of latent rules $\mathbf{z}$ for answering the query. Specifically, a chain-like Horn rule $r_h(x, y) \leftarrow r_{b_1}(x, z_1) \wedge \cdots \wedge r_{b_n}(z_{n-1}, y)$ can be viewed as a sequence of relations $[r_h, r_{b_1}, r_{b_2}, \ldots, r_{b_n}, r_{\text{END}}]$, where r_h is the query relation or the rule head, $\mathbf{r_b} = [r_{b_1}, \ldots, r_{b_n}]$ represents the rule body, and r_{END} is a special relation indicating the end of the relation sequence. Combining the rule head and rule body, we denote a chain-like Horn rule as $(r_h, \mathbf{r_b})$. RNN is the natural choice to model a relation sequence. Therefore, we have

$$p_\theta(\mathbf{z}|\mathbf{q}) = \text{Mult}(\mathbf{z}||\Delta|, \text{RNN}_\theta(\cdot|r_h)), \tag{5.19}$$

where Mult stands for multinomial distributions, $|\Delta|$ is the size of the set of logical rules $\mathbf{z}$, and $\text{RNN}_\theta(\cdot|r_h)$ denotes the probability vector for each rule.

Reasoning Predictor. The reasoning predictor aims to predict the answer a for the query $\mathbf{q} = (e_i, r_h, ?)$ using a set of rules $\mathbf{z}$ to preform reason. Let $\mathcal{A} \subseteq \mathcal{E}$ be the set of candidate answers which can be discovered by any logic rule in the set $\mathbf{z}$. For each candidate answer $e_j \in \mathcal{A}$, we compute the following scalar score for that candidate:

$$\text{score}_w(e_j) = \sum_{\mathbf{r_b} \in \mathbf{z}} \text{score}_w(e_j|\mathbf{r_b}) = \sum_{\mathbf{r_b} \in \mathbf{z}} \sum_{p \in \mathcal{P}(e_i, \mathbf{r_b}, e_j)} \psi_w(\mathbf{r_b}) \qquad (5.20)$$

where $\mathcal{P}(e_i, \mathbf{r_b}, e_j)$ is the set of grounding paths that start at e_i and end at e_j following the rule body $\mathbf{r_b}$, and $\psi_w(\mathbf{r_b})$ denotes the scalar weights of rule $(r_h, \mathbf{r_b})$. Once we have the score for every candidate's answer, we can further define the probability that the answer a of the query $\mathbf{q}$ is entity e_j by using a softmax function as follows:

$$p_w(a = e_j|\mathcal{G}, \mathbf{q}, \mathbf{z}) = \frac{\exp(\text{score}_w(e_j))}{\sum_{e' \in \mathcal{A}} \exp(\text{score}_w(e'))} \qquad (5.21)$$

RNNLogic optimizes the reasoning predictor and rule generator in order to maximize the objective defined in Eq. 5.18. In each training iteration, the algorithm first maximizes the objective in Eq. 5.18 with respect to the reasoning predictor p_w. The parameter w of the reasoning predictor $p_w(a|\mathcal{G}, \mathbf{q}, \mathbf{z})$ is updated to maximize the log-likelihood of the answer a based on rules $\hat{\mathbf{z}} \sim p_\theta(\mathbf{z}|\mathbf{q})$ generated by the rule generator. Then, it updates the rule generator using the Expectation-Maximization (EM) algorithm. In the *E-step*, a set of high-quality rules $\mathbf{z}_I$ is identified from all generated rules through posterior inference $p_{\theta,w}(\mathbf{z}_I|\mathcal{G}, \mathbf{q}, \mathbf{z}) \propto p_w(a|\mathcal{G}, \mathbf{q}, \mathbf{z}_I) p_\theta(\mathbf{z}_I|\mathbf{q})$, using the rule generator as the prior and the reasoning predictor as the likelihood. In the *M-step*, the parameters θ of the rule generator p_θ are updated to be consistent with the high-quality rules $\mathbf{z}_I$ selected in the E-step.

Despite introducing a rule generator to reduce the search space, the reasoning predictor in RNNLogic still requires the counting of all ground rules or path instances based on the generated rules. This limits the efficiency of the algorithm. As a result, scaling RNNLogic to handle KGs with hundreds of relations (such as FB15K-237) or millions of entities (such as YAGO3-10) remains a challenging task.

R5

Although the RNNLogic model has been successful in predicting missing links in benchmark KG datasets, it lacks a key aspect of machine intelligence known as *systematicity*. Systematicity involves a model's capacity to recombine established parts and rules to create novel sequences while reasoning over relational data. For example, by combining logical rules δ_1 and δ_2 in Fig. 5.4 we can successfully obtain rule δ_3 for prediction. This ability is critical for real-world applications, where data may be complex and varied, and the model must be able to reason over a wide range of scenarios.

$\delta_1 := \text{hasDaughter}(x, y) \leftarrow \text{hasGranddaughter}(x, z) \wedge \text{hasMother}(z, y)$

$\delta_2 := \text{hasDaughter}(x, y) \leftarrow \text{hasDaughter}(x, z) \wedge \text{hasSister}(z, y)$

$\delta_3 := \text{hasDaughter}(x, y) \leftarrow \text{hasGranddaughter}(x, z_1) \wedge \text{hasMother}(z_1, z_2) \wedge \text{hasSister}(z_2, y)$

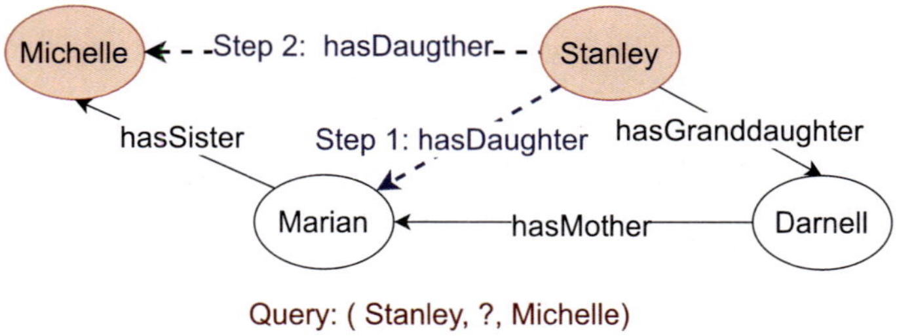

Query: (Stanley, ?, Michelle)

Fig. 5.4 This example demonstrates how R5 simplifies a relation path to deduce the direct link between two entities, *Stanley* and *Michelle*, highlighted in red. In the provided example, two steps of inference are required. Initially, R5 applies the rule δ_1 to simplify the relation path between *Stanley* and *Michelle*. This reduction transforms the path into Stanley $\xrightarrow{\text{hasDaughter}}$ Marian $\xrightarrow{\text{hasSister}}$ Michelle. In the subsequent step, R5 utilizes rule δ_2 to further deduce a direct relationship, Stanley $\xrightarrow{\text{hasDaughter}}$ Michelle. This logical progression effectively demonstrates R5's capability at recurrent relational reasoning

Recently, R5 [14] has been proposed as a solution to overcome the lack of systematicity in RNNLogic. R5 formulates the task of relational reasoning as a sequential decision-making problem and employs *a reasoning agent* in combination with a *dynamic rule memory* to perform logical reasoning and rule extraction. Specifically, it initially converts a KG into a collection of paths linking the queried entity pairs. Note in R5, a query is in the form of $(h, ?, t)$, i.e., query the relation for a given pair of entities. Subsequently, R5 repeatedly employs learned rules to merge a pair of relations along the paths, substituting them with a singular relation. This process continues iteratively until it derives a final relation that links the two queried nodes as shown in Fig. 5.4.

Reasoning Agent. To begin, we introduce the reasoning agent which is trained with deep reinforcement learning (RL) and Monte Carlo Tree Search (MCTS) [15]. It models logical rule learning as a sequential decision-making problem. In this scenario, given a sequence of relations $[r_{b_1}, \ldots, r_{b_l}]$, the agent systematically selects relation pairs $(r_{b_i}, r_{b_{i+1}})$. Following the selection of a relation pair, the agent applies the learned rule $r_h \leftarrow (r_{b_i}, r_{b_{i+1}})$ to merge the two relations into one. This process iterates, employing the learned rules to progressively simplify the sequence into a single relation. The training objective is to optimize a reward function based on accurate predictions of the links directly connecting the queried entities. To offer more comprehensive detail, we present the key components of the reasoning agent as follows:

- **Reasoning as sequential decision-making**: The reasoning agent is trained based on a policy value network combined with MCTS [15]. In this setup, MCTS leverages the policy network to guide its simulations towards selecting the best action at each step. It outputs a vector π representing the search probabilities of the available actions. The policy-value network is denoted as $(\rho, v) = f_\theta(s)$ in R5. When fed the current state s, the network outputs both the probabilities of taking each possible action ρ and a predicted state value v. During training, the policy-value network aims to align the predicted state value v with the actual reward z obtained at the conclusion of each episode. Additionally, it strives to enhance the congruence between the probability vectors ρ and π, optimizing the policy network for efficient search.

$$\mathcal{L} = (z - v)^2 - \pi^{\mathsf{T}} \log \rho + a \, \|\theta\|^2 \tag{5.22}$$

where a is a hyper-parameter and θ is the parameter of the policy network.
- **Action**: At each step of an episode, MCTS selects a relation pair $(r_{b_i}, r_{b_{i+1}})$ from the relation path $[r_{b_1}, \ldots, r_{b_l}]$, which can be denoted as the action a_B. Then, the model references the dynamic rule memory to obtain a rule of the form $r_h \leftarrow (r_{b_i}, r_{b_{i+1}})$, which implies that the relation pair $(r_{b_i}, r_{b_{i+1}})$ in the path will be replaced with r_h. We will address the implementation of the dynamic rule memory at a later point.
- **State**: As the path between two queried nodes get reduced step by step, the state aims to record the details concerning the current paths between query nodes at each step. This can be represented by considering all potential pairs of relations among the current paths, $s \in \mathbb{R}^{(m+n) \times (m+n) \times k}$, where m is the number of observed relations, n is the number of invented relations, and k is the dimension of features of each relation pair.
- **Reward**: Within an episode, actions are iteratively applied to a relation path until the path is reduced to a single relation r_h and a reward value, $z_T \in \{-1, 0, +1\}$, is assigned to all states in the episode, where

$$z_T = \begin{cases} -1 & \text{if } r_h \text{ is a known relation, but is not the target relation} \\ 0 & \text{if } r_h \text{ is an invented relation} \\ 1 & \text{if } r_h \text{ is the target relation} \end{cases} \tag{5.23}$$

By optimizing the reward function, the goal is to ensure that the resulting relation precisely corresponds to the observed ground truth links directly connecting the queried nodes.

Dynamic Rule Memory. Dynamic rule memory module aims to store and update candidate rules and interact with the reasoning agent during training, whose design can be interpreted as two hash tables: one hash table D_{rl} in the form of $r_h \leftarrow (r_{b_i}, r_{b_{i+1}})$ is used to memorize the candidate rules, and another hash table D_{rls} in the form of $score \leftarrow (r_{b_i}, r_{b_{i+1}})$ to track the rule scores. Specifically, the MCTS obtains a rule $r_h \leftarrow (r_{b_i}, r_{b_{i+1}})$ from the hash table D_{rl}, and replaces the current relation pair $(r_{b_i}, r_{b_{i+1}})$ in the path with the rule head r_h. If the rule is not found in the hash table D_{rl}, the MCTS adds an invented relation to the buffer r_{unkn} and uses it as the rule head r_h. During training, the dynamic rule memory module is updated to keep track of the score of each rule.

Despite providing a promising approach for learning first-order logical rules, R5 faces limitations in its scalability and ability to generalize to the KG completion task. This is due to the requirement for pre-sampling the paths that entail the query, which can be impractical even for small-scale KGs due to the large number of paths that need to be considered. Furthermore, R5 employs a hard decision mechanism for merging a relation pair into a single relation, which makes it challenging to handle the uncertainty that exists in KGs. For example, given the rule body hasAunt$(x, z) \wedge$ hasSister(z, y), both hasMother(x, y) and hasAunt(x, y) can be derived as the rule head. The inaccurate merging of a relation pair may lead to error propagation when generalizing to longer paths.

Summary

Learning-based methods provide a flexible and adaptable approach to combining symbolic logical rule learning with neural network models by leveraging various learning paradigms. The effectiveness of the rule learning process depends heavily on the choice of the learning algorithm, as these methods rely on the algorithm to discover rules from the data. Hence, it is crucial to carefully select an appropriate algorithm that is tailored to the specific application and characteristics of the data being analyzed.

5.4 RLogic: A Representation-Learning Based Model For Logical Rule Learning

Although many efforts have been made to learn logical rules automatically, there are two limitations to the existing studies. First, most existing methods entirely rely on observed rule instances to define the score function for rule evaluation. They are unable to mine rules that have no support from rule instances. For example, due to the lack of supportive evidence, the following rule cannot be learned from Fig. 5.3:

$$\delta_3 := \text{hasUncle}(x, y) \leftarrow \text{hasGrandma}(x, z) \wedge \text{hasSon}(z, y) \qquad (5.24)$$

Second, the number of rule instances is extremely large for a big KG, thus scalability is another central challenge. Instead of completely relying on rule instances for rule evaluation, RLogic [1] proposes to learn logical rules directly at the *schema level* via a representation learning-based model. For more discussions of template rules (i.e., logical rules at the schema level) and ground rules (i.e., instance rules), the readers can check Sect. 2.3. As a small amount of sampled closed paths is enough for training such a model, it greatly improves the efficiency. To push deductive reasoning deeper into rule learning, RLogic breaks a big sequential model into small atomic models in a recursive way, which is essential for us to detect rules without the direct support from rule instances.

5.4.1   Framework of RLogic

RLogic aim to learn chain-like Horn rules in the following form:

$$r_h(x, y) \leftarrow r_{b_1}(x, z_1) \wedge \cdots \wedge r_{b_n}(z_{n-1}, y) \qquad (5.25)$$

We previously introduced chain-like Horn rules in Sect. 2.3, where $r_h(x, y)$ is called **rule head** and $r_{b_1}(x, z_1) \wedge \cdots \wedge r_{b_n}(z_{n-1}, y)$ is called **rule body**. Combining rule head and rule body, we denote a Horn rule as $(r_h, \mathbf{r_b})$ where $\mathbf{r_b} = [r_{b_1}, \ldots, r_{b_n}]$. The fundamental idea of RLogic is to assign a plausibility score $s(r_h, \mathbf{r_b})$ to each rule $(r_h, \mathbf{r_b})$ in **rule space**. $s(\cdot)$ is called the score function.

5.4.1.1   From Counting-Based Measure to Model-Based Measure for Rule Evaluation

The ratio that a body path can be closed is usually utilized to define the score function $s(r_h, \mathbf{r_b})$ (e.g., the confidence for association rule mining as discussed in Sect. 5.2.2 and the percentage of triples of the rule head to be satisfied for Neural-LP as discussed in Sect. 5.3.1.2). During rule extraction, the top k rules with the highest score will be selected as the learned rules.

Existing Counting-based Measure for Rule Evaluation

Among several possible measures, *confidence* is the most representative one widely used by association rule mining. As mentioned in Sect. 2.3.2, a chain-like Horn rule instance can be easily identified as a "closed path" in a KG. Here, the rule body represents a relation path in the KG, and the rule head represents the target relation that connects the starting and ending entities in the rule body. Consequently, the confidence measure is defined as the ratio of the number of times the target relation can close a body path. Given an arbitrary rule defined in Eq. 5.3, its confidence can be calculated as:

$$s(r_h, \mathbf{r_b}) = \frac{|\{(x, z_1, \ldots, z_{n-1}, y) : r_h(x, y) \leftarrow r_{b_1}(x, z_1) \wedge \cdots \wedge r_{b_n}(z_{n-1}, y)\}|}{|\{(x, z_1, \ldots, z_{n-1}, y) : r_{b_1}(x, z_1) \wedge \cdots \wedge r_{b_n}(z_{n-1}, y)\}|} \qquad (5.26)$$

where the numerator is the number of its rule instances (i.e., closed paths) and the denominator is the number of its body instances (i.e., relation paths). The confidence measure is purely based on counting on observed rule instances, and it is very sensitive to the quality and completeness of the KG. For example, if the KG contains noises, it might bring in false-positive rules. If the KG contains similar entities and relations with different names (e.g., "Anthony" vs. "Tony"), it might miss some rules due to undercounting the rule instances. Similarly, if the KG misses any facts, it might miss some rules due to the low support of the rule instances.

Proposed Model-based Measure for Rule Evaluation

As discussed above, the calculation of confidence entirely relies on observed rule instances, which is sensitive to the quality of the KG. In addition, enumerating rule instances is usually time-consuming. Instead, we propose a new measure for rule evaluation based on the model-based probability that the rule head can be predicted by the rule body:

$$s(r_h, \mathbf{r_b}) = q(r_h | \mathbf{r_b}) \tag{5.27}$$

For a rule with body length n, we need a tensor with $|\mathcal{R}|^{(n+1)}$ dimension to store all the probabilities. It is too expensive and impossible to get enough data points to estimate each entry in the tensor using counting-based approach.

Model-based approaches can alleviate this issue by fitting a function with observed instances, which can infer the probability for any entry with the body and head inputs. For example, a sequential model, such as RNN, is a natural option to learn $q(r_h | \mathbf{r_b})$ by encoding the relation sequence $\mathbf{r_b}$ into a representation with fixed dimension.

5.4.1.2 The RLogic Framework

In RLogic, we combine representation learning and logical deduction to effectively and efficiently learn rules from KG.

First, each relation r_i is associated with a learnable embedding vector $\mathbf{r_i} \in \mathbb{R}^d$. With the representation of relations, RLogic can identify similar relations like *GrandPa* and *GrandFather* even though they are lexically different. A relation path $\mathbf{r_b}$ is encoded by a vector iteratively via path deduction. It is important to note that it is not always possible to infer an existing relation from a relation path. For example, consider the relation path [*hasMother, hasMother, hasDaughter*], which is inferred to be *hasAunt*, but the relation *hasAunt* is not present in the KG. To accommodate unseen relations, we introduce a "null" predicate into the prediction set $\mathcal{R}$, which is denoted as r_0. The score function $s(r_h, \mathbf{r_b})$ in Eq. 5.27 can be computed based on the representation of relations.

Next, we propose to incorporate the *deductive nature* of the logical rules into the modeling process, which significantly improves the performance due to its capability in combining learning and reasoning, especially when the evidence is sparse. Deductive nature, as one of the most significant properties of logical rules, allows us to decompose the inference of long rules on the basis of the shorter rules. Given a short Horn rule that is in the form $r_k \leftarrow r_i \wedge r_j$, we can reduce the long logical body $r_{b_1} \wedge r_{b_2} \wedge \cdots \wedge r_{b_n}$ by replacing the relation pair $r_i \wedge r_j$ with their head r_k. By recursively applying different short Horn rules to a relation path (body-based path), it will be transformed into a single head at the end. Following the same idea, we can use $q(r_h | r_i, r_j)$ to compute $q(r_h | \mathbf{r_b})$ in a recursive way. For example, given a relation path $[r_{b_1}, r_{b_2}, r_{b_3}]$, $q(r_h | r_{b_1}, r_{b_2}, r_{b_3})$ can be computed as follows if we follow the order from left to right to reduce the path:

$$q(r_h | r_{b_1}, r_{b_2}, r_{b_3}) = \sum_k q(r_h | r_k, r_{b_3}) q(r_k | r_{b_1}, r_{b_2}) \tag{5.28}$$

In other words, we reduce the first two relations r_{b_1}, r_{b_2} into some possible relation $r_k \in \mathcal{R} \cup \{r_0\}$, where r_0 denotes an unknown relation. Then we further reduce the intermediate relation r_k with r_{b_3} into the head relation r_h. We aggregate all the possible cases for r_k, and the final probability for the body to predict the head is a weighted average over each case. As for every step we only need to model a sequence with length 2, this significantly reduces the computational burden caused by long sequence modeling, such as RNN.

Although we can follow logical deduction to reduce a relation path into one single head, this head relation may not always be observed due to the sparsity of real-world KGs. We thus introduce $p(r_t|r_h)$ to bridge the gap between the logical rule-based "ideal prediction" and the "real observation" in KGs, which is the probability that we can observe a triple with relation r_t given r_h is true for the same head and tail entity. Then the ratio that a relation path $\mathbf{r_b}$ can be closed with relation r_t can be defined as:

$$p(r_t|\mathbf{r_b}) = \sum_h p(r_t|r_h)q(r_h|\mathbf{r_b}) \tag{5.29}$$

Following the proposed idea, we introduce a (1) *recursive relation path reduction module* for relation path encoding and a (2) *close ratio predictor* to predict the ratio that a path will close.

(1) Recursive Relation Path Reduction ($q(r_h|\mathbf{r_b})$). The goal here is to model the score for any relation path $\mathbf{r_b}$ for a given head relation r_h, which can be interpreted as the probability of the head to be true if the body is true. As the score function has $|\mathcal{R}|^{n+1}$ entries for a rule with a length n body, it is impractical to estimate each entry independently. Model-based approach can capture the correlation between these entries with a much smaller parameter space. A natural sequence model is RNN and Transformer, but they still heavily relied on the observed closed paths. If no instances are observed for a rule, there is no way for these models to produce a high score for the body and head combination.

We propose to reduce long relation path into shorter ones by pushing reasoning into the prediction. Specifically, we recursively reduce two adjacent relations in the body into one, until two relations are left. In this case, we only need to model the probability for a length-2 body to a relation head, $q(r_k|r_i, r_j)$, for which it is easy to collect more evidences due to their relative short length.

This idea requires (1) deciding the order to reduce a relation path (i.e., selecting the appropriate relation pair in each step) to a single relation and (2) learning the probability of predicting a single relation from a relation pair (i.e., $q(r_k|r_i, r_j)$).

- **Deciding the next pair of relations for deduction**. As shown in Fig. 5.5, there are many different ways to deduct a relation path. Determining the best order involves searching over a potentially large problem space. Given a relation path with length n, there are $C_{n-1} = \frac{1}{n}\binom{2(n-1)}{n-1} = \prod_{k=2}^{n-1} \frac{n-1+k}{k}$ (Catalan number) different ways to decompose the relation path. To alleviate the high computational complexity, instead of enumerating all possible deduction orders to find the global optimal, we adopt a greedy algorithm to select the optimal relation pair at each step, which reduces the complexity into $(n-1) + (n-2) + \cdots + 1$.

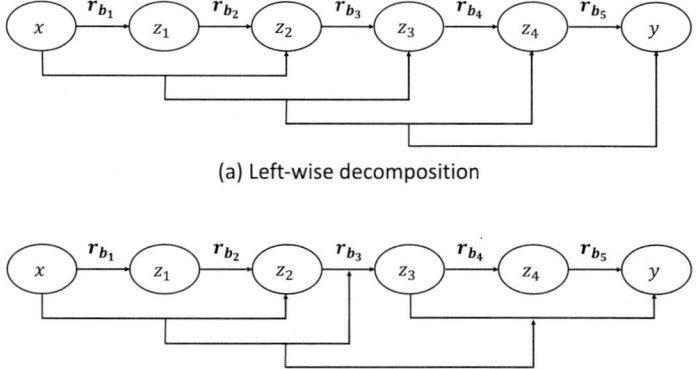

(a) Left-wise decomposition

(b) Decomposition following an irregular order

Fig. 5.5 Different order to deduct a relation path. **a** left-wise decomposition; **b** irregular decomposition

Considering that the ground truth deduction order is unavailable in our problem, we propose to use entropy to measure the uncertainty of the reduction. The entropy of a relation pair (r_i, r_j) to be merged is defined as follows:

$$E((r_i, r_j)) = \sum_{r_k \in \mathcal{R}} -q(r_k|r_i, r_j) \log q(r_k|r_i, r_j) \tag{5.30}$$

When the entropy is lower, we can be more certain that the relation pair can be reduced by one relation. By selecting the relation pair with the lowest entropy at every step, we always pick the pair of relation with the highest confidence for deduction.

- **Probabilistic deduction to a single relation from a relation path**. The next question is to how to model $q(r_k|r_i, r_j)$ and encode the relation path recursively. In RLogic, $q(r_k|r_i, r_j)$ is approximated via a multilayer perceptron (MLP) classifier, denoted as $f_\theta(\mathbf{r_i}, \mathbf{r_j})$, where θ denotes the parameters of the MLP. It takes the embedding of predicate r_i, r_j as input, and outputs the probability of predicting each relation in the KG, including the "null" predicate (i.e., unknown relation). Considering that $q(r_k|r_i, r_j)$ follows categorical distribution, the MLP classifier uses softmax as the activation function for the final layer.

For a rule body $\mathbf{r}_b = [r_{b_1}, r_{b_2}, \ldots, r_{b_n}]$, assuming (r_{b_1}, r_{b_2}) is selected for deduction first, they lead to each relation $r_k \in \mathcal{R}$ in KG with different probability (i.e., $q(r_k|r_{b_1}, r_{b_2})$). For example, given the rule body $hasAunt(x, z) \wedge hasSister(z, y)$, both $hasMother(x, y)$ and $hasAunt(x, y)$ can be derived as the rule head with different probabilities. It is important to include all these possibilities in computation to model complex logical deduction. We propose to encode the relation pair (r_{b_1}, r_{b_2}) as the weighed average over different relations, including the unknown relation r_0:

$$\tilde{\mathbf{r}} = \sum_{k=0}^{|\mathcal{R}|} q(r_k | r_{b_1}, r_{b_2}) \cdot \mathbf{r_k}, \tag{5.31}$$

We can observe that $\tilde{\mathbf{r}}$ is a "weighted average" representation, which is learned by "softly" adding up representations of all predicates in a KG. The relation path encoder will recursively decide the next best pairs to deduct, and compute the embedding for the newly generated relation. When there are only two relations left in the rule body, we can use the MLP to predict the probability for it to reduce to any relation r_h. For example, a relation path in their embedding $[\mathbf{r}_{b_1}, \mathbf{r}_{b_2}, \mathbf{r}_{b_3}]$ may be reduced to $[\tilde{\mathbf{r}}, \mathbf{r}_{b_3}]$, and the probability for the body to imply any relation can be computed as:

$$q(\cdot | \mathbf{r}_{b_1}, \mathbf{r}_{b_2}, \mathbf{r}_{b_3}) = q(\cdot | \tilde{\mathbf{r}}, \mathbf{r}_{b_3}) = f_\theta(\tilde{\mathbf{r}}, \mathbf{r}_{b_3}) \tag{5.32}$$

(2) Close Ratio Predictor ($p(r_t | r_h)$). Although we can follow logical deduction to reduce a relation path into one single head relation probabilistically, this head relation may not always be observed due to the sparsity of real-world KGs. To bridge the gap between "ideal prediction" following logical rules and "real observation", the close-ratio predictor is proposed to predict the ratio that a path will close. A two-layer fully-connected neural network (MLP) is introduced to model $p(r_t | r_h)$. In particular, it uses ReLU as the activation function for the first layer and adds sigmoid as the activation function for the second layer. The "weighted average" $\tilde{\mathbf{r}}^*$ learned by the relation path encoder at the final step and the embedding $\mathbf{r_t}$ are taken as input to decide the close ratio, where $\tilde{\mathbf{r}}^* = \sum_{k=0}^{|\mathcal{R}|} q(r_k | \tilde{\mathbf{r}}, \mathbf{r}_{b_3}) \cdot \mathbf{r_k}$ in our above example.

5.4.1.3 Model Training

This section discusses the training procedure for RLogic. We first introduce our proposed closed path sampler for training data generation. Then we give the objective functions for training relation path encoder and close ratio predictor.

Closed path sampler for training data generation. Rather than enumerate all closed paths in KG, we utilize a closed path sampler to sample only a small portion of closed paths to train the model. We propose a random walk [16] based procedure to efficiently sample the closed paths. Formally, given a source entity x_0, we simulate a random walk of fixed length n. Let x_l denote the lth node in the walk, they are generated by the following distribution:

$$p(x_l = e_i | x_{l-1} = e_j) = \begin{cases} \frac{1}{|\mathcal{N}(e_j)|}, & \text{if } (e_i, e_j) \in \mathcal{E} \\ 0, & \text{otherwise} \end{cases} \tag{5.33}$$

where $|\mathcal{N}(e_j)|$ is the neighbor size of entity e_j. Different from a random walk, each time after we sample the next node x_l, we add an edge from x_0 to x_l if they are connected in KG to construct the closed paths.

Objective function for training relation path encoder. The relation path encoder aims to predict a head relation r_h for a given relation path $\mathbf{r_b}$. Each sampled closed path can be regarded as a positive example, whose target relation gives the ground truth of head relation r_h. Negative examples can be generated by corrupting positive examples. Note that KGs operate under the Open World Assumption (OWA): a statement that is not contained in the KG is not necessarily false; it is just unknown. Therefore, we choose to use ranking-based loss. To make the scores of positive examples higher than those of negative ones, we employ a pairwise margin-based ranking loss function to learn $q(r_k|\mathbf{r_b})$.

$$\sum_{(r_h,\mathbf{r_b})\in\mathcal{P}} \sum_{(r_h',\mathbf{r_b})\in\mathcal{N}(r_h,\mathbf{r_b})} [\gamma - q(r_h|\mathbf{r_b}) + q(r_h'|\mathbf{r_b}))]_+ \qquad (5.34)$$

where $[x]_+ = \max\{0, x\}$, the score function $q(\cdot|\cdot)$ is parameterized by the relation path encoder, and $\gamma > 0$ is the margin hyperparameter. To reduce the effects of randomness, we sample multiple negative examples for each positive closed path. We denote the set of negative samples of a closed path $(r_h, \mathbf{r_b})$ as $\mathcal{N}(r_h, \mathbf{r_b})$, which is constructed by replacing the head relation of the closed path $(r_h, \mathbf{r_b})$ with a relation sampled randomly from relation set $\mathcal{R}$:

$$\mathcal{N}(r_h, \mathbf{r_b}) \subset \{(r_h', \mathbf{r_b})|r_h' \in \mathcal{R}\}\} \qquad (5.35)$$

Objective function for training close ratio predictor. Close ratio predictor bridges the gap between "ideal prediction" following logical rules and "real observation" by predicting the ratio that a path $\mathbf{r_b}$ wll close. Each closed path in KG can be regarded as a positive example while the paths that fail to be closed by any relation are regarded as negative examples. The training objective for learning $p(r_t|r_h)$ is incorporated in learning a good $p(r_t|\mathbf{r_b})$, which can be formulated as the binary cross-entropy loss:

$$\sum_{(r_t,\mathbf{r_b})\in\mathcal{P}} \log p(r_t|\mathbf{r_b}) + \sum_{(r_t,\mathbf{r_b})\in\mathcal{N}} \log(1 - (p(r_t|\mathbf{r_b})) \qquad (5.36)$$

where $\mathcal{P}$ stores positive examples, $\mathcal{N}$ stores negative examples, and $\mathbf{r_b}$ denotes the relation path.

The RLogic framework is summarized in Fig. 5.6.

5.4.1.4 Rule Extraction

To recover logical rules from RLogic, we calculate the score $s(r_h, \mathbf{r_b})$ for each rule $(r_h, \mathbf{r_b})$ in rule space when the model has finished training. Unlike most of the existing neural symbolic methods for rule learning, such as Neural-LP and RNNLogic, which learn rules for a specified head relation, our model can learn rules with different heads simultaneously and thus can provide a holistic ranking among them. With such scores, we can select the most important rules to interpret the whole KG rather than select the ones to infer a certain relation.

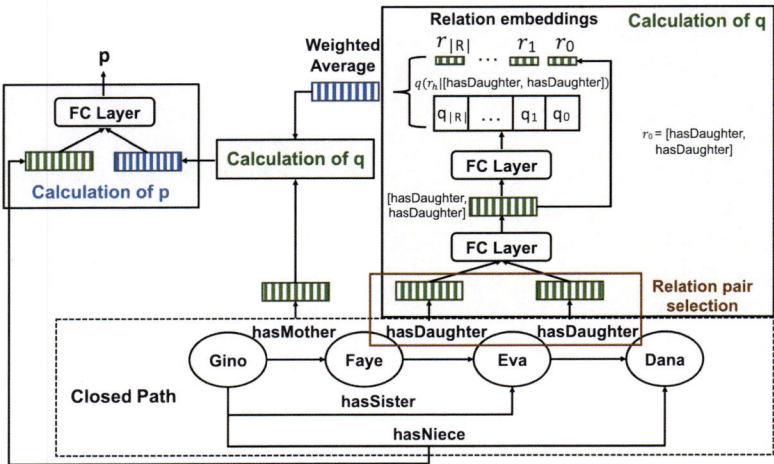

Fig. 5.6 Illustration of the RLogic framework. It contains two main components: (1) a relation path encoder to model $q(r_h|\mathbf{r_b})$; and (2) a close ratio predictor to model $p(r_t|r_h)$. Given a path $\mathbf{r_b}$, the relation path encoder reduces $\mathbf{r_b}$ into a single head r_h by recursively merge relation pairs in path $\mathbf{r_b}$ according to $q(r_h|r_i, r_j)$. Then, the close ratio predictor bridges the gap between "ideal prediction" following logical rules and "real observation" by predicting the ratio that the relation path $\mathbf{r_b}$ will close

The detailed procedure to extract rules is presented below. Given a candidate rule body $\mathbf{r_b}$, we reduce $\mathbf{r_b}$ into a single head r_k by recursively merge relation pairs in path $\mathbf{r_b}$ according to $q(r_k|r_i, r_j)$. Every step, the relation pair (r_i, r_j) with minimum entropy will be selected and replaced by an intermediate representation $\tilde{\mathbf{r}}$ according to Eq. (5.31). At the end of the deduction, we obtain the vector $[q(r_0|\mathbf{r_b}), q(r_1|\mathbf{r_b}), \ldots, q(r_{|R|}|\mathbf{r_b})]$ where $q(r_k|\mathbf{r_b})$ are the score of rule $(r_k, \mathbf{r_b})$. Top k rules with highest score will be selected as learned rules.

5.4.2   Connection to Existing Approaches

Note that logical rule is a schema-level concept, while only instance-level evidence can be directly observed from KGs. To bridge this gap, the frequency of rule instances is commonly used to determine the plausibility of logical rules. For example, traditional methods such as association rule mining [6, 17] define the score as the ratio of the total number of rule instances to the total number of body instances for the corresponding rule. Then the rule mining process is to search over the rule space and select the rules with the highest score. For example, given the KG in Fig. 5.3, the rule space with length 2 to predict head relation r_2 (hasGrandma) can be represented as a tree structure, and each path from the root to a leaf corresponds to a rule body. Two rules with high scores can be learned in Fig. 5.3 (δ_1 has a score of 0.75 and δ_2 has a score of 1), which are:

$$\delta_1 := \text{hasGrandma}(x, y) \leftarrow \text{hasMother}(x, z) \wedge \text{hasMother}(z, y)$$
$$\delta_2 := \text{hasUncle}(x, y) \leftarrow \text{hasMother}(x, z_1) \wedge \text{hasMother}(z_1, z_2) \wedge \text{hasSon}(z_2, y) \tag{5.37}$$

In recent years, there have been proposals for neural symbolic approaches [9, 18, 19] to learn logical rules by integrating symbolic logical rule learning with neural network models. A notable example of such an approach is Neural-LP, which enables the soft counting of rule instances through differentiable tensor multiplication rather than discrete counting. To identify useful rules from the rule space, these methods also search for rule bodies (or proof paths) that maximize the observations (i.e., triples) of the rule head.

Although many efforts have been made to learn logical rules automatically, there are two limitations to the existing studies. First, most existing methods rely on observed rule instances entirely to define the score function for rule evaluation. They are unable to mine rules that have no support from rule instances. For example, due to the lack of supportive evidence, the following rule cannot be learned from Fig. 5.3:

$$\delta_3 := \text{hasUncle}(x, y) \leftarrow \text{hasGrandma}(x, z) \wedge \text{hasSon}(z, y) \tag{5.38}$$

Note that the number of rule instances is extremely large for a big KG, scalability is another central challenge. Instead of completely relying on rule instances for rule evaluation, we propose to learn logical rules directly at the schema level via a representation learning-based model. The score of a rule can be calculated based on the learned predicate representations. In this way, a rule can be evaluated without direct support from rule instances. Since a small amount of sampled rule instances is enough for training such a model, it greatly improves the efficiency.

Second, a majority of existing methods learn logical rules by assuming that logical rules are independent of each other, which seriously contradicts the *deductive nature* of logical rules. The deductive nature of logical rules describes the capability to combine existing rules for deriving new rules. For example, given two short rules δ_1 and δ_3, we can infer a long rule δ_2. The inference of δ_2 can be decomposed into recursive steps as shown in Fig. 5.7. Starting from the first two predicates, we can derive an intermediate conclusion $hasGrandma(x, z_2)$ following δ_1. Then, by replacing the first two predicates with the derived relation, we rewrite the rule body as $hasGrandma(x, z_2) \wedge hasMother(z_2, y)$ and derive the final conclusion according to δ_3. Because deductive nature describes the logical dependency among rules, it can be considered as "higher-order constraints" over rules, which is essential for us to validate rules without enough support from rule instances. For example, although we cannot rely on rule instances to evaluate δ_3 due to the lack of supportive evidence, as long as we can see evidence from Fig. 5.3 to support δ_1 and δ_2, by pushing deduction deeper into δ_2, δ_3 is forced to be true to make δ_2 true. To incorporate deductive nature into rule learning, we propose to break a big sequential model to small atomic models in a recursive way following logical deduction. We summarize the advantage of RLogic compared to SOTA below.

Fig. 5.7 Deduction from δ_1
and δ_3 to δ_2

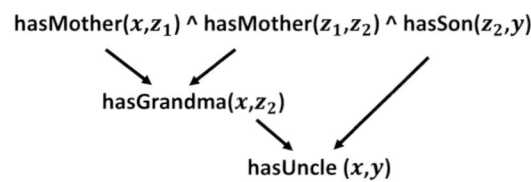

- **Stronger generalization ability**: Rule is an abstract level concept, which consists of only predicates and variables. Since we cannot directly observe abstract rules in KGs, existing methods, such as AMIE and Neural-LP, rely on the rule instances to define the score function of rules. Such definitions lack generalizability. Instead, RLogic proposed to learn the representation of predicates (i.e., relations) to define the score of a rule as shown in Eq. 5.27 and thus show stronger generalization ability. In this way, a rule can be detected without the need to see a rule instance. Besides, RLogic can identify similar predicates like *Mother* and *Mom* even though they are lexically different.
- **Pushing deductive reasoning deeper into rule learning**: Most existing methods, such as Neural-LP and RNNLogic learn logical rules by assuming that logical rules are independent of each other, which seriously contradicts the deductive nature of logical rules. Instead, RLogic is able to follow logical deductions to validate a rule by pushing deductive reasoning deeper into rule learning, which is critical when a rule lacks supporting evidence. For example, although we cannot rely on rule instances to evaluate δ_3 due to the lack of supportive evidence, as long as we can see evidence from Fig. 5.3 to support δ_1 and δ_2, by pushing deduction deeper into δ_2, δ_3 is forced to be true to make δ_2 true.

5.4.3   Experiments

5.4.3.1 Datasets

Four widely used benchmark datasets are used to evaluate our proposed RLogic, which includes WN18RR [10], FB15K-237 [11], YAGO3-10 [12] and Family [20]. The detailed statistics of the datasets are summarized in Table 5.2.

Table 5.2 Data statistics

Dataset	# Triple	# Relation	# Entity
FB15K-237	310,116	237	14,541
WN18RR	93,003	11	40,943
YAGO3-10	1,089,040	37	123,182
Family	28,356	12	3,007

5.4.3.2 Quality of Learned Rules in Terms of KG Completion Task

KG completion is a classic task widely used by logical rule learning methods such as Neural-LP [9], DRUM [18], and NLIL [19] to evaluate the quality of learned rules. We use *forward chaining* [21] to derive missing facts from logical rules after rules are learned. The top 2400 rules with the highest score learned by RLogic are selected for the KG completion task.

Evaluation Metrics. RLogic mask the head or tail entity of each test triple and require each method to predict the masked entity. During the evaluation, the filtered setting [22] and three evaluation metrics, i.e., Hit@1, Hit@10, and MRR are used. To break ties for triples with the same score, RLogic follows *random protocol* [23] to rank the triples with the same score.

Comparing with Other Methods. RLogic is evaluated against SOTA algorithms, including (1) traditional KG embedding (KGE) methods (e.g., TransE [22], DistMult [24], ConvE [10], ComplEx [25] and RotatE [26]); (2) logical rule learning methods (e.g., Neural-LP [9], NLIL [19], DRUM [18], AMIE [6] and RNNLogic [13]). The comparison results are presented in Table 5.3. We can observe that: (1) Although RLogic is not designed specifically for KG completion tasks, compared with traditional KGE models, it still achieves comparable results on all datasets; (2) RLogic outperforms most logical rule learning methods with significant performance gain in most cases; (3) RNNLogic shows great performance over KG completion tasks because it jointly trains a powerful reasoning predictor to predict missing links. To fairly compare with RNNLogic, RLogic+ is proposed to incorporate an

Table 5.3 Transductive link prediction. The bold numbers represent the best performed method(s) while the underlined numbers represent the second best performed method(s)

Category	Model	WN18RR			FB15K-237			YAGO3-10		
		MRR	Hit@1	Hit@10	MRR	Hit@1	Hit@10	MRR	Hit@1	Hit@10
KGE	TransE	0.23	2.2	52.4	0.29	18.9	46.5	<u>0.36</u>	25.1	<u>58.0</u>
	DistMult	0.42	38.2	50.7	0.22	13.6	38.8	0.34	24.3	53.3
	ConvE	0.43	40.1	52.5	**0.32**	<u>21.6</u>	<u>50.1</u>	<u>0.36</u>	<u>26.5</u>	55.6
	ComplEx	0.44	41.0	51.2	0.24	15.8	42.8	0.34	24.8	54.9
	RotatE	**0.47**	<u>42.9</u>	**55.7**	**0.32**	**22.8**	**52.1**	**0.49**	**40.2**	**67.0**
Rule learning	Neural-LP[†]	0.38	36.8	40.8	0.24	17.3	36.2	–	–	–
	NLIL[†]	0.30	20.1	33.5	0.25	13.8	32.4	–	–	–
	DRUM[†]	0.38	36.9	41.0	0.23	17.4	36.4	–	–	–
	AMIE	0.36	39.1	48.5	0.23	14.8	41.9	0.25	20.6	34.3
	RNNLogic (w/o emb)[‡]	<u>0.46</u>	41.4	53.1	0.29	20.8	44.5	–	–	–
	RLogic	**0.47**	**44.3**	<u>53.7</u>	<u>0.31</u>	20.3	<u>50.1</u>	<u>0.36</u>	25.2	50.4

[†] Neural-LP, NLIL and DRUM exceeds the capacity of our machines on YAGO3-10 dataset

[‡] Results on RNNLogic are taken from the original papers

improved reasoning predictor for prediction. The results of RLogic+ on KG completion task are shown in the following section.

Inductive Link Prediction. It is important to note that comparing logical rule learning methods with KGE methods solely on transductive KG completion tasks is not fair. Different from KGE methods, which are not capable of reasoning on unseen entities, logical rules are more powerful in an inductive setting. The results for the inductive link prediction experiment are shown in Table 5.4. We observe that all rule learning algorithms still achieve similar performances as they did in the transductive settings.

RLogic+. Unlike other baseline methods, RLogic directly learns rules without enhancing KG completion tasks as a side product. Although RLogic is able to generate high-quality logic rules, its performance over KG completion task is severely limited by the coverage of rules and the incompleteness of KGs due to the lack of a good reasoning predictor. Following UniKER [27], we resolve the KG sparsity issue by adding additional triples with the high score using RotatE [26], and then conduct forward chaining to predict missing triples. The methods that extending RNNLogic and RLogic in this way are denoted as RNNLogic+ and RLogic+. The results are shown in Table 5.5. We can see that with the help of KG embedding, the performance of RLogic+ over KG completion task gets significantly improved on all datasets, especially on FB15k237.

Table 5.4 Inductive link prediction. The bold numbers represent the best performances among all methods

Model	WN18RR			FB15K-237			YAGO3-10		
	MRR	Hit@1	Hit@10	MRR	Hit@1	Hit@10	MRR	Hit@1	Hit@10
KGE[†]	–	–	–	–	–	–	–	–	–
Neural-LP[‡]	0.23	20.3	33.1	0.14	9.3	27.6	–	–	–
DRUM[‡]	0.23	20.5	34.4	0.16	10.8	29.3	–	–	–
AMIE	0.32	33.6	45.5	0.19	13.9	38.0	0.21	15.8	30.1
RLogic	**0.43**	**42.1**	**50.8**	**0.29**	**18.4**	**48.7**	**0.32**	**22.8**	**47.2**

† KGE methods are not applicable in an inductive setting
‡ Neural-LP, NLIL, and DRUM exceed the capacity of our machines on YAGO3-10 dataset

Table 5.5 Combine learned rules with KG embedding for KG completion task

Model	WN18RR			FB15K-237			YAGO3-10		
	MRR	Hit@1	Hit@10	MRR	Hit@1	Hit@10	MRR	Hit@1	Hit@10
RNNLogic+ (with emb.)	0.51	**47.1**	59.7	0.35	25.8	53.3	–	–	–
RLogic	0.43	42.1	50.8	0.29	18.4	48.7	0.32	22.8	47.2
RLogic+	**0.52**	46.6	**60.4**	**0.55**	**51.1**	**64.3**	**0.53**	**42.6**	**70.3**

5.4.3.3 Quality of Learned Rules in Terms of Rule Head Prediction Task

In addition to the promising performance in terms of the KG completion task, *we also directly evaluate the correctness of rules learned by each system on Family dataset.* In particular, we propose a novel task **rule head prediction** to predict the heads of a set of rule bodies. *Human annotations are used to label the rule bodies for ground truth preparation.* Mean Average Precision (MAP) is taken as an evaluation metric.

Task 1: Learn Equal-length Rules. We evaluate RLogic against a number of logical rule learning methods. Each method is given a set of closed paths with length 2 as training data and required to predict the rule head of *equal-length* rule bodies. The comparison results are presented in Fig. 5.8. We observed that RLogic outperforms all other logical rule learning methods with significant gain.

Task 2: Learn Longer Rules. RLogic incorporates the deductive nature into rule learning and thus can learn longer rules with only shorter closed paths observed in the training stage. In this experiment, we allow only closed paths with length 2 to be observed in the training stage and require each system to predict rule heads of *longer rule bodies* whose lengths range from 2 to 6.

Comparing with Other Methods. Considering that most of the existing logical rule learning methods rely on rule instances to define the score function for rule evaluation and thus cannot handle such a difficult setting, we construct two baselines by replacing the relation path encoder in RLogic with RNN and LSTM. Experiment results are shown in the left figures of Fig. 5.9. We observe that: (1) RLogic performs the best in rule head prediction tasks, giving almost completely correct predictions; (2) LSTM performs better than RNN, as it naturally can handle longer sequential data better compared with RNN.

Effect of Rule Length. To further investigate how the length of the rule body affects the performance, we vary the lengths of rule bodies among $n \in \{2, 3, 4, 5, 6\}$ and report corresponding MAP. As depicted in the right figure of Fig. 5.9, the performances of RNN and LSTM drop severely when the rule bodies grow longer while RLogic is less affected by the length of rule body.

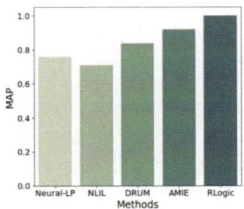

Fig. 5.8 Equal-length rule detection comparison on Family dataset (The code provided by RNNLogic didn't output the learned rules. Without the learned rules, we are unable to include RNNLogic in this experiment)

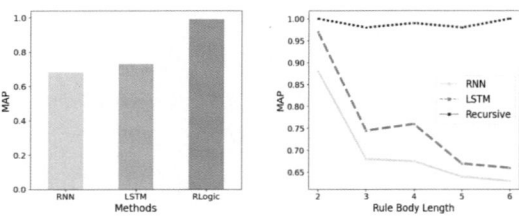

Fig. 5.9 Longer-length rule detection comparison on Family dataset. Left: overall rule detection performance, where the lengths of rule bodies are varied among $\{2, 3, 4, 5, 6\}$. Right: rule detection performance w.r.t body length

Query 1 $?\,(x, y) \leftarrow hasBrother(x, z_1) \wedge hasSister(z_1, y)$

Query 2 $\begin{aligned} ?\,(x, y) \leftarrow\ & hasBrother(x, z_1) \wedge hasSister(z_1, z_2) \\ & \wedge hasFather(z_2, z_3) \wedge hasWife(z_3, z_4) \\ & \wedge hasHusband(z_4, y) \end{aligned}$

Query 3 $\begin{aligned} ?\,(x, y) \leftarrow\ & hasBrother(x, z_1) \wedge hasSister(z_1, z_2) \\ & \wedge hasFather(z_2, z_3) \wedge hasWife(z_3, z_4) \\ & \wedge hasHusband(z_4, z_5) \wedge hasBrother(z_5, y) \end{aligned}$

Query	RNN	LSTM	RLogic
Query 1	**hasSister 0.7** hasBrother 0.1 hasMother 0.1	**hasSister 0.9** hasBrother 0.0 hasNiece 0.0	**hasSister 0.9** hasDaughter 0.0 hasBrother 0.0
Query 2	hasSister 0.8 **hasFather 0.1** hasUncle 0.0	**hasFather 0.8** hasMother 0.1 hasDaughter 0.1	**hasFather 1.0** hasSon 0.0 hasMother 0.0
Query 3	hasBrother 0.3 hasDaughter 0.3 hasSon 0.2	hasMother 0.8 hasBrother 0.1 hasFather 0.1	**hasUncle 0.8** hasBrother 0.1 hasAunt 0.0

Fig. 5.10 Case study of RLogic in inferring rules with different lengths. The figure on the top gives rule bodies with different lengths (i.e., 2, 5, 6). The table at the bottom presents predicted rule heads ranked by probabilities. The bold predicates correspond to the ground truth answers

Case Studies. In addition, we conduct a case study to show the power of the recursive mechanism which enables RLogic to give the right predictions when the rule body grows longer. As shown in the figure on the top of Fig. 5.10, three queries are manually designed with rule bodies of length 2, 5, and 6 respectively. The longer queries are formed by adding new predicates to the end of the rule body of the shorter ones. The top three rule heads inferred are given in the table at the bottom of Fig. 5.10, associated with their probabilities (rounded). We observed that RLogic consistently performs well in all cases while it is more and more challenging for RNN and LSTM to provide correct prediction with the increase of body length.

5.4.3.4 Training Efficiency

RLogic learns rules directly at the schema level while other existing methods learn rules based on instance-level ground rules. Therefore, RLogic is much more efficient than all existing methods. To demonstrate the scalability of RLogic, we show the training time of RLogic and other logical rule learning methods on three benchmark datasets in Table 5.6. Considering that it is challenging for baseline methods to learn long rules, to fairly compare with different methods, we limit the maximum length of learned rules to 2. We can observe that: (1) Neural-LP, NLIL, and DRUM do not perform well in terms of efficiency as they involve large matrix multiplication. They cannot handle YAGO3-10 dataset due to the memory issue. (2) It is also challenging for RNNLogic to scale to large-scale KGs. It can neither handle KG with hundreds of relations (e.g., FB15K-237) nor KG with million entities (e.g., YAGO3-10). (3) Although performances of RLogic and AMIE are on the same scale, AMIE is less efficient as it relies on all rule instances for rule evaluation.

5.4.3.5 Quality and Interpretability of the Rules

To demonstrate the quality and interpretability of rules mined by RLogic, we show some logic rules generated on the FB15k-237 dataset in Table 5.7. Two rules with different lengths are presented for each head predicate. We highlight the predicates which convey the same semantic meaning with boldface. We can observe that the boldfaced predicates in longer rules can be used to infer the boldfaced predicate in shorter rules. This observation again validates that RLogic is able to capture the deductive nature of logical rules.

Table 5.6 Training time (minutes) of logical rule learning methods on WN18-RR, FB15K-237, and YAGO3-10 datasets

Methods	WN18-RR	FB15K-237	YAGO3-10
Neural-LP[†]	21.8	395.0	–
NLIL[†]	14.9	108.3	–
DRUM[†]	19.1	373.8	–
AMIE	0.5	13.9	41.3
RNNLogic[†]	17.4	–	>4 days
RLogic	**0.2**	**5.2**	**17.3**

† Neural-LP, NLIL, and DRUM exceed the capacity of our machines on YAGO3-10 dataset and RNNLogic exceeds the capacity of our machines on FB15K-237 dataset

Table 5.7 Top rules learned by RLogic on FB15K-237. We highlight the predicates which convey the same semantic meaning with boldface

speak_language(x, y) ← geographic_distribution(x, z) ∧ **phone_service_language**(z, y)
speak_language(x, y) ← geographic_distribution(x, z_1) ∧ **tv_network_programs**(z_1, z_2)∧ **program_language**(z_2, y)
location_at_time_zones(x, y) ← county_at_location(x, z) ∧ **location_at_time_zones**(z, y)
location_at_time_zones(x, y) ← county_at_location(x, z_1) ∧ **location_partially_contains**(z_1, z_2)∧ **location_at_time_zones**(z_2, y)
has_nationality(x, y) ← write_tv_programs(x, z) ∧ **tv_programs_in_country**(z, y)
has_nationality(x, y) ← write_tv_programs(x, z_1) ∧ **has_regular_tv_appearance**(z_1, z_2)∧ **headquarters_in_country**(z_2, y)

5.5   Summary and Discussions

The goal of logical rule learning is to discover a set of logical rules that can be used to represent the underlying structure of a given domain or to make accurate predictions about new, unseen data. By representing knowledge in a logical format, logical rule learning approaches allow human experts to understand and reason about the learned models and integrate them with existing KGs. Two broad categories of methods used for logical rule learning are traditional search-based methods and modern neuro-symbolic integration.

Traditional search-based methods involve exploring the space of possible rules to identify the best ones based on specific criteria, such as accuracy. These methods offer various benefits, such as expressive knowledge representation and generalization capability. However, they also face challenges such as computational complexity, sensitivity to noise, and difficulties in integrating background knowledge or managing complex relationships.

Modern neuro-symbolic integration offers an alternative approach to learning logical rules by combining symbolic logical rule learning with neural network models. The incorporation of neural network models allows neuro-symbolic integration methods to handle the challenges of learning from real-world KGs. Existing neuro-symbolic integration approaches can be divided into two categories: differentiable searching-based methods and learning-based methods. Differentiable searching-based methods extend traditional searching-based methods by using a differentiable loss function to optimize the search in a continuous search space, while learning-based methods combine various learning paradigms to learn rules from data, where the rules are represented in a symbolic form. By combining the benefits of symbolic reasoning and neural networks, these methods provide increased adaptability in representing and learning logical rules from data, as well as harnessing the scalability of neural networks. However, they may require more data for learning precise rules and may be less interpretable compared to traditional search-based strategies.

Neuro-symbolic integration is heavily relied on observed data to learn rules, which makes it difficult for the method to identify rules that lack enough supported instances. To address this limitation, RLogic proposes a different approach. Rather than relying solely on rule instances for evaluation, RLogic suggests learning logical rules directly at the schema level using a representation learning-based model. The efficiency of this approach is greatly improved because only a small number of closed paths are required for model training. Additionally, RLogic recursively decomposes a large sequential model into smaller atomic models, enabling the detection of rules without the need for direct supporting rule instances. This step is crucial in embedding deductive reasoning more deeply into the rule-learning process.

Due to space limitations, we can only cover the primary approaches to rule learning. However, it is essential to acknowledge that there are other promising directions in this field, which we will discuss below.

Compositional Rule Learning

Logical rules naturally have an interesting property—called *compositionality*: where the meaning of a whole logical expression is a function of the meanings of its parts and of the way they are combined [28].

Although RLogic attempts to learn the compositional structure, it adopts a heuristic method to find the order to deduct a relation path. Due to the limited modeling capability of the heuristic method, it is likely to lead to errors or biases because it is based on incomplete or inaccurate information. NCRL [29] extends RLogic to *explicitly learns a hierarchical tree* to express the rule composition in an *end-to-end* way. NCRL starts by sampling a set of paths from a given KG, and further splitting each path into short compositions using a sliding window. Then, NCRL uses a reasoning agent to reason over all the compositions to select one composition. NCRL uses a recurrent attention unit to transform the selected composition into a single relation represented as a weighted combination of existing relations. By recurrently merging compositions in the path, NCRL finally predicts the rule head.

References

1. K. Cheng, J. Liu, W. Wang, and Y. Sun. Rlogic: Recursive logical rule learning from knowledge graphs. In *Proceedings of the ACM SIGKDD International Conference on Knowledge Discovery and Data Mining (KDD)*, pages 179–189, 2022.
2. N. Lavrac and S. Dzeroski. Inductive logic programming. In *WLP*, pages 146–160. Springer, 1994.
3. S. Muggleton and L. De Raedt. Inductive logic programming: Theory and methods. *The Journal of Logic Programming*, 19:629–679, 1994.
4. J. R. Quinlan. Learning logical definitions from relations. *Machine learning*, 5(3):239–266, 1990.
5. L. Galárraga, C. Teflioudi, K. Hose, and F. M. Suchanek. Fast rule mining in ontological knowledge bases with amie+. *The VLDB Journal*, 24(6):707–730, 2015.

6. L. A. Galárraga, C. Teflioudi, K. Hose, and F. Suchanek. Amie: association rule mining under incomplete evidence in ontological knowledge bases. In *Proceedings of the International World Wide Web Conference (WWW)*, pages 413–422. ACM, 2013.

7. T. Rocktäschel and S. Riedel. End-to-end differentiable proving. In *Advances in Neural Information Processing Systems (NeurIPS)*, pages 3788–3800, 2017.

8. W. W. Cohen. Tensorlog: A differentiable deductive database. *arXiv preprint* arXiv:1605.06523, 2016.

9. F. Yang, Z. Yang, and W. W. Cohen. Differentiable learning of logical rules for knowledge base reasoning. In *Advances in Neural Information Processing Systems (NeurIPS)*, pages 2319–2328, 2017.

10. T. Dettmers, P. Minervini, P. Stenetorp, and S. Riedel. Convolutional 2d knowledge graph embeddings. In *Proceedings of AAAI Conference on Artificial Intelligence (AAAI)*, 2018.

11. K. Toutanova and D. Chen. Observed versus latent features for knowledge base and text inference. In *Proceedings of the 3rd Workshop on Continuous Vector Space Models and Their Compositionality*, pages 57–66, 2015.

12. F. M. Suchanek, G. Kasneci, and G. Weikum. YAGO: a core of semantic knowledge. In *Proceedings of the International World Wide Web Conference (WWW)*, pages 697–706. ACM, 2007.

13. M. Qu, J. Chen, L.-P. Xhonneux, Y. Bengio, and J. Tang. Rnnlogic: Learning logic rules for reasoning on knowledge graphs. *arXiv preprint* arXiv:2010.04029, 2020.

14. S. Lu, B. Liu, K. G. Mills, S. JUI, and D. Niu. R5: Rule discovery with reinforced and recurrent relational reasoning. In *International Conference on Learning Representations (ICLR)*, 2022.

15. C. B. Browne, E. Powley, D. Whitehouse, S. M. Lucas, P. I. Cowling, P. Rohlfshagen, S. Tavener, D. Perez, S. Samothrakis, and S. Colton. A survey of monte carlo tree search methods. *IEEE Transactions on Computational Intelligence and AI in games*, 4(1):1–43, 2012.

16. F. Spitzer. *Principles of random walk*, volume 34. Springer Science & Business Media, 2013.

17. C. Meilicke, M. W. Chekol, D. Ruffinelli, and H. Stuckenschmidt. Anytime bottom-up rule learning for knowledge graph completion. In *Proceedings of the International Joint Conferences on Artificial Intelligence (IJCAI)*, pages 3137–3143, 2019.

18. A. Sadeghian, M. Armandpour, P. Ding, and D. Z. Wang. Drum: End-to-end differentiable rule mining on knowledge graphs. *arXiv preprint* arXiv:1911.00055, 2019.

19. Y. Yang and L. Song. Learn to explain efficiently via neural logic inductive learning. *arXiv preprint* arXiv:1910.02481, 2019.

20. G. E. Hinton et al. Learning distributed representations of concepts. In *Proceedings of the Eighth Annual Conference of the Cognitive Science Society*, volume 1, page 12. Amherst, MA, 1986.

21. E. Salvat and M.-L. Mugnier. Sound and complete forward and backward chainings of graph rules. In *International Conference on Conceptual Structures*, pages 248–262. Springer, 1996.

22. A. Bordes, N. Usunier, A. Garcia-Duran, J. Weston, and O. Yakhnenko. Translating embeddings for modeling multi-relational data. In *Advances in Neural Information Processing Systems (NeurIPS)*, pages 2787–2795, 2013.

23. Z. Sun, S. Vashishth, S. Sanyal, P. Talukdar, and Y. Yang. A re-evaluation of knowledge graph completion methods. *arXiv preprint* arXiv:1911.03903, 2019.

24. B. Yang, W.-t. Yih, X. He, J. Gao, and L. Deng. Embedding entities and relations for learning and inference in knowledge bases. *arXiv preprint* arXiv:1412.6575, 2014.

25. T. Trouillon, J. Welbl, S. Riedel, É. Gaussier, and G. Bouchard. Complex embeddings for simple link prediction. In *International Conference on Machine Learning (ICML)*, pages 2071–2080, 2016.

26. Z. Sun, Z.-H. Deng, J.-Y. Nie, and J. Tang. Rotate: Knowledge graph embedding by relational rotation in complex space. In *International Conference on Learning Representations (ICLR)*, 2018.

27. K. Cheng, Z. Yang, M. Zhang, and Y. Sun. Uniker: A unified framework for combining embedding and definite horn rule reasoning for knowledge graph inference. In *Proceedings of the Conference on Empirical Methods in Natural Language Processing (EMNLP)*, 2021.

28. D. Hupkes, V. Dankers, M. Mul, and E. Bruni. Compositionality decomposed: How do neural networks generalise? *Journal of Artificial Intelligence Research*, 67:757–795, 2020.

29. K. Cheng, N. Ahmed, and Y. Sun. Neural compositional rule learning for knowledge graph reasoning. In *International Conference on Learning Representations (ICLR)*, 2023.

Incorporating Ontology to Knowledge Graph Reasoning

6

> *"Science is organized knowledge. Wisdom is organized life."—Immanuel Kant*

6.1   Overview

Many large-scale knowledge graphs (KGs), such as DBPedia [2], YAGO [3], and Concept-Net [4], have two distinct views: (1) an ontology view comprising meta-relations of abstract concepts (illustrated in the top of Fig. 6.1); and (2) an instance view containing relations between specific entities (illustrated in the bottom of Fig. 6.1). For instance, *(Politician, IsLeaderOf, City)* represents a triple within the ontology-view KG, which is a relation between two concepts; while *(Barack Obama, WasBornIn, Honolulu)* constitutes a triple in the instance-view KG, which is a relation between two entities. The ontology view and instance view of a KG are interconnected seamlessly through cross-view links. For example, the cross view triple *(Honolulu, IsA, City)* between "*Honolulu*" and "*City*" denotes "*Honolulu is a City*". Despite the two views, the majority of existing methods primarily focus on representing instance-view KGs, neglecting the information in the ontology view. In this chapter, we delve into the methods that jointly consider both views in KGs to enhance KG reasoning.

Since the instance-view KGs have already been thoroughly introduced in previous sections, we now provide a detailed introduction to the ontology-view KG.

Ontology-view Knowledge Graph

The concept of ontology and its significance in knowledge representation has a long history. Early advances in Artificial Intelligence (AI) research during the 1970 and 1980s laid the foundation for ontologies, aiming to create structured knowledge representations for automated reasoning. In the 1990s, the advent of the Semantic Web initiative propelled the development of ontologies and their integration into knowledge representation on the web.

Ontology–view Knowledge Graph

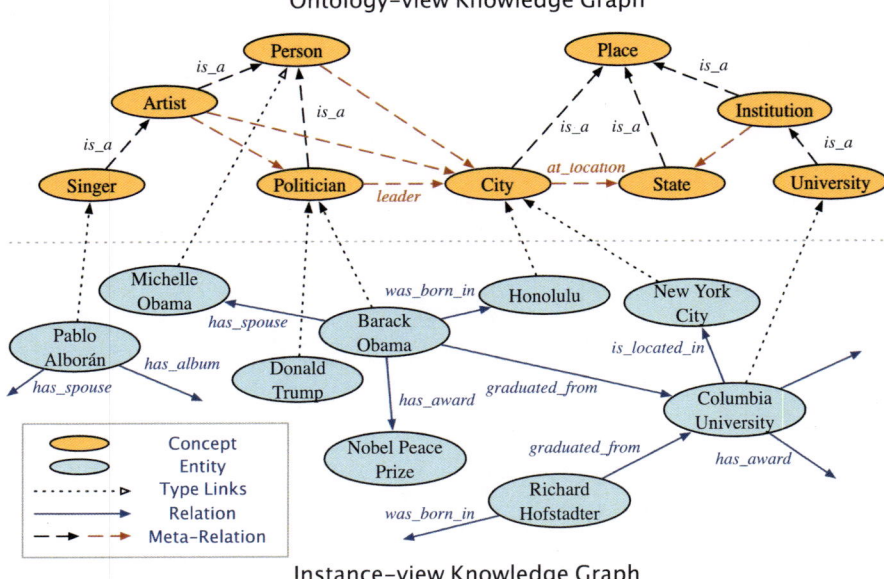

Fig. 6.1 An example of two-view KG. Regular meta-relations and hierarchical meta-relations are denoted as orange and black dashed lines respectively in the ontology view

This led to the creation of languages such as RDF (Resource Description Framework) [5] and OWL (Web Ontology Language) [6], which facilitated the formal representation of knowledge and ontologies in a machine-readable format. With the growth of large-scale Knowledge Graphs (KGs) like DBpedia [7] and Freebase [8], the inclusion of ontological concepts and relationships became increasingly crucial.

The inclusion of ontological concepts allows for a more structured and comprehensive representation of knowledge. Consider the ontological concept of "*Author*", which represents a generalization that encompasses properties common to all authors. This concept provides a framework for organizing and categorizing information about authors within the KG. It is important to note that ontologies do not contain specific information about individual entities. Instead, concrete instances such as "*Albert Einstein*" are considered specific entities that belong to the "*Author*" concept, inheriting properties from their parent concept. This distinction between ontological concepts and specific entities allows ontology-view KGs to achieve a more structured and comprehensive representation of knowledge, facilitating better generalization of knowledge.

In addition to defining the entity types and properties, ontology can also define the relationships between concepts. For example, a "*Write*" relationship can be defined between "*Author*" and "*Book*", and a "*PublishedBy*" relationship can be defined between the "*Book*" and "*Publisher*".

In general, there are three main components to an ontology, which are usually described as *classes*, *attributes*, and *relations*.

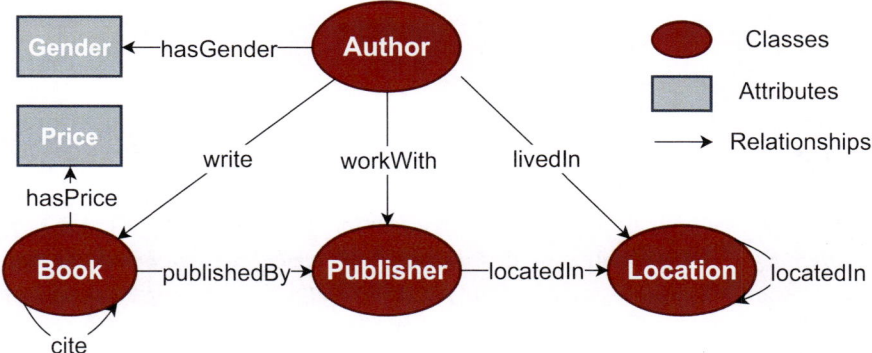

Fig. 6.2 An example of KG ontology. Each ellipse in the figure represents a class in an ontology-view KG and each rectangle in the figure represents an attribute that describes a property of an individual class

- **Classes**: the distinct types of entities that exist in KG.
- **Attributes**: properties that describe an individual class.
- **Relations**: links that connect two classes.

For example, as shown in Fig. 6.2, we have four classes to represent entities in a KG: *"Book"*, *"Author"*, *"Publisher"* and *"Location"*. Every class possesses its unique properties. For instance, all entities within the *"Book"* class have a price attribute. Relations establish connections between two classes. Taking *"authors"* class as an example, it interacts with other classes through various relations.

- Authors *write* Books
- Authors *work with* Publishers
- Authors *live in* Locations.

Ontology serves as a general data model for KGs that provides a reusable framework to describe entities and properties in the KG. By not including information about specific entities, ontology ensures consistency and accuracy in the representation of information in the KG. This common framework enables effective reasoning and manipulation of the information stored in the KG and facilitates the development of applications that can utilize the information. Due to its high generalizability, ontology is often stable and does not change frequently. To account for the varying evolvement speeds of ontology and data, it is common practice to keep ontology and data as separate resources and combine them in applications. This approach allows for easy modification of data while preserving the consistency of the ontology. In recent years, the integration of ontologies into Knowledge Graphs (KGs) has expanded to encompass a wide range of domains and applications. This integration has proven valuable in various fields, and numerous ontologies have been developed to support knowledge representation and reasoning in specific domains. Here are a few examples of ontologies that have been employed across different domains:

- **Amazon Catalogue**: The Amazon Catalogue ontology is a critical aspect of the Amazon e-commerce platform. It defines the hierarchical structure and relationships of products, facilitating efficient browsing, searching, and recommendation systems [9].
- **Taxonomy of research areas**: The ACM (Association for Computing Machinery) maintains a taxonomy of research areas that organizes and categorizes various fields within computer science [10]. This ontology aids in the classification and retrieval of research papers, conferences, and researchers.
- **Gene Ontology**: Gene ontology is a widely used ontology in biomedicine [11]. It categorizes genes and their functions across different species, facilitating gene annotation, analysis, and biological knowledge discovery.
- **Disease Ontology**: The disease ontology provides a structured representation of diseases and their relationships, aiding in the organization and retrieval of biomedical information related to diseases, including symptoms, causes, and treatments [12].

These examples highlight the practical applications of ontologies in different domains, demonstrating their role in organizing and leveraging information for effective reasoning.

Formalization of Instance-view KG and Ontology-view KG

We use $\mathcal{G}_I$ and $\mathcal{G}_O$ to denote the *instance-view KG* and *ontology-view KG*, respectively.

- The instance-view KG $\mathcal{G}_I = (\mathcal{E}, \mathcal{R}_I, \mathcal{O}_I)$ contains a set of entities $\mathcal{E}$, a set of relations $\mathcal{R}_I$, and a set of facts $\mathcal{O}_I$, where a fact is a triple $(h^{(I)} \in \mathcal{E}, r^{(I)} \in \mathcal{R}_I, t^{(I)} \in \mathcal{E})$.
- The ontology-view KG $\mathcal{G}_O = (\mathcal{C}, \mathcal{R}_O, \mathcal{O}_O)$ contains a set of concepts $\mathcal{C}$, a set of relations $\mathcal{R}_O$, and a set of facts $\mathcal{O}_O$, where a fact is a triple $(h^{(O)} \in \mathcal{C}, r^{(O)} \in \mathcal{R}_O, t^{(O)} \in \mathcal{C})$.

Specifically, for each view in the KB, a dedicated low-dimensional space is assigned to embed nodes and edges. Boldfaced $\mathbf{h}^{(I)}, \mathbf{t}^{(I)}, \mathbf{r}^{(I)}$ represent the embedding vectors of head entity $h^{(I)}$, tail entity $t^{(I)}$ and relation $r^{(I)}$ in instance-view triples. Similarly, $\mathbf{h}^{(O)}, \mathbf{t}^{(O)}$, and $\mathbf{r}^{(O)}$ denote the embedding vectors for the corresponding concepts and their meta-relation in the ontology-view graph.

Besides the notations for two views, $\mathcal{S}$ is used to denote the set of known cross-view links in the KB, which contains associations between instances and concepts such as "*type_of*". We use $(e, c) \in \mathcal{S}$ to denote a link between $e \in \mathcal{E}$ and its corresponding concept $c \in \mathcal{C}$. For example, (*e*: Los Angeles International Airport, *c*: airport) denotes that "*Los Angeles International Airport*" is an instance of the concept "*airport*". Looking into the nature of the ontology view, we also have hierarchical substructures identified by "*subclass_of*" (or other similar meta-relations). That is, we can observe concept pairs $(c_l, c_h) \in \mathcal{C}$ that indicate a finer (more specific) concept belongs to a coarser (more general) concept. One aforementioned example is (c_l: singer, c_h: person).

Incorporating Ontology to Knowledge Graph Reasoning

Incorporating ontology information into knowledge graph reasoning has become increasingly important for improving the accuracy and effectiveness of KG embedding methods. Ontology information provides a semantic structure for the KG, which includes entity and relationship types, as well as their hierarchies.

By leveraging ontology information, KG embedding methods can resolve ambiguities in entity and relationship meanings, which can arise due to the use of different names or labels for the same entity or relationship in different parts of the KG. Let's use an example to illustrate this. Assume we have two triples in the KG: *(Michael Jordan, PlayFor, Chicago Bulls)* and *(Michael Jordan, Field, Machine Learning)*. Although both triples share the same head entity, Michael Jordan, they refer to different individuals. The first relation, *"PlayFor"*, is associated with the schema *(Athlete, PlayFor, Team)*, indicating that it pertains to the domain of sports. On the other hand, the second relation, *"Field"*, is related to the schema *(Scientist, Field, Domain area)*, suggesting a connection to scientific disciplines. Based on the ontology, we can determine that the first *"Michael Jordan"* is an athlete, while the second *"Michael Jordan"* is a scientist. By incorporating this ontology knowledge, KG embedding methods can learn to represent these two individuals separately in the embedding space, taking into account their distinct roles and associated relationships, thereby resolving the ambiguity in their interpretations, and leading to better performance on downstream tasks such as link prediction, entity classification, and KG completion.

Furthermore, the incorporation of ontology brings benefits to the reasoning process. As exemplified in the example from Sect. 2.2.1, *"All men are mortal; Socrates is a man; therefore Socrates is mortal"*, we can deduce the properties and relationships of an instance based on its parent class. This deductive approach differs from relying solely on instance-level information, which may require a substantial amount of evidence to make reasonable inferences. From this perspective, ontology provides a valuable foundation for deduction, enabling more efficient and accurate reasoning. It allows us to leverage the knowledge and relationships defined at the class level to infer properties and relationships of specific instances. Therefore, ontology plays a crucial role in enhancing reasoning capabilities and enabling more informed decision-making, especially in scenarios involving cold-start and long tail entities, as well as common sense reasoning.

Methods that integrate ontology schemas into KG reasoning can be classified into two main types, depending on the links they use: (1) those utilizing *cross-view* links, and (2) those utilizing *intra-view* links.

- **Leveraging Cross-view Hierarchies for KG Representation Learning**: These techniques aim to establish connections between different views by using entity-type information to bridge the gap between the ontology schema and instance-level data.
- **Leveraging Intra-view Hierarchies for KG Representation Learning**: These methods primarily focus on exploiting information from the same view of the ontology schema by utilizing hierarchy information. Depending on the type of hierarchy information used, this

category can be further divided into two subcategories: (1) techniques that use concept hierarchies, and (2) techniques that use relation hierarchies.

We will provide a more detailed explanation of these two categories below.

6.2   Leveraging Cross-View Links for KG Representation Learning

Cross-view links bridge the gap between the instance view and the ontology view of KG by associating entities with their corresponding classes. For example, as illustrated in Fig. 6.1, the entity "Barack Obama" in the instance-view KG belongs to the "Polititian" class in the ontology-view KG, and the entity "Honolulu" in the instance-view KG is a class of "City" in the ontology-view KG. This cross-view links are found in many KGs, allowing for seamless integration of the ontology view's abstract knowledge with the instance view's specific knowledge.

Cross-view links are essential in KG embedding learning because they supply valuable contextual and structural information that can enhance the quality and expressiveness of the resulting embeddings. By inferring relationships between entities based on their types, a more comprehensive understanding of the domain can be achieved, leading to improved reasoning capabilities. For instance, the cross-view links help resolve ambiguities and potential confusion surrounding entities. By associating entities with their respective classes, their roles and relationships become clearer, which in turn aids the reasoning process. Furthermore, cross-view links enable the identification of common patterns and relationships between entities of the same type, leading to better generalizations that can be applied across various instances and assist in discovering new relationships and insights within the KG. Additionally, cross-view links help to ensure consistency within the KG by identifying discrepancies in entity classifications. This not only improves the overall data quality but also strengthens the reasoning capabilities and usefulness of the KG.

In this subsection, we highlight the crucial role of cross-view links (i.e., entity-type information) for KG embedding and offer a brief overview of some key methods and techniques for leveraging entity-type information in KG embedding. These methods can be categorized into three primary groups: (1) *modeling cross-view links as additional relations*; (2) *modeling cross-view links using regularization terms*; and (3) *modeling cross-view links using type embeddings*.

6.2.1   Modeling Cross-View Links as Additional Relations

The most straightforward way to incorporate entity type information is to integrate both views of KG into a unified graph by representing the cross-view links as an additional relation "IsA". For instance, the cross-view links between concrete entity "Barack Obama" and entity type "Polititian" in Fig. 6.1 can be formulated as a triple ("Barack Obama", "IsA", "Polititian"). The entity type information can be naturally captured by including all triples in the unified KG for training. For example, YAGO contains a rich ontology that captures various types of relationships between entities and their properties. To exploit this information, Nickel et al. [13] represent both classes and entities into the same latent space and models cross-view links as a special type of relation. Then, The bilinear model RESCAL, discussed earlier in Sect. 3.3.3.1, is employed to factorize the KG for learning KG embeddings and predicting unknown triples. In other words, this approach simply ignores the differences in both views, and treat the integrated KG as a regular KG.

6.2.2   Modeling Cross-View Links Using Regularization Terms

Another way is to take entity type information as guidance to enforce entities of the same type to be close in the embedding space. For example, entity "cat" is supposed to stay closer to entity "dog" than entity "computer" as entities belonging to the same semantic category (i.e., animal) will lie close to each other in the embedding space. Semantically Smooth Embedding (SSE) [14] employs two manifold learning algorithms, i.e., (1) Laplacian eigenmaps and (2) locally linear embedding to model this smoothness assumption. Both methods are formulated as manifold regularization terms to constrain the KG embedding objective function. The Laplacian eigenmaps require an entity to lie close to every other entity in the same category. To achieve this goal, SSE incorporates $\mathcal{R}_1$ as a regularization term into the margin-based ranking loss adopted in KG embedding methods:

$$\mathcal{R}_1 = \frac{1}{2} \sum_{i=1}^{n} \sum_{j=1}^{n} \left\| \mathbf{e}_i - \mathbf{e}_j \right\|_2^2 w_{ij}^{(1)} \tag{6.1}$$

where $w_{ij}^{(1)}$ is defined as:

$$w_{ij}^{(1)} = \begin{cases} 1 & \text{if } c_{e_i} = c_{e_j} \\ 0 & \text{otherwise} \end{cases} \tag{6.2}$$

where c_{e_i} and c_{e_j} denote the category label of entity e_i and e_j.

The locally linear embedding represents that entity as a linear combination of its nearest neighbors (i.e. entities within the same category), where nearest neighbors refer to entities belonging to the same semantic category:

$$\mathcal{R}_2 = \sum_{i=1}^{n} \left\| \mathbf{e}_i - \sum_{e_j \in \mathcal{N}(e_i)} w_{ij}^{(2)} \mathbf{e}_j \right\|_2^2 \tag{6.3}$$

where $w_{ij}^{(2)}$ is defined as:

$$w_{ij}^{(2)} = \begin{cases} 1 & \text{if } e_j \in \mathcal{N}(e_i) \\ 0 & \text{otherwise} \end{cases} \tag{6.4}$$

where $\mathcal{N}(e_i)$ is a set of randomly sampled K entities uniformly from the category to which e_i belongs, then we normalize the rows so that $\sum_{j=1}^{n} w_{ij}^{(2)} = 1$ for each row i.

By incorporating $\mathcal{R}_1$ and $\mathcal{R}_2$ as a regularization term into the margin-based ranking loss defined in conventional KG embedding loss, SSE obtains an embedding space that is semantically smooth and at the same time compatible with observed facts. SSE has proven to be a superior method for KG embedding; however, it has a notable limitation in that it disregards the hierarchical nature of entities' semantic categories and assumes that each entity only belongs to a single category. This shortcoming will be further elaborated in the upcoming Sect. 6.3.1.

6.2.3   Summary

Cross-view links are connections that bridge the gap between the ontology view and the instance view of a KG. These links play a crucial role in integrating the abstract knowledge from the ontology view with the specific entities and relationships from the instance view. By associating entities with their respective types, cross-view links facilitate a better understanding of the roles and relationships of entities within the KG and thus improve the overall quality and expressiveness of the generated KG embeddings.

6.3   Leveraging Intra-View Hierarchies for KG Representation Learning

In addition to the cross-view connections between specific entities in the instance view KG and their corresponding types in the ontology view, the ontology view alone contains hierarchical organization. For instance, considering Fig. 6.1, "Singer", "Artist", and "Person" forms a hierarchy within the ontology view, as a "Singer" falls under the category of an "Artist", and an "Artist" is a type of "Person."

The ontology view features two primary types of hierarchy: *entity hierarchy* and *relation hierarchy*. The entity hierarchy captures the hierarchical relationships among entities in the KG, while the relation hierarchy focuses on the hierarchical relationships among relations in the KG. In the following section, we will discuss how to utilize these two types of hierarchy information to enhance the embedding model.

6.3.1 Entity Type Hierarchies

Entity type hierarchy refers to the hierarchical relationships between different types of entities in a KG. It defines a tree-like structure where each node represents a type of entity, and the relationships between the nodes indicate the parent-child relationships between entity types. In other words, the hierarchy defines subtypes and supertypes of entities, where subtypes inherit properties and relationships from their parent supertype, while also having their own unique properties and relationships.

The entity type hierarchy can be used to improve the performance of KG embedding by enabling inheritance and generalization of properties and relationships, facilitating more advanced reasoning operations. For example, if "Jazz Musician" is a subclass of "Musician", and a Musician can be related to "Club" by a relation "performs in", then it can be inferred that "Jazz Musician" is also related to "Club" by the same relationship. This inheritance and generalization of properties can be captured by embedding methods that use entity hierarchy information, allowing them to better capture the semantics of the KG.

The most notable method for incorporating entity hierarchy into KG embedding learning is the Type-based Knowledge Representation Learning (TKRL) method [15]. TKRL employs a translational distance model that features type-specific entity projections. Given a fact represented as (e_i, r_k, e_j), the model first projects entities e_i and e_j using type-specific projection matrices. Then, it models the relation r_k as a translation between the two projected entities. The scoring function for this model can be expressed as:

$$f_{r_k}(e_i, e_j) = \left\| \mathbf{M}_{r_k e_i} \mathbf{e}_i + \mathbf{r}_k - \mathbf{M}_{r_k e_j} \mathbf{e}_j \right\| \tag{6.5}$$

where $\mathbf{M}_{r_k e_i}$ and $\mathbf{M}_{r_k e_j}$ denote distinct projection matrices for entities e_i and e_j. As an entity in a KG can have multiple types, the projection matrix $\mathbf{M}_e$ for a given entity e is modeled as the weighted summation of all type matrices:

$$\mathbf{M}_e = \alpha_1 \mathbf{M}_{c_1} + \alpha_2 \mathbf{M}_{c_2} + \cdots + \alpha_n \mathbf{M}_{c_n} \tag{6.6}$$

where α_d represents the weight assigned to the type matrix $\mathbf{M}_{c_d}$ that corresponds to the type c_d the entity e belongs to.

In certain situations, it is important for entities to have different representations that emphasize specific attributes. Fortunately, relation-specific type information in KGs can provide possible types an entity may belong to in a particular relation, aiding the creation of multiple entity representations. The projection matrix $\mathbf{M}_{r_k e_i}$ can be computed as:

$$\mathbf{M}_{r_k e_i} = \frac{\sum_{d=1}^{n} \alpha_d \mathbf{M}_{c_d}}{\sum_{d=1}^{n} \alpha_d} \, , \quad \alpha_d = \begin{cases} 1 & \text{if } c_d \in C_{r_k e_i} \\ 0 & \text{if } c_d \notin C_{r_k e_i} \end{cases} \tag{6.7}$$

where $C_{r_k e_i}$ denotes the type set of the head entity in relation r_k, as provided by the relation-specific type information. Projection matrices $\mathbf{M}_{r_k e_j}$ for tail entities will have the same form as those for head entities. $\mathbf{M}_c$ represents the projection matrix for type c, which can be constructed using the following two encoders:

- **Recursive Hierarchy Encoder (RHE)**: The RHE defines the matrix $\mathbf{M}_c$ as the product of projection matrices for all the sub-types in the hierarchical structure:

$$\mathbf{M}_c = \prod_{d=1}^{m} \mathbf{M}_{c^{(d)}} = \mathbf{M}_{c^{(1)}} \mathbf{M}_{c^{(2)}} \ldots \mathbf{M}_{c^{(m)}} \qquad (6.8)$$

- **Weighted Hierarchy Encoder**: This encoder calculates the hierarchical type matrix $\mathbf{M}_c$ by summing up the projection matrices of all sub-types, each with a different weight:

$$\mathbf{M}_c = \sum_{d=1}^{m} \beta_d \mathbf{M}_{c^{(d)}} = \beta_1 \mathbf{M}_{c^{(1)}} + \beta_2 \mathbf{M}_{c^{(2)}} + \cdots + \beta_m \mathbf{M}_{c^{(m)}} \qquad (6.9)$$

In both cases, m is the number of layers for type c in the hierarchical structure, $\mathbf{M}_{c^{(d)}}$ denotes the projection matrix of the d-th sub-type $c^{(d)}$, and $c^{(d+1)}$ is the parent sub-type of $c^{(d)}$. While TKRL has demonstrated great performance in downstream tasks, such as link prediction and triple classification, its space complexity is relatively high. This is due to its association of each class with a particular projection matrix.

6.3.2 Relation Hierarchies

In addition to entity type hierarchy, relation hierarchies are another important aspect of KGs. A relation hierarchy represents the hierarchical structure of relationships or properties in a KG, where higher-level relationships subsume more specific relationships. For example, in the movie KG, the relation hierarchy might have "cast" and "crew" as the highest-level relationships. "Cast" could have sub-relations such as "actor", "actress", "voice actor", and so on; while "crew" could have sub-relations such as "director", "producer", "writer", and so on. This hierarchy can lead to a more comprehensive understanding of the domain and facilitate more advanced reasoning operations. For example, by leveraging relation hierarchy, KG embedding methods can better infer the unobserved relations between entities and their properties, leading to more accurate and expressive embeddings. Relation hierarchy can also help in the generalization and inheritance of relationships, making it easier to reason about entities and their relationships at different levels of abstraction.

However, relation hierarchies can be complex and difficult to manage, particularly for large and heterogeneous KGs. It may be difficult to explicitly define the relation hierarchy given a KG. In the absence of an explicit relation hierarchy, Zhang et al. [16] propose a three-layer Hierarchical Relation Structure (HRS) consisting of (1) relation clusters, (2) relations, and (3) subrelations in KGs. Relation clusters are groups of semantically similar relations. For instance, the relations "producerOf" and "directorOf" might be semantically related because they both describe a relationship between a person and a film. Since some relations can have multiple semantic meanings, subrelations are employed to distinguish the different meanings of a specific relation. For example, the relation "partOf" has at least two semantics: location-related (New York, partOf, USA) and composition-related (monitor, partOf, television). Subrelations offer fine-grained descriptions for each relation.

In the HRS model, the embedding of a relation $\mathbf{r_k}$ for a triple (e_i, r_k, e_j) comprises three components: the relation cluster embedding $\mathbf{r_k^c}$, the relation-specific embedding $\mathbf{r_k^0}$, and the subrelation embedding $\mathbf{r_k^s}$. This can be represented as:

$$\mathbf{r_k} = \mathbf{r_k^c} + \mathbf{r_k^0} + \mathbf{r_k^s} \tag{6.10}$$

The k-means algorithm is applied to the relation embeddings obtained from TransE to create relation clusters $\mathbf{r_k^c}$. TransE assumes that $\mathbf{e}_i - \mathbf{e}_j \approx \mathbf{r}_k$ when the triple (e_i, r_k, e_j) is valid. To learn subrelations for relation r_k, all the $\hat{\mathbf{r}}_k = \mathbf{e}_i - \mathbf{e}_j$ values for each triple (e_i, r_k, e_j) are collected and clustered using the k-means algorithm into several groups. Each group corresponds to a fine-grained subrelation. The scoring function for the HRS model is given as:

$$f_{r_k}(e_i, e_j) = \left\| \mathbf{e}_i + \mathbf{r_k^c} + \mathbf{r_k^0} + \mathbf{r_k^s} - \mathbf{e}_j \right\| \tag{6.11}$$

While RHS proposes a three-layer structure to represent relation hierarchy, this may not be universally applicable given the complexity of relations in KGs. To address this limitation, TransRHS introduces a more general RHS, which is constructed using a generalization relationship called *subRelationOf* between relations (e.g., the relation labeled as "is_a" in Fig. 6.1 could be considered a *subRelationOf* relation). For example, a subRelationOf triple (actor, subRelationOf, cast) indicates the semantic relevance between the relation "actor" and the relation "cast" with the former being a subrelation of the latter. With the introduction of the subRelationOf relation, the triple set $\mathcal{O}$ in a KG can be divided into two corresponding disjoint subsets:

- **subRelationOf triple set** $\mathcal{O}_r = \{(r_k, sro, r_p)|r_k, r_p \in \mathcal{R}\}$, where r_k, r_p are relations in KGs and sro is the generalization relationship *subRelationOf*.
- **relational triple set** $\mathcal{O}_e = \{(e_i, r_k, e_j)|e_i, e_j \in \mathcal{E}, r_k \in \mathcal{R}\}$, where e_i, e_j represents head entity and tail entity, respectively, and r_k represents a relation between entities.

Note that when $(r_k, sro, r_p) \in \mathcal{O}_r$ holds and $(e_i, r_k, e_j) \in \mathcal{O}_e$ is a positive triple, then (e_i, r_p, e_j) must also be a positive triple. Following the principle of TransE, the embedding should satisfy that if $\mathbf{e}_i + \mathbf{r}_k \approx \mathbf{e}_j$, then $\mathbf{e}_i + \mathbf{r}_p \approx \mathbf{e}_j$. In TransRHS, each entity is learned as a low-dimensional vector, and each relation is encoded as a low-dimensional vector along with a *relation-specific sphere*. We denote the embedding of r_p and r_k as $\mathbf{r}_p$ and

$\mathbf{r}_k$, and their corresponding spheres as s_1 with radius m_1, and s_2 with radius m_2. TransRHS define the loss functions for different cases as follows:

$$L_{RHS} = \begin{cases} \alpha_1 \left[\left\| \mathbf{e}_i + \mathbf{r}_p - \mathbf{e}_j \right\|_2 - m_1 \right]_+ & \text{if } d_1 > m_1 \\ \alpha_2 \left[\left\| \mathbf{e}_i + \mathbf{r}_k - \mathbf{e}_j \right\|_2 - m_2 \right]_+ & \text{if } d_2 > m_2 \\ \alpha_3 \left[m_1 - \left\| \mathbf{e}_i + \mathbf{r}_k - \mathbf{e}_j \right\|_2 \right]_+ & \text{if } d_2 < m_1 \\ \alpha_4 \left[m_1 - m_2 \right]_+ & \text{if } m_1 > m_2 \end{cases} \qquad (6.12)$$

where $d_1 = \left\| \mathbf{e}_i + \mathbf{r}_p - \mathbf{e}_j \right\|$, $d_2 = \left\| \mathbf{e}_i + \mathbf{r}_k - \mathbf{e}_j \right\|$, and α's denote the weights to each case.

6.3.3 Summary

The hierarchical structure present in the ontology view of a KG also plays a significant role in capturing the relationships between entities and relations. This structure can be leveraged to improve the quality of embeddings and enhance the accuracy of downstream tasks like link prediction and entity classification. By incorporating hierarchy information into KG embedding methods, the ambiguity between entities or relations with similar labels can be resolved, leading to improved interpretability of KG embeddings. The utilization of hierarchy information is vital in advancing the state-of-the-art in knowledge representation and reasoning, which in turn enables more accurate and interpretable AI applications.

6.4 JOIE: Jointly Combining Ontology View and Instance View for KG Embedding

Note that both cross-view connection and intra-view structures in KG are significant for KG reasoning. To jointly leverage both types of information, we introduce the model JOIE [1], which jointly embeds entities and concepts using two model components: *cross-view association model* and *intra-view model*, where the cross-view association model enables the connection and information flow between the two views by capturing the instantiation of entities from corresponding concepts, and the intra-view model encodes the entities/concepts and relations/meta-relations on each view of the KG. The illustration of these model components for learning different aspects of the KG is shown in Fig. 6.3. In the following subsections, we first discuss the cross-view association model and intra-view model for each view, then combine them into variants of the proposed JOIE model.

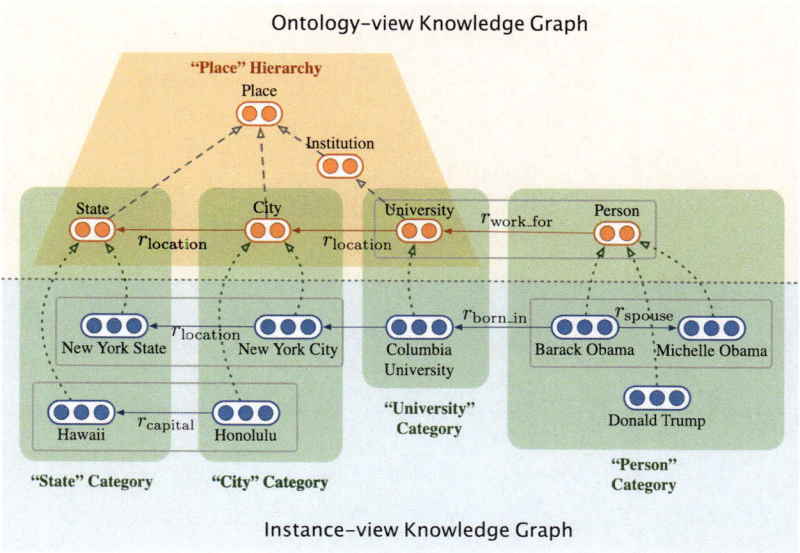

Fig. 6.3 JOIE learns two aspects of a KG. The cross-view association model learns embeddings from cross-view links (dash arrows in green "category" box). The default intra-view model learns embeddings from triples (grey box) in each view; Besides, hierarchy-aware intra-view models the meta-relation facts that form hierarchies in the ontology (orange "Hierarchy" trapezoid)

6.4.1   Framework of JOIE

6.4.1.1 Cross-View Association Model

The goal of the cross-view association model is to capture the associations between the entity embedding space and the concept embedding space, based on the cross-view links in KBs, which will be our key contributions. We propose two techniques to model such associations: *Cross-view Grouping (CG)* and *Cross-view Transformation (CT)*. These two techniques are based on different assumptions and thus optimize different objective functions.

Cross-view Grouping (CG). The cross-view grouping method can be considered as grouping-based regularization, which assumes that the ontology-view KG and instance-view KG can be embedded into the same space, and forces any instance $e \in \mathcal{E}$ to be close to its corresponding concept $c \in \mathcal{C}$, as shown in Fig. 6.4. This requires the embedding dimensionalities for the instance-view and ontology-view graphs to be the same, i.e. $d = d_c = d_e$. Specifically, the categorical association loss for a given pair of cross-view link (e, c) is defined as the distance between the embeddings of e and c compared with margin γ^{CG}, and the loss is defined as,

$$J_{Cross}^{CG} = \frac{1}{|\mathcal{S}|} \sum_{(e,c) \in \mathcal{S}} \left[||\mathbf{c} - \mathbf{e}||_2 - \gamma^{CG} \right]_+, \tag{6.13}$$

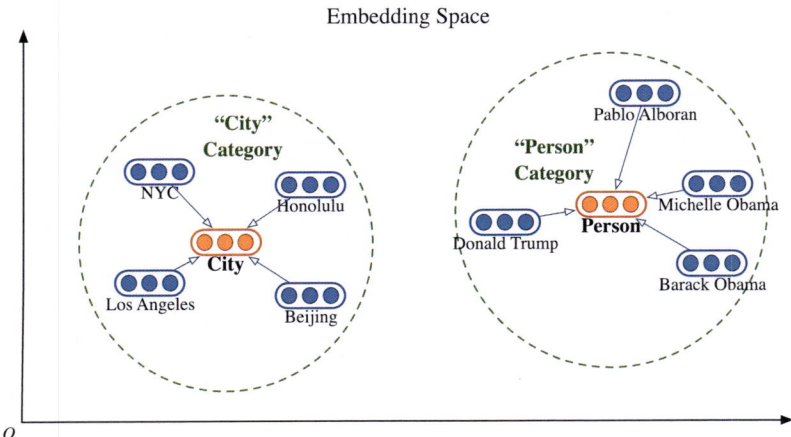

Fig. 6.4 Intuition of the cross-view association model: Cross-view Grouping (CG)

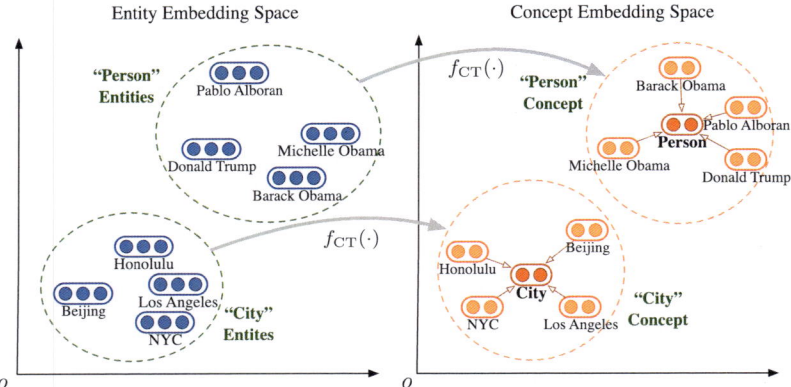

Fig. 6.5 Intuition of the cross-view association model: Cross-view Transformation (CT)

where $[x]_+$ is the positive part of the input x, i.e., $[x]_+ = \max\{x, 0\}$. This penalizes the case where the embedding of e falls out the γ^{CG}-radius[1] neighborhood centered at the embedding of c. CG has a strong clustering effect that makes entity embeddings close to their concept embeddings in the end.

Cross-view Transformation (CT). We also propose a cross-view transformation technique, which seeks to transform information between the entity embedding space and the concept space. Unlike CG which requires the two views to be embedded into the same space, the CT technique allows the two embedding spaces to be completely different from each other, which will be aligned together via a transformation, as shown in Fig. 6.5. In

---

[1] Typically, margin hyperparameter γ in the hinge loss can be chosen as 0.5 or 1 for different model settings. However, it is not a sensitive hyperparameter in our models.

other words, after the transformation, an instance will be mapped to an embedding in the ontology-view space, which should be close to the embedding of its corresponding concept:

$$\mathbf{c} \leftarrow f_{\text{CT}}(\mathbf{e}), \forall (e, c) \in \mathcal{S}, \tag{6.14}$$

where $f_{\text{CT}}(\mathbf{e}) = \sigma(\mathbf{W}_{\text{ct}} \cdot \mathbf{e} + \mathbf{b}_{\text{ct}})$ is a non-linear affine transformation, $\mathbf{W}_{\text{ct}} \in \mathbb{R}^{d_2 \times d_1}$ is a weight matrix and $\mathbf{b}_{\text{ct}}$ is a bias vector, and $\sigma(\cdot)$ is a non-linear activation function, for which we use tanh. Note d_1 denotes the embedding dimension for entities and d_2 denotes the embedding dimension for concepts, and these two do not have to be the same. Intuitively, there are much fewer concepts than entities, and thus d_2 can be set smaller than d_1.

The total loss of the cross-view association model is formulated as Eq. 6.15, which aggregates the CT objectives for all concepts involved in $\mathcal{S}$.

$$J_{\text{Cross}}^{\text{CT}} = \frac{1}{|\mathcal{S}|} \sum_{\substack{(e,c) \in \mathcal{S} \\ \wedge (e,c') \notin \mathcal{S}}} \left[\gamma^{\text{CT}} + ||\mathbf{c} - f_{\text{CT}}(\mathbf{e})||_2 - ||\mathbf{c}' - f_{\text{CT}}(\mathbf{e})||_2 \right]_+ \tag{6.15}$$

6.4.1.2 Intra-View Model

The aim of intra-view model is to preserve the original structural information in each view of the KB separately in two embedding spaces. Because of the different semantic meanings of relations in the instance view and meta-relations in the ontology view, it helps to give each view separate treatment rather than combining them into a single representation schema, improving the performance of downstream tasks, as shown in Sect. 6.4.3.2. In this section, we provide two intra-view model techniques for encoding heterogeneous and hierarchical graph structures.

Default Intra-view Model. To embed such a triple (h, r, t) in one KG, a score function $f(\mathbf{h}, \mathbf{r}, \mathbf{t})$ measures the plausibility of it. A higher score indicates a more plausible triple. Any triple embedding technique is applicable in our intra-view framework. In this paper, we adopt three representative techniques, i.e. TransE [17], DistMult [18] and HolE [19]. The score functions of these techniques are given as follows.

$$f_{\text{TransE}}(\mathbf{h}, \mathbf{r}, \mathbf{t}) = -||\mathbf{h} + \mathbf{r} - \mathbf{t}||_2$$
$$f_{\text{DistMult}}(\mathbf{h}, \mathbf{r}, \mathbf{t}) = (\mathbf{h} \circ \mathbf{t}) \cdot \mathbf{r} \tag{6.16}$$
$$f_{\text{HolE}}(\mathbf{h}, \mathbf{r}, \mathbf{t}) = (\mathbf{h} \star \mathbf{t}) \cdot \mathbf{r}$$

where $\circ$ denotes the Hadamard product, $\cdot$ dentoes the dot product, and $\star : \mathbb{R}^d \times \mathbb{R}^d \to \mathbb{R}^d$ denotes the circular correlation defined as $[\mathbf{a} \star \mathbf{b}]_k = \sum_{i=0}^{d} a_i b_{(k+i) \mod d}$.

To learn embeddings of all nodes in one graph $\mathcal{G}$, a hinge loss is minimized for all triples in the graph:

$$J_{\text{Intra}}^{\mathcal{G}} = \frac{1}{|\mathcal{G}|} \sum_{\substack{(h,r,t)\in\mathcal{G} \\ \wedge(h',r,t')\notin\mathcal{G}}} \left[\gamma^{\mathcal{G}} + f(\mathbf{h}',\mathbf{r},\mathbf{t}') - f(\mathbf{h},\mathbf{r},\mathbf{t})\right]_{+}, \tag{6.17}$$

where $\gamma^{\mathcal{G}} > 0$ is a positive margin, and (h',r,t') is one sample from the set of corrupted triples that replace either head or tail entity and does not exist in $\mathcal{G}$.

The aforementioned techniques, losses, and learning objectives for embedding graphs are naturally applicable to both instance-view graph and ontology-view graph. In the default intra-view model setting, for triples $(h^{(I)},r^{(I)},t^{(I)}) \in \mathcal{G}_I$ or $(h^{(O)},r^{(O)},t^{(O)}) \in \mathcal{G}_O$, we can compute $f_I(\mathbf{h}^{(I)},\mathbf{r}^{(I)},\mathbf{t}^{(I)})$ and $f_O(\mathbf{h}^{(O)},\mathbf{r}^{(O)},\mathbf{t}^{(O)})$ with the same techniques when optimizing $J_{\text{Intra}}^{\mathcal{G}_I}$ and $J_{\text{Intra}}^{\mathcal{G}_O}$. Combining the losses from instance-view and ontology-view graphs, the joint loss of the intra-view model is given below,

$$J_{\text{Intra}} = J_{\text{Intra}}^{\mathcal{G}_I} + \alpha_1 \cdot J_{\text{Intra}}^{\mathcal{G}_O}, \tag{6.18}$$

where a positive hyperparameter α_1 weighs between the structural loss of the instance-view graph and ontology-view graph.

In default Intra-view model, we employ the same triple encoding technique to represent both views of the KG. The purpose of doing so is to enforce the same paradigm of characterizing relational inferences in both views. It is noteworthy that there are other triple encoding techniques for KG embeddings, which can potentially be used in our intra-view model.

Hierarchy-Aware Intra-view Model for the Ontology. It is observed that the ontology views of some KGs form hierarchies, which are typically constituted by a meta-relation with the hierarchical property, such as "*subclass_of*" and "*is_a*" [7, 20]. We can define such meta-relation facts as $(c_l, r_{\text{meta}} = \text{"subclass\_of"}, c_h)$. For example, "*musician*" and "*singer*" belong to "*artist*" and "*artist*" is also a subclass of "*person*". Such semantic ontological features require additional modeling than other meta-relations. In other words, we further distinguish between meta-relations that form the ontology hierarchy and those regular semantic relations (such as "*related_to*") in our intra-view model.

To address this problem, we propose the hierarchy-aware (HA) intra-view model by extending a similar method to that of cross-view transformation as defined in Eq. 6.14. Given concept pairs (c_l, c_h), we model such hierarchies into a non-linear transformation between coarser concepts and associated finer concepts by

$$g_{\text{HA}}(\mathbf{c}_h) = \sigma(\mathbf{W}_{\text{HA}} \cdot \mathbf{c}_l + \mathbf{b}_{\text{HA}}) \tag{6.19}$$

where $\mathbf{W}_{\text{HA}} \in \mathbb{R}^{d_2 \times d_2}$ and $\mathbf{b}_{\text{HA}} \in \mathbb{R}^{d_2}$ are defined similarly. Also, we use tanh function as $\sigma(\cdot)$ option. This will introduce a new loss term, ontology hierarchy loss inside the ontology view, which is similar to Eq. 6.15,

$$J_{\text{Intra}}^{\text{HA}} = \frac{1}{|\mathcal{T}|} \sum_{\substack{(c_l,c_h)\in\mathcal{T} \\ \wedge(c_l,c_h')\notin\mathcal{T}}} \left[\gamma^{\text{HA}} + ||\mathbf{c}_h - g(\mathbf{c}_l)||_2 - ||\mathbf{c_h}' - g(\mathbf{c_l})||_2\right]_{+} \tag{6.20}$$

Therefore, the total training loss of the hierarchy-aware intra-view model for both views changes slightly,

$$J_{\text{Intra}} = J_{\text{Intra}}^{\mathcal{G}_I} + \alpha_1 \cdot J_{\text{Intra}}^{\mathcal{G}_O \setminus \mathcal{T}} + \alpha_2 \cdot J_{\text{Intra}}^{\text{HA}} \quad (6.21)$$

where positive α_1 and α_2 are two weighing hyperparameters. In Eq. 6.21, $J_{\text{Intra}}^{\mathcal{G}_O \setminus \mathcal{T}}$ refers to the loss of the default intra-view model that is only trained on triples with regular semantic relations. $J_{\text{Intra}}^{\text{HA}}$ is explicitly trained on the triples with meta-relations that form the ontology hierarchy, which is a major difference from Eq. 6.18.

As the conclusion of this subsection, in JOIE, the basic assumption is that KGs have ontology hierarchy and rich semantic relational features compared to social or citation networks. JOIE is able to encode such KG properties in its model architecture. Note that we are also aware of the fact that there are more comprehensive properties of relations and meta-relations in the two views such as logical rules of relations and entity types. Incorporating such properties into the learning process is left as future work.

6.4.1.3 Joint Training on Two-View KGs

Combining the intra-view model and cross-view association model, JOIE minimizes the following joint loss function:

$$J = J_{\text{Intra}} + \omega \cdot J_{\text{Cross}}, \quad (6.22)$$

where $\omega > 0$ is a positive hyperparameter that balances between J_{Intra} and J_{Cross}.

Instead of directly updating J, our implementation optimizes $J_{\text{Intra}}^{\mathcal{G}_I}$, $J_{\text{Intra}}^{\mathcal{G}_O}$ and J_{Cross} alternately. In detail, we optimize $\theta^{\text{new}} \leftarrow \theta^{\text{old}} - \eta \nabla J_{\text{Intra}}$ and $\theta^{\text{new}} \leftarrow \theta^{\text{old}} - (\omega\eta)\nabla J_{\text{Cross}}$ in successive steps within one epoch. η is the learning rate, and ω differentiates between the learning rates for intra-view and cross-view losses.

We use the AMSGrad optimizer [21] to optimize the joint loss function. We initialize vectors by drawing from a uniform distribution on the unit spherical surface, and initialize matrices using random orthogonal initialization [22]. During the training, we enforce the constraint that the L2 norm of all entity and concept vectors to be 1, in order to prevent them from shrinking to zero. This follows the setting by [17–19, 23]. Negative sampling is used on both intra-view model and cross-view association model with a ratio of 1 (number of negative samples per positive one). A hinge loss is applied for both models with all variants.

6.4.1.4 Variants of JOIE and Complexity Analysis

Without considering the HA technique, we have six variants of JOIE given two options of cross-view association models in Sect. 6.4.1.1 and three options of intra-view models in Sect. 6.4.1.2. For simplicity, we use the names of its components to denote specific variants of JOIE, such as "JOIE-TransE-CT" representing JOIE with the cross-view transformation and TransE-based default intra-view embeddings. In addition, we incorporate the hierarchy-aware intra-view model for the ontology view into cross-view transformation model,[2] which produces three additional model variants denoted as JOIE-HATransE-CT, JOIE-HAMult-CT, and JOIE-HAHolE-CT.

The model complexity depends on the cross-view association model and intra-view model for learning two-view KGs. We denote n_e, n_c, n_r, n_m as the number of total entities, concepts, relations, and meta-relations (typically $n_e \gg n_c$) and d_e, d_c as embedding dimensions ($d_e = d_c$ if CG is used). The model complexity of parameter sizes is $O(n_e d_e + n_c d_c)$ for all CG-based variants and $O(n_e d_e + n_c d_c + d_e d_c)$ for all CT-based variants. An additional parameter size of $O(d_c^2)$ is needed if the hierarchy-aware intra-view model applies. Because of $n \gg d_e$ (or d_c), the parameter complexity is approximately proportional to the number of entities and the model training runtime complexity is proportional to the number of triples in the KG. For the task of triple completion in the KG, the time complexity for all variants is $O(n_e d_e)$ for the instance-view graph or $O(n_c d_c)$ for the ontology-view graph. To process each prediction case in the entity typing task, the time complexity is $O(n_c d_e)$ for CG and $O(n_c d_c d_e)$ for CT. Details about each task are curated in Sects. 6.4.3.2 and 6.4.3.3.

6.4.2   Connection to Existing Approaches

Although a few approaches have been proposed to incorporate complex type information of entities into KG embedding techniques [15, 24–26], from which our settings are substantially different from two perspectives:

- These studies utilize the proximity of entity types to strengthen the learning of instance-level entity similarity, while do not capture the semantic relations between such types;
- They mostly focus on improving instance-view triple completion, but do not leverage instance-view knowledge to improve ontology population, nor support cross-view association to bridge instances and ontological concepts.

To address the above limitations of the existing works, JOIE is proposed to jointly encode both the ontology and instance views of a KG. JOIE contains two components. First, a *cross-view association model* is designed to associate the instance embedding to its corresponding concept embedding. Second, the *intra-view embedding model* characterizes the relational facts of ontology and instance views in two separate embedding spaces. For the cross-view association model, we explore two techniques to capture the cross-view links. The *cross-view grouping* technique assumes that the two views can be forced into the same embedding space, while the *cross-view transformation* technique enables non-linear transformations from the instance embedding space to the ontology embedding space. As for the intra-view embedding model, in particular, we use three state-of-the-art translational or similarity-based relational

---

[2] We later show in the experiments that CT-based variants consistently outperform CG-based variants and thus we only apply HA intra-view model settings to CT-based model variants.

embedding techniques to capture the multi-relational structures of each view. Additionally, for some KGs where ontologies contain hierarchical substructures, we employ a *hierarchy-aware* embedding technique based on intra-view non-linear transformations to preserve such substructures.

Another related branch of approaches leverages logic rules [27, 28] to incorporate ontology into knowledge graph reasoning. We have introduced some of the methods in Sect. 3.3. However, they require additional information that typically is not provided in two-view KGs.

6.4.3   Experiments

In this section, we evaluate JOIE with two groups of tasks: the triple completion task on both instance-view and ontology-view KGs and the entity typing task to bridge two views of the KG. Besides, we provide a case study on ontology population and long-tail entity typing.

6.4.3.1 Datasets

To the best of our knowledge, existing datasets for KG embeddings consider only an instance view (e.g. FB15k [17]) or an ontology view (e.g. WN18 [29]). Hence, we prepare two new datasets: *YAGO26K-906* and *DB111K-174*, which are extracted from the connected subsets of YAGO [20] and DBpedia [7] respectively. The datasets are constructed through the following steps:

1. We first filter out all attribute triples, since such triples do not represent the relations of entities or concepts. We then randomly sample some relational triples from the rest of the filtered dataset since the original YAGO and DBpedia both have large collections of instance-view triples.
2. After we obtain the entity set of instance view, we extract the cross-view alignment of those entities to the ontology view of the two KGs. As a result, a portion of entities are linked to the associated concepts, which are naturally the nodes in the ontology view.
3. Given all the associated concepts from step (2), we construct the corresponding ontology view based on the intersecting subgraph of the original ontologies.

It is noteworthy that the original YAGO has a taxonomical ontology with only three types of semantic relations, which casts limitations on semantic relations among concepts. We enrich the ontology view of YAGO using the knowledge from ConceptNet [4], which is another KG containing a large collection of meta-relations among concepts. The concepts in ConceptNet and YAGO are easily aligned by the shared WordNet-based IDs or concept names. Consequently, we obtain two datasets that are much larger than FB15K—the widely adopted instance KG benchmark dataset by many recent works [17–19, 30].

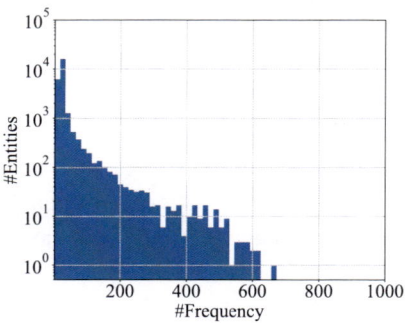

Fig. 6.6 Entity frequency distribution of YAGO26K-906

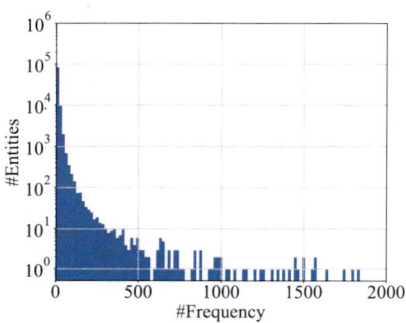

Fig. 6.7 Entity frequency distribution of DB111K-174

Table 6.1 Statistics of datasets

Dataset	Instance graph $\mathcal{G}_I$			Ontology graph $\mathcal{G}_O$			Type links $\mathcal{S}$
	#Entities	#Relations	#Triples	#Concepts	#Meta-relations	#Triples	
YAGO26K-906	26,078	34	390,738	906	30	8,962	9,962
DB111K-174	111,762	305	863,643	174	20	763	99,748

As stated in Sect. 6.4.3.4, the frequency of entities and relations often follow a long-tail distribution (Zipf's law) in both YAGO26K-906 and DB111K-174 datasets, which is confirmed by the histogram in Figs. 6.6 and 6.7.

Table 6.1 provides the statistics of both datasets. Normally, the instance-view KG is significantly larger than the ontology-view graph. Also, we notice that the two KGs are different in the density of type links, i.e., DB111K-174 has a much higher entity-to-concept ratio (643.4) than YAGO26K-906 (28.7). Datasets are available at https://github.com/JunhengH/joie-kdd19.

6.4.3.2 KG Triple Completion

The objective of triple completion is to construct the missing relation facts in a KG structure, which directly tests the quality of learned embeddings. In our experiment, this task spans into two sub-tasks for instance-view KG completion and ontology population. We perform the sub-tasks on both datasets with all JOIE variants compared with baseline models.

Evaluation Protocol. First, we separate the instance-view triples into training set $\mathcal{G}_I^{\text{train}}$, validation set $\mathcal{G}_I^{\text{valid}}$ and test set $\mathcal{G}_I^{\text{test}}$, as well as separate similarly the ontology-view triples to $\mathcal{G}_O^{\text{train}}$, $\mathcal{G}_O^{\text{valid}}$ and $\mathcal{G}_O^{\text{test}}$. The percentage of the training, validation, and test cases is 85%, 5%, and 10%, which is consistent with that of the widely used benchmark dataset [17] for instance-only KG embeddings. Each JOIE variant is trained on $\mathcal{G}_I^{\text{train}}$ and $\mathcal{G}_O^{\text{train}}$ triples along with all cross-view links $\mathcal{S}$. In the testing phase, given each query $(h, r, ?t)$, the plausibility scores $f(\mathbf{h}, \mathbf{r}, \tilde{\mathbf{t}})$ for triples formed with every $\tilde{t}$ in the test candidate set are computed and ranked by the intra-view model. We report three metrics for testing: mean reciprocal ranks (MRR), accuracy ($Hits@1$), and the proportion of correct answers ranked within the top 10 ($Hits@10$). All three metrics are preferred to be higher, so as to indicate better triple-completion performance. Also, we adopt the filtered metrics as suggested in previous work which are aggregated based on the premise that the candidate space has excluded the triples that have been seen in the training set [17, 18].

As for the hyperparameters in training, we select the dimensionality d among {50, 100, 200, 300} for concepts and entities, learning rate among {0.0005, 0.001, 0.01}, margin γ among {0.5, 1}. We also use different batch sizes according to the sizes of the graphs. We fix the best configuration $d_e = 300, d_c = 50$ for CT and $d_e = d_c = 200$ for CG with $\alpha_1 = 2.5, \alpha_2 = 1.0$. We set $\gamma^{\mathcal{G}_I} = \gamma^{\mathcal{G}_O} = 0.5$ as the default for all TransE variants and $\gamma^{\mathcal{G}_I} = \gamma^{\mathcal{G}_O} = 1$ for all DistMult and HolE variants. The training processes on all datasets and models are limited to 120 epochs.

Baselines. We compare our model with TransE, DistMult, and HolE as well as TransC [31]. We deploy the following variants of baselines: (i) We train these mono-graph models (TransE, DistMult, and HolE) either on instance-view triples or ontology-view triples separately, denoted as (*base*) in Table 6.2; (ii) We also train TransE, DistMult, and HolE based on all triples in both $\mathcal{G}_I^{\text{train}}$ and $\mathcal{G}_O^{\text{train}}$. For the second setting thereof, we incorporate cross-view links by adding one additional relation "*type_of*" to them, denoted as (*all*) in Table 6.2. (iii) TransC is trained on both views of a KG. TransC is a recent work that differentiates the encoding process of concepts from instances. Note that TransC is equivalent to a simplified case of our JOIE-TransE-CG where no semantic meta-relations in the ontology view are included. For that reason, TransC does not apply to the completion of the ontology view.

Results. As reported in Table 6.2, we categorize the results into three different groups based on the intra-view models. Though three intra-view models have different capabilities, among all the baselines in same group, JOIE notably outperforms others by 6.8% on MRR, and 14.8% on $Hit@10$ on average. A significant improvement is achieved on the ontology-view of DB111K-174 with JOIE, compared to concept embeddings trained with

Table 6.2 Results of KG triple completion. H@1 and H@10 denote $Hit@1$ and $Hit@10$ respectively. For each group of model variants with the same intra-view model, the best results are bold-faced. The overall best results on each dataset are underscored

Datasets	YAGO26K-906						DB111K-174					
Graphs	$\mathcal{G}_I$ KG completion			$\mathcal{G}_O$ KG completion			$\mathcal{G}_I$ KG completion			$\mathcal{G}_O$ KG completion		
Metrics	MRR	H@1	H@10	MRR	H@1	H@10	MRR	H@1	H@10	MRR	H@1	H@10
TransE (base)	0.195	14.09	34.51	0.145	12.29	20.59	0.327	22.26	49.01	0.313	23.22	46.91
TransE (all)	0.187	13.73	35.05	0.189	14.72	24.36	0.318	22.70	48.12	0.539	47.90	61.84
TransC	0.252	15.71	37.79	–	–	–	0.359	24.83	49.31	–	–	–
JOIE-TransE-CG	0.264	16.38	35.45	0.189	11.16	29.44	0.394	27.75	51.20	0.598	53.84	71.79
JOIE-TransE-CT	0.292	**18.72**	44.14	0.240	14.49	33.47	0.443	32.10	67.89	**0.622**	**58.10**	72.97
JOIE-HATransE-CT	**0.306**	18.62	**51.72**	**0.263**	16.72	**38.46**	**0.473**	**33.79**	**71.37**	0.591	52.07	**79.65**
DistMult (base)	0.253	22.91	28.76	0.197	**17.72**	25.08	0.265	25.95	27.63	0.235	15.18	29.11
DistMult (all)	0.288	**24.06**	31.24	0.156	14.32	16.54	0.280	27.24	29.70	0.501	45.52	64.73
JOIE-Mult-CG	0.274	18.80	37.45	0.198	11.16	27.91	0.320	23.44	49.49	0.532	46.15	68.91
JOIE-Mult-CT	**0.309**	20.40	**46.15**	**0.207**	14.71	30.43	**0.404**	**26.55**	**60.86**	**0.563**	**50.50**	71.62
JOIE-HAMult-CT	0.296	19.39	45.48	0.202	13.72	**31.10**	0.369	24.82	55.86	0.521	38.46	**77.25**
HolE (base)	0.265	**25.90**	28.31	0.192	18.70	20.29	0.301	29.24	31.51	0.227	18.91	32.83
HolE (all)	0.252	24.22	26.56	0.138	11.29	14.43	0.295	28.70	30.32	0.432	38.80	56.05
JOIE-HolE-CG	0.253	18.75	34.11	0.167	13.04	22.33	0.361	24.13	46.15	0.469	41.89	62.16
JOIE-HolE-CT	0.313	20.40	47.80	0.229	**20.85**	28.42	0.425	29.09	66.88	**0.514**	**43.24**	69.23
JOIE-HAHolE-CT	**0.327**	22.42	**52.41**	**0.236**	16.72	**30.96**	**0.464**	**33.11**	**69.56**	0.503	40.80	**71.03**

only ontology-view triples: 10.4% average increase compared to "all"-setting baselines and 34.97% compared to "base"-setting baselines. These results indicate that JOIE has a better ability to utilize information from the instance view to promote the triple completion in the ontology view. Comparing different intra-view models, translation-based models performs better than similarity-based models on ontology population and instance-view KG completion on the DB111K-174 dataset. This is because these graphs are sparse, and TransE is less hampered by the sparsity in comparison to the similarity-based techniques [32]. By applying the HA technique in the intra-view models with CT, the performance on instance-view triple completion is noticeably improved in most cases in comparison to the default intra-view CT-based models, especially in variants with translation and circular correlation based intra-view models.

Generally, JOIE provides an effective method to train two-view KG separately, and both $\mathcal{G}_I$ and $\mathcal{G}_O$ benefit each other in learning better embeddings, producing promising results in the triple completion task.

6.4.3.3 Entity Typing

The entity typing task seeks to predict the associating concepts of certain given entities. Similar to the triple completion task, we rank all candidates and report the top-ranked answers for evaluation.

Evaluation Protocol. We separate the cross-view links of each dataset into training and test sets with the ratio of 60 to 40%, denoted as $\mathcal{S}^{train}$ and $\mathcal{S}^{test}$ respectively. Each model is trained on the entire instance-view and ontology-view graphs with cross-view links $\mathcal{S}^{train}$. Hyperparameters are carried forward from the triple completion task, in order to evaluate under controlled variables. In the test phase, given a specific entity e_q, we rank the concepts based on their embedding distances from the projection of $\mathbf{e}_q$ in the concept embedding space, and calculate MRR, $Hit@1$ (i.e. accuracy) and $Hit@3$ on the test queries. We perform the entity typing task on both datasets with all JOIE variants compared with these baselines.

Baselines. We compare with TransE, DistMult, HolE and MTransE. For baselines other than MTransE, we convert the cross-view links (e, c) to triples $(e, r_T = \text{``type\_of''}, c)$. Therefore, entity typing is equivalent to the triple completion task for these baseline models. For MTransE, we treat concepts and entities as different views (originally input as knowledge bases of two languages in [33]) in their model and test with distance-based ranking.

Results. Results are reported in Table 6.3. All JOIE variants perform significantly better than the baselines. The best JOIE model, i.e. JOIE-TransE-CT, outperforms the best baseline model MTransE by 15.4% in terms of accuracy and 14.4% in terms of MRR on

Table 6.3 Results of entity typing

Datasets	YAGO26K-906			DB111K-174		
Metrics	MRR	Acc.	Hit@3	MRR	Acc.	Hit@3
TransE	0.144	7.32	35.26	0.503	43.67	60.78
MTransE	0.689	60.87	77.64	0.672	59.87	81.32
JOIE-TransE-CG	0.829	72.63	93.35	0.828	70.58	95.11
JOIE-TransE-CT	0.843	75.31	93.18	0.846	74.41	94.53
JOIE-HATransE-CT	**0.897**	**85.60**	**95.91**	**0.857**	**75.55**	**95.91**
DistMult	0.411	36.07	55.32	0.551	49.83	68.01
JOIE-Mult-CG	0.762	62.62	87.82	0.764	60.83	91.80
JOIE-Mult-CT	0.805	70.83	89.25	**0.791**	65.30	**93.47**
JOIE-HAMult-CT	**0.865**	**81.63**	**91.83**	0.778	**69.38**	85.71
HolE	0.395	34.83	54.79	0.504	44.75	65.38
JOIE-HolE-CG	0.777	65.30	87.89	0.784	66.75	89.37
JOIE-HolE-CT	0.813	72.27	88.71	0.805	68.84	**91.22**
JOIE-HAHolE-CT	**0.888**	**83.67**	**93.87**	**0.808**	**72.51**	89.79

YAGO26K-906. The improvement on accuracy and MRR are 14.3 and 14.5% on DB111K-174 compared to MTransE. The results by other baselines confirm that the cross-view links, which apply to all entities and concepts, cannot be properly captured as a regular relation and requires a dedicated representation technique.

Considering different JOIE variants, our observation is that using translation-based intra-view model and CT as the cross-view association model (JOIE-TransE-CT) is consistently better than other settings on both datasets. It has an average of 4.1% performance gain in MRR over JOIE-HolE-CT and JOIE-DistMult-CT, and an average of 2.17% performance gain in accuracy over the best of the rest variants (JOIE-TransE-CG). We believe that, compared with similarity-based intra-view models, translation based intra-view model better differentiates between different entities and different concepts in KGs with directed relations and meta-relations in the KG [32]. The results by CT-based model variants are generally better than those by CG-based ones. We believe this is due to two reasons: (i) CT allows the two embedding spaces have different dimensionalties, and hence better characterizes the ontology-view that is smaller and sparser than the instance view; (ii) As the topological structures of the two views may exhibit some inconsistency, CT adapts well and is less sensitive to such inconsistency than CG.

In terms of different intra-view models, it is also observed that HA intra-view model with CT settings can drastically enhance entity typing task and achieve the best performance, especially for YAGO26K-906 with relatively rich ontology, which improves an average of 6.0% on MRR and 10.5% in accuracy compared with the default intra-view settings. The reason that the HA technique does not have similar effects on DB111K-174 is that DB111K-174 contains a small ontology with much smaller hierarchical structures.[3] Comparing the two datasets, our experiments show that, JOIE generally achieves similar accuracies and MRR scores on YAGO26K-906 and DB111K-174, but slightly better $Hit@3$ on DB111K-174 due to its smaller candidate space.

Our method opens up a new direction that the learned embedding may help guide labeling entities with unknown types.

6.4.3.4 Case Study

In this section, we provide two case studies for ontology population and entity typing for long-tail entities.

Ontology Population. By embedding the meta-relations and concepts in the ontology view, the triple completion process can already populate the ontology view with seen meta-relations, by answering the query like (*"Concert"*,*"Related to"*,*?t*) in the KG completion task. Given the top answers to the query, we can reconstruct triples like (*"Concert"*,*"Related to"*,*"Ballet"*) and (*"Concert"*,*"Related* to*"*,*"Musical"*) with high confidence. However, this process does not resolve the zero-shot cases where some concepts may satisfy some meta-

---

[3] DB111K-174 contains 164 ontology-view triples for meta-relations with the hierarchical property, while YAGO26K-906 contains 1,411.

relations that have not pre-existed in the vocabulary of meta-relations. We cannot predict the potentially new meta-relation "is Politician of" directly with triple completion by answering the following query: ("*Office Holder*", *?r*, "*Country*").

Our proposed JOIE provides a feasible solution by leveraging the cross-view association model that bridges the two views of the KG and migrates proper instance-view relations to ontology-view meta-relations. This is realized by transforming the concept embeddings in the query to the entity embedding space, and selecting candidate relations from the instance-view. Considering the previous query ("*Office Holder*", *?r*, "*Country*"), we first find the concept embeddings of "*Office Holder*" and "*Country*" (denoted as c_{office} and c_{country} respectively), and then transform them to the entity space. Specifically, for JOIE variants with the translational intra-view model, we find the instance-view relations that are closest to $f_{\text{CT}}^{\text{inv}}(c_{\text{country}}) - f_{\text{CT}}^{\text{inv}}(c_{\text{office}})$. Figure 6.8 shows the PCA projections of the top 10 relation prediction results for this query. The top 3 relations are "*is Politician of*", "*is Leader of*", and "*is Citizen of*", which are all reasonable answers.

Table 6.4 shows some examples of newly discovered meta-relation facts that have not pre-existed in the ontology views of the two datasets. Five predictions with the highest

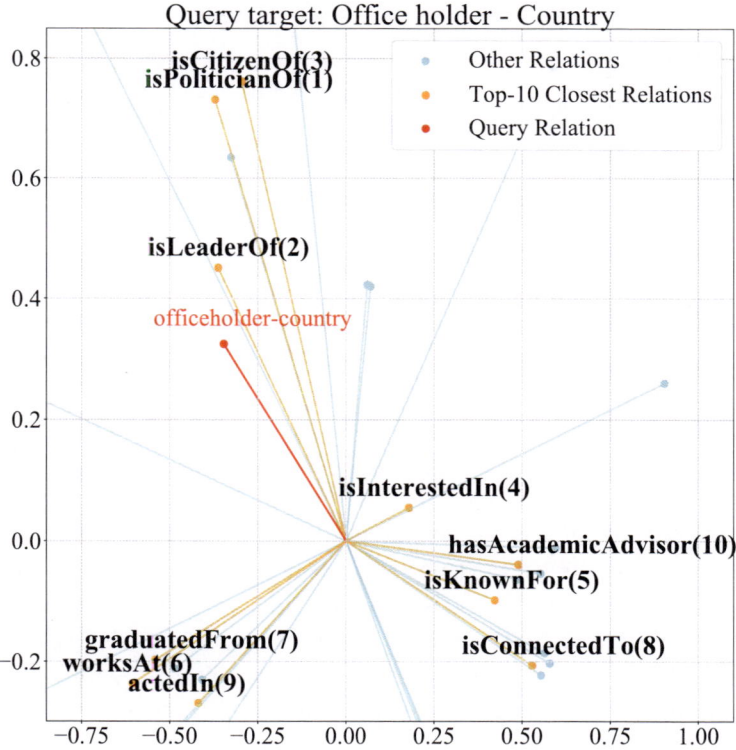

Fig. 6.8 Examples of ontology population by finding the closest relations in the instance view for the query "Office Holder-Country". The top 10 predicted relations are plotted with their ranks

Table 6.4 Examples of ontology population from JOIE-TransE-CT. The top 5 Populated Triples with the smallest L2-norm distances are provided with reasonable answers bold-faced

Query	Top 5 Populated triples with distances
(scientist,?r, university)	scientist, *graduated from*, university (0.499)
	scientist, *isLeaderOf*, university (1.082)
	scientist, *isKnownFor*, university (1.098)
	scientist, *created*, university (1.119)
	scientist, *livesIn*, university (1.141)
(boxer, ?r, club)	boxer, *playsFor*, club (1.467)
	boxer, *isAffiliatedTo*, club (1.474)
	boxer, *worksAt*, club (1.479)
	boxer, *graduatedFrom*, club (1.497)
	boxer, *isConnectedTo*, club (1.552)
(TV station, ?r, country)	TV station, *headquarter*, country (1.221)
	TV station, *parentOrganisation*, country (1.246)
	TV station, *appointer*, country (1.253)
	TV station, *broadcastArea*, country (1.266)
	TV station, *principalArea*, country (1.271)
(scientist, ?r, scientist)	scientist, *deputy*, scientist (0.204)
	scientist,*doctoralAdvisor*, scientist (0.218)
	scientist, *doctoralStudent*, scientist (0.221)
	scientist, *relative*, scientist (0.228)
	scientist, *spouse*, scientist (0.230)

plausibility (smallest distance) are provided for each query from the ontology-view graph. From these top predictions, we observe that most populated ontology triples migrated from the instance view are meaningful.

Long-tail entity typing. In KGs, the frequency of entities and relations often follow a long-tail distribution (Zipf's law). As shown in Figs. 6.6 and 6.7, both YAGO26K-906 and DB111K-174 discover such a property. Over 75% of the total entities has less than 15 occurrences. Those long-tails entities, types, and relations are difficult for representation learning algorithms to capture due to being few-shot in training cases.

In this case study, we select the entities with considerably low frequency,[4] which involve around 15–30% of total entities in the instance view of the two KG datasets. Then, we evaluate the entity typing task for these long-tail entities. Table 6.5 shows the results by the best baselines (DistMult, MTransE) and a group of our best JOIE variants. Similar to our previous

---

[4] In this experiment, we select entities in YAGO26K-906 which occurs less than 8 times and entities in DB111K-174 which occurs less than 3 times.

Table 6.5 Results of long-tail entities typing

Datasets	YAGO26K-906			DB111K-174		
Metrics	MRR	Acc.	Hit@3	MRR	Acc.	Hit@3
DistMult	0.156	10.89	25.33	0.219	16.48	33.71
MTransE	0.526	46.45	67.25	0.505	46.67	64.36
JOIE-TransE-CG	0.708	59.97	79.80	0.741	64.45	83.05
JOIE-TransE-CT	0.737	62.05	82.60	0.758	66.35	83.80
JOIE-HATransE-CT	**0.802**	**69.66**	**87.75**	**0.760**	**67.34**	**89.79**

Table 6.6 Examples of long-tail entity typing. The top 3 predictions are provided with the correct type bold-faced

Entity	Model	Top 3 Concept prediction
Laurence Fishburne	DistMult	Football team, Club, Team
	MTransE	Writer, **Person**, Artist
	JOIE	**Person**, Artist, Philosopher
Warangal City	DistMult	Country, Village, **City**
	MTransE	Administrative region, **City**, Settlement
	JOIE	**City**, Town, Country
Royal Victorian Order	DistMult	Person, Writer, Administrative region
	MTransE	Election, Award, **Order**
	JOIE	Award, **Order**, Election

observation, JOIE significantly outperforms other baselines. Compared with the results in Sect. 6.4.3.3, we observe the decrease of performance for all models, while JOIE variants only have an average of 12.5% decrease in MRR with CG models and 12.3% decrease in MRR with CT models while other baselines suffer over 20% on long-tail entity prediction. There is also an interesting observation that, for long-tails entities, smaller embeddings for both CG ($d_1 = d_2 = 100$) and CT ($d_1 = 100, d_2 = 50$) models are beneficial for associated concept prediction. We hypothesize that this is caused by overfitting on long-tail entities if high dimensionality is used for training without enough training data.

In Table 6.6, we include some examples of the top 3 predicted categories of long-tail entities by DistMult, MTransE and JOIE (using JOIE-HATransE-CT variant) from DB111K-174, when the instance-view graph and ontology-view graph are relatively sparser. JOIE is still able to make correct predictions of low-frequency entities while other baseline models can only output inaccurate predictions.

6.5   Summary and Discussions

The representation of a knowledge graph (KG) involves two main views, the ontology view and the instance view. The ontology view describes abstract concepts such as entity types and relation hierarchies, while the instance view contains specific entities and their relationships. Integrating these two views is crucial for generating more comprehensive and semantically meaningful embeddings that can benefit a wide range of downstream tasks. In this chapter, we explore different approaches to integrate both views for reasoning, which can be broadly classified into two categories based on the links they use: (1) those using cross-view links and (2) those using intra-view links.

Cross-view links serve as a vital connection between the instance view and the ontology view of KG, associating entities with their corresponding classes such as people, places, and organizations. These links enable the model to discern common patterns and relationships among entities of the same type, resulting in improved generalizations that can be applied across various instances to uncover new relationships and insights within the KG. By integrating cross-view links into the embedding process, the quality and expressiveness of the generated embeddings are significantly enhanced.

Apart from cross-view links, the ontology view alone exhibits a prominent hierarchical structure. Methods that employ intra-view links within the ontology view KG leverage either the entity or the relation hierarchy to boost embedding performance. Entity type hierarchy injection requires defining hierarchies of entity types, including sub-types and super-types, which facilitate more sophisticated reasoning operations by allowing inheritance and generalization of properties and relationships. Relation hierarchy injection, on the other hand, involves establishing hierarchies of relationships between entities, such as sub-relations and super-relations, which promote advanced reasoning operations by enabling the deduction of implicit relationships among entities. By using intra-view links, the embeddings can capture more fine-grained semantic information about entities or relations.

Given the importance of both cross-view connections and intra-view structures in KG ontologies for KG reasoning, a state-of-the-art method JOIE uses both types of information to improve KG embedding. The cross-view association model learns to connect the embeddings of ontological concepts and their corresponding instance-view entities. Intra-view models are trained jointly to capture the structured knowledge of instance and ontology views in separate embedding spaces. JOIE also employs a hierarchy-aware encoding technique for ontologies with hierarchies. The combination of cross-view connections and intra-view structures enables JOIE to outperform previous models on the instance-view triple prediction task and ontology population on ontology view KG.

We have only covered the fundamental techniques for integrating ontology into KG reasoning in this chapter. Nevertheless, it is vital to recognize that there are other potential avenues in this area that we can delve into as follows.

Ontology Embedding in Hyperbolic Space

Hyperbolic space is a non-Euclidean space with constant negative curvature, which allows for a more efficient representation of hierarchical structures in an ontology view compared to Euclidean space. In hyperbolic space, points that are far away from the origin can be represented using a small number of dimensions. This is particularly useful for hierarchical structures, where nodes at different levels of the hierarchy are at varying distances from the root node.

Several approaches have been proposed for ontology embedding in hyperbolic space, one of which is the dual-geometric space embedding model for two-view knowledge graphs (DGS) [34]. The DGS model extends JOIE by combining hyperbolic space and spherical space to create a dual-geometric space. It uses hyperbolic space to represent ontology-view concepts for hierarchical relations, spherical space for instance-view entities for cyclic relations, and a specially designed intersection bridge space for entities that are involved in both cyclic and hierarchical structures. Hyperbolic space plays a key role in the DGS model as it allows for an efficient representation of the hierarchical structure of the KG. By using hyperbolic space in conjunction with spherical space, the DGS model can capture both the hierarchical and semantic relationships in the graph, providing a more complete representation of the KG.

Hyperbolic ontology embedding is still a relatively new area of research with many open questions and challenges to be addressed. These include handling large-scale ontologies effectively and incorporating additional sources of information, such as textual data, into the embedding process. As research in this area continues, it is likely that we will see more approaches that combine different geometric spaces to effectively model the diverse relationships in KGs.

Application of Ontology in Biology Ontology has emerged as a valuable resource in various domains, such as biology. For instance, the knowledge obtained from studies on viruses in the realm of biological research is often limited. Therefore, it becomes crucial to leverage the extensive biological knowledge from closely related species to infer the molecular impact of new species, such as SARS-CoV-2. Recognizing this need, Bio-JOIE [35] extends the JOIE model to facilitate joint embedding learning across multiple domains of biological knowledge bases (KBs). The primary contribution of Bio-JOIE lies in its ability to integrate information from diverse biological knowledge bases, enabling the improvement of predictions related to protein-protein interactions (PPIs).

Specifically, Bio-JOIE accomplishes this by simultaneously learning two essential model components. The first component is a knowledge model that characterizes different domain-specific knowledge graphs (KGs) within separate low-dimensional embedding spaces. The second component is a transfer model that captures associations and shared knowledge between different domains. By combining these two components, Bio-JOIE effectively harnesses the integrated knowledge to enhance the prediction of PPIs.

In addition to biology, ontology embedding also has many other applications in various domains. For instance, in healthcare informatics, the embedding of medical ontologies like

SNOMED CT or Gene Ontology simplifies the capture of relationships between medical concepts, aids in disease diagnosis, and enhances patient outcome prediction models. Furthermore, embedding ontologies that represent user interests and item attributes enables recommendation algorithms to produce more precise and personalized recommendations in domains ranging from e-commerce, music, and movies to news.

References

1. J. Hao, M. Chen, W. Yu, Y. Sun, and W. Wang. Universal representation learning of knowledge bases by jointly embedding instances and ontological concepts. In *Proceedings of the ACM SIGKDD International Conference on Knowledge Discovery and Data Mining (KDD)*, pages 1709–1719. ACM, 2019.
2. S. Auer, C. Bizer, G. Kobilarov, J. Lehmann, R. Cyganiak, and Z. Ives. Dbpedia: A nucleus for a web of open data. In *Proceedings of the International Semantic Web Conference (ISWC)*, pages 722–735. Springer, 2007.
3. F. M. Suchanek, G. Kasneci, and G. Weikum. YAGO: a core of semantic knowledge. In *Proceedings of the International World Wide Web Conference (WWW)*, pages 697–706. ACM, 2007.
4. R. Speer, J. Chin, and C. Havasi. Conceptnet 5.5: An open multilingual graph of general knowledge. In *Proceedings of AAAI Conference on Artificial Intelligence (AAAI)*, 2017.
5. Wikipedia. Resource description framework. https://en.wikipedia.org/wiki/Resource_Description_Framework. [Online].
6. Wikipedia. Owl. https://en.wikipedia.org/wiki/Owl. [Online].
7. J. Lehmann, R. Isele, M. Jakob, A. Jentzsch, D. Kontokostas, P. N. Mendes, S. Hellmann, M. Morsey, P. Van Kleef, S. Auer, et al. Dbpedia–a large-scale, multilingual knowledge base extracted from wikipedia. *Semantic Web*, 6(2):167–195, 2015.
8. K. Bollacker, C. Evans, P. Paritosh, T. Sturge, and J. Taylor. Freebase: a collaboratively created graph database for structuring human knowledge. In *Proceedings of ACM SIGMOD International Conference on Management of Data (SIGMOD)*, pages 1247–1250. ACM, 2008.
9. A. P. Taxonomy. Amazon store taxonomy: Definition, importance & best practices. https://www.amazonlistingservice.com/blog/amazon-store-taxonomy-organization/, 2023. [Online].
10. Wikipedia. Acm computing classification system. https://en.wikipedia.org/wiki/ACM_Computing_Classification_System. [Online].
11. Wikipedia. Gene ontology. https://en.wikipedia.org/wiki/Gene_Ontology. [Online].
12. D. Ontology. Disease ontology. https://disease-ontology.org/.
13. M. Nickel, V. Tresp, and H.-P. Kriegel. Factorizing yago: scalable machine learning for linked data. In *Proceedings of the International World Wide Web Conference (WWW)*, pages 271–280, 2012.
14. S. Guo, Q. Wang, B. Wang, L. Wang, and L. Guo. Semantically smooth knowledge graph embedding. In *Proceedings of the 53rd Annual Meeting of the Association for Computational Linguistics and the 7th International Joint Conference on Natural Language Processing (ACL-IJCNLP)*, pages 84–94, 2015.
15. R. Xie, Z. Liu, M. Sun, et al. Representation learning of knowledge graphs with hierarchical types. In *Proceedings of the International Joint Conferences on Artificial Intelligence (IJCAI)*, pages 2965–2971, 2016.

16. Z. Zhang, F. Zhuang, M. Qu, F. Lin, and Q. He. Knowledge graph embedding with hierarchical relation structure. In *Proceedings of the Conference on Empirical Methods in Natural Language Processing (EMNLP)*, pages 3198–3207, 2018.

17. A. Bordes, N. Usunier, A. Garcia-Duran, J. Weston, and O. Yakhnenko. Translating embeddings for modeling multi-relational data. In *Advances in Neural Information Processing Systems (NeurIPS)*, pages 2787–2795, 2013.

18. B. Yang, W.-t. Yih, X. He, J. Gao, and L. Deng. Embedding entities and relations for learning and inference in knowledge bases. *arXiv preprint* arXiv:1412.6575, 2014.

19. M. Nickel, L. Rosasco, T. A. Poggio, et al. Holographic embeddings of knowledge graphs. In *Proceedings of AAAI Conference on Artificial Intelligence (AAAI)*, pages 1955–1961. AAAI Press, 2016.

20. F. Mahdisoltani, J. Biega, et al. Yago3: A knowledge base from multilingual Wikipedias. In *Proceedings of the Conference on Innovative Data Systems Research (CIDR)*, 2015.

21. S. J. Reddi, S. Kale, and S. Kumar. On the convergence of adam and beyond. In *International Conference on Learning Representations (ICLR)*, 2018.

22. A. M. Saxe, J. L. McClelland, et al. Exact solutions to the nonlinear dynamics of learning in deep linear neural networks. *International Conference on Learning Representations (ICLR)*, 2014.

23. Z. Wang, J. Zhang, J. Feng, and Z. Chen. Knowledge graph embedding by translating on hyperplanes. In *Proceedings of AAAI Conference on Artificial Intelligence (AAAI)*, pages 1112–1119. AAAI Press, 2014.

24. D. Krompaß, S. Baier, V. Tresp, et al. Type-constrained representation learning in knowledge graphs. In *Proceedings of the International Semantic Web Conference (ISWC)*, 2015.

25. S. Ma, J. Ding, W. Jia, et al. Transt: Type-based multiple embedding representations for knowledge graph completion. In *Proceedings of the European Conference on Machine Learning and Knowledge Discovery in Databases (ECML-PKDD)*, 2017.

26. J. Ma, P. Cui, X. Wang, and W. Zhu. Hierarchical taxonomy aware network embedding. In *Proceedings of the ACM SIGKDD International Conference on Knowledge Discovery and Data Mining (KDD)*. ACM, 2018.

27. T. Rocktäschel, S. Singh, and S. Riedel. Injecting logical background knowledge into embeddings for relation extraction. In *Proceedings of the Conference of the North American Chapter of the Association for Computational Linguistics: Human Language Technologies (NAACL-HLT)*, pages 1119–1129, 2015.

28. S. Guo, Q. Wang, L. Wang, B. Wang, and L. Guo. Jointly embedding knowledge graphs and logical rules. In *Proceedings of the Conference on Empirical Methods in Natural Language Processing (EMNLP)*, pages 192–202, 2016.

29. A. Bordes, X. Glorot, J. Weston, and Y. Bengio. A semantic matching energy function for learning with multi-relational data. *Machine Learning*, 94(2):233–259, 2014.

30. Y. Lin, Z. Liu, M. Sun, Y. Liu, and X. Zhu. Learning entity and relation embeddings for knowledge graph completion. In *Proceedings of AAAI Conference on Artificial Intelligence (AAAI)*, 2015.

31. X. Lv, L. Hou, J. Li, and Z. Liu. Differentiating concepts and instances for knowledge graph embedding. In *Proceedings of the Conference on Empirical Methods in Natural Language Processing (EMNLP)*, 2018.

32. J. Pujara, E. Augustine, and L. Getoor. Sparsity and noise: Where knowledge graph embeddings fall short. In *Proceedings of the Conference on Empirical Methods in Natural Language Processing (EMNLP)*, 2017.

33. M. Chen, Y. Tian, M. Yang, and C. Zaniolo. Multilingual knowledge graph embeddings for cross-lingual knowledge alignment. In *Proceedings of the International Joint Conferences on Artificial Intelligence (IJCAI)*, 2017.

34. R. G. Iyer, Y. Bai, W. Wang, and Y. Sun. Dual-geometric space embedding model for two-view knowledge graphs. In *Proceedings of the ACM SIGKDD International Conference on Knowledge Discovery and Data Mining (KDD)*, pages 676–686, 2022.

35. J. Hao, C. J.-T. Ju, M. Chen, Y. Sun, C. Zaniolo, and W. Wang. Bio-joie: Joint representation learning of biological knowledge bases. In *Proceedings of the 11th ACM International Conference on Bioinformatics, Computational Biology and Health Informatics*, pages 1–10, 2020.

Conclusion and Research Frontiers

7

In this book, we have conducted an extensive investigation into the fascinating domain of integrating neural networks with symbolic reasoning for Knowledge Graph (KG) reasoning. Our focus has been directed toward three primary categories of reasoning tasks: knowledge graph completion, complex query answering, and logical rule learning. Furthermore, we have thoroughly explored the utilization of KG ontology as a valuable resource to enhance the reasoning capabilities of KGs. For each task, we have provided a comprehensive overview of both symbolic and neural methodologies, delving into the synergistic potential that arises from their combined utilization, where a neuro-symbolic reasoning system can exhibit enhanced accuracy and interpretability. A succinct summary of each task is presented below.

- **Knowledge Graph Completion**: The objective of knowledge graph completion revolves around predicting missing facts by leveraging existing facts. We have introduced various approaches for KG completion, including (1) traditional symbolic reasoning techniques, (2) recent representation learning-based methods, and (3) neuro-symbolic approaches. While attempts have been made to combine neural and symbolic methods through probabilistic programming frameworks, scalability issues have hindered their effectiveness. To address these limitations, we introduce the UniKER algorithm [1] that seamlessly combines symbolic reasoning and representation learning for KG completion tasks, achieving both effectiveness and efficiency.
- **Complex Query Answering**: In contrast to KG completion, complex query answering presents a more challenging problem of responding to complex queries defined in First-Order Logical (FOL) format, involving multiple entities and relations. We present two primary approaches for addressing complex query answering in KGs: (1) traditional sub-

K. Cheng and Y. Sun, *Knowledge Graph Reasoning*, Synthesis Lectures on Data, Semantics, and Knowledge, https://doi.org/10.1007/978-3-031-72008-6_7

graph matching techniques and (2) more recent logical query embedding methods. While logical query embedding has witnessed significant progress, many existing models fail to conform to logical laws with their logical operations, leading to subpar performance. To overcome this challenge, we introduce the FuzzQE algorithm [2] as a state-of-the-art approach to logical query embedding. By employing fuzzy logic to define logical operators within the embedding space, FuzzyQE ensures adherence to logical laws, resulting in improved performance.

- **Logical Rule Learning**: The goal of Logical Rule Learning is to automatically derive logical rules from KGs, which can be broadly classified into two categories: (1) traditional search-based methods and (2) more recent neuro-symbolic approaches. Despite achieving remarkable performance in learning logical rules, neuro-symbolic integration methods heavily rely on observed data for rule identification. This poses challenges when attempting to identify rules that lack sufficient instances for support. To address this limitation, we present the state-of-the-art RLogic approach [3]. RLogic pushes deductive reasoning into the learning process, and thus reduce the reliance on direct evidence support.
- **Incorporating Ontology into Knowledge Graph Reasoning**: Knowledge graphs typically encompass two perspectives: (1) an ontology view for meta-level abstraction and (2) an instance view for instance-level instantiation. The inclusion of the ontology view provides additional valuable information for KGs, and the joint consideration of both views can significantly enhance KG reasoning performance. Techniques that incorporate ontology schemas for KG reasoning can be categorized into two groups based on their integration of schema information: those utilizing cross-view connections and those utilizing intra-view connections. It is crucial to acknowledge that both cross-view connections and intra-view structures within KG ontologies play pivotal roles in KG reasoning. Therefore, we introduce JOIE [4] as the most representative work that effectively integrates both sources of information in a joint manner.

We have also discussed the challenges and limitations of neuro-symbolic reasoning systems, such as the interpretability issues associated with neural networks and the scalability concerns when handling large-scale data. However, we believe that the potential benefits of combining neural networks with symbolic reasoning for KG reasoning far outweigh the challenges and that this approach will continue to be an active area of research in the coming years. There are many exciting research frontiers and potential future directions in this field. We illustrate a few of them here:

- **Explainable neuro-symbolic reasoning**: Improving the interpretability of neuro-symbolic reasoning systems is a crucial direction for advancing the field. Users need to understand the reasoning behind the system's decisions to build trust in it. While logical rule learning is one way to generate explanations, there are other possible ways that have not been explored in this book. For instance, attention mechanisms can identify the most critical input data that led to a particular output, generating explanations that are easy to understand and helping users build trust in the system. Additionally, visualization techniques can be used to display the internal workings of the neuro-symbolic reasoning system. For example, representing the decision-making process as a graph can enable users to understand how the system arrived at a specific conclusion. By exploring these and other approaches, the interpretability of neuro-symbolic reasoning systems can be improved, leading to more trust and acceptance of the system in real-world applications.

- **Multi-modal reasoning**: Another crucial direction for advancing neuro-symbolic reasoning systems is to develop multi-modal systems that can handle multiple types of data. In many real-world applications, such as autonomous driving or medical diagnosis, reasoning systems need to analyze data from different modalities, including text, image, and video. Developing multi-modal neuro-symbolic reasoning systems that can handle and integrate different data types is therefore essential. Future research could focus on developing techniques for multi-modal feature extraction, where features are extracted from each modality and combined into a joint representation that can be used for reasoning. This can be achieved by using neural networks to extract features from each modality, then combining them using techniques such as late fusion or cross-modal attention mechanisms. These systems can provide more accurate and comprehensive reasoning capabilities and have the potential to impact a wide range of applications in fields such as healthcare, finance, and autonomous systems.

- **Combining KGs with Large Language Models**: Large language models, such as GPT-4, are revolutionizing the field of natural language processing and artificial intelligence, showcasing their impressive ability to generate human-like text across a wide range of tasks. However, despite their remarkable performance, LLMs have limitations when it comes to accessing and incorporating factual knowledge. These models primarily rely on patterns learned from massive amounts of text data, which may result in inaccuracies or the propagation of false information. This is where Knowledge Graphs (KGs), such as Wikipedia, come into play. KGs serve as structured repositories of factual knowledge, explicitly representing relationships and semantic connections between entities. By integrating KGs with LLMs, we can address the limitations of both approaches and leverage their respective advantages. LLMs can benefit from the external knowledge provided by KGs, enabling them to access accurate and reliable information for inference and improving their interpretability. This integration allows LLMs to go beyond the limitations of their training data and make more informed and contextually grounded responses. For example, OreoLM [5] introduces a Knowledge Interaction Layer (KIL) that is inserted between the layers of a Language Model (LM). The KIL interacts with a KG reasoning module, enabling the discovery of various reasoning paths. These paths are then utilized by the reasoning module to generate answers. On the other hand, KGs face their own challenges. Constructing KGs requires significant manual effort and expertise, and they need to constantly evolve to capture new facts and represent previously unseen knowledge. Existing methods for KG construction may struggle to keep up with the rapid growth and dynamic nature of knowledge. By unifying LLMs and KGs, we can address these challenges by leveraging the language generation capabilities of LLMs to generate new facts and extend the representation of KGs. The integration of LLMs and KGs allows researchers to create more robust and knowledgeable AI systems that can leverage both structured knowledge and the generative power of language models.

- **Incorporating temporal reasoning**: Many real-world applications involve reasoning about changes over time, such as in financial markets or epidemiological models. Future research could focus on developing techniques to incorporate temporal reasoning into neuro-symbolic reasoning systems, allowing them to reason over dynamic KGs and make predictions about future trends. This work would involve addressing the challenges of representing and reasoning with temporal information within KGs, as well as designing algorithms that can effectively capture and utilize temporal dependencies. Additionally, efforts could be directed towards developing methods for learning temporal patterns and trends from historical data, enabling the system to extrapolate and forecast future states of the KG. By incorporating temporal reasoning into KG reasoning, researchers can enhance the capabilities of existing neuro-symbolic systems and empower them to provide more accurate and informed predictions, thereby facilitating better decision-making in various domains.

- **Federated KG reasoning**: Traditional KG reasoning approaches typically rely on centralized data repositories, where the entire KG is stored and processed in a single location. However, in real-world scenarios, KGs are often distributed across multiple sources due to privacy concerns, ownership constraints, or scalability issues. Federated KG reasoning addresses this challenge by enabling reasoning and inference across distributed KGs without centralizing the data. Instead of sharing the complete KG, participants can selectively share specific parts or perform reasoning tasks locally on their private KGs. This approach ensures data privacy and allows participants to retain control over their sensitive or proprietary information while still benefiting from collective reasoning capabilities. By embracing federated KG reasoning, collaboration and knowledge sharing can thrive among diverse organizations or entities. Each participant in the federation can contribute their local KG, which may contain unique or domain-specific information. By federating these KGs, reasoning can be performed across multiple sources, resulting in a more comprehensive and diverse knowledge base. This collaborative aspect facilitates the generation of cross-domain insights and a broader understanding of complex phenomena.

Overall, combining neural networks with symbolic reasoning for KG reasoning is a rich and rapidly evolving research area. These additional future directions demonstrate the broad range of applications and challenges that these systems can address, and highlight the potential for continued innovation and impact in this field. We hope this book has provided readers with a comprehensive understanding of this field and we encourage readers to explore further the exciting possibilities of neuro-symbolic reasoning.

References

1. K. Cheng, Z. Yang, M. Zhang, and Y. Sun. Uniker: A unified framework for combining embedding and definite horn rule reasoning for knowledge graph inference. In *Proceedings of the Conference on Empirical Methods in Natural Language Processing (EMNLP)*, 2021.
2. X. Chen, Z. Hu, and Y. Sun. Fuzzy logic based logical query answering on knowledge graphs. In *Proceedings of AAAI Conference on Artificial Intelligence (AAAI)*, volume 36, pages 3939–3948, 2022.
3. K. Cheng, J. Liu, W. Wang, and Y. Sun. Rlogic: Recursive logical rule learning from knowledge graphs. In *Proceedings of the ACM SIGKDD International Conference on Knowledge Discovery and Data Mining (KDD)*, pages 179–189, 2022.
4. J. Hao, M. Chen, W. Yu, Y. Sun, and W. Wang. Universal representation learning of knowledge bases by jointly embedding instances and ontological concepts. In *Proceedings of the ACM SIGKDD International Conference on Knowledge Discovery and Data Mining (KDD)*, pages 1709–1719. ACM, 2019.
5. Z. Hu, Y. Xu, W. Yu, S. Wang, Z. Yang, C. Zhu, K.-W. Chang, and Y. Sun. Empowering language models with knowledge graph reasoning for question answering. *arXiv preprint* arXiv:2211.08380, 2022.

Knowledge Graph Completion

A

A.1 Representation Learning Based KG Completion

A.1.1 Variants of TransE

Translating on Hyperplanes: TransH

To address the limitations of TransE, TransH [1] allows entities to have different representations when involved in different relations. Specifically, each entity $e_i \in \mathcal{E}$ has a general representation vector $\mathbf{e}_i \in \mathbb{R}^d$; each relation r_k is associated with a relation-specific hyperplane with a unit-length normal vector $\mathbf{w}_{r_k} \in \mathbb{R}^d$ ($||\mathbf{w}_{r_k}|| = 1$) and a relation-specific translation vector $\mathbf{r}_k \in \mathbb{R}^d$ on the hyperplane. For a triple (e_i, r_k, e_j), the entities are first projected to the r_k-specific hyperplane:

$$\mathbf{e}'_i = \mathbf{e}_i - \mathbf{w}_{r_k}^{\mathsf{T}} \mathbf{e}_i \mathbf{w}_{r_k}$$
$$\mathbf{e}'_j = \mathbf{e}_j - \mathbf{w}_{r_k}^{\mathsf{T}} \mathbf{e}_j \mathbf{w}_{r_k}$$

(A.1)

Then the translation is defined on the hyperplane, which maps the projected head entity $\mathbf{e}'_i$ into the projected tail entity on the hyperplane as $\mathbf{e}'_i + \mathbf{r}_k$, and the score function can be defined as:

$$f_{r_k}(e_i, e_j) = - \left\| \mathbf{e}'_i + \mathbf{r}_k - \mathbf{e}'_j \right\|_2^2.$$

(A.2)

The idea is illustrated in Fig. A.1b. In this way, even if the embeddings of "*Mary Stilwell*" and "*Mina Miller*" are close given the relation "*isMarriedTo*", they could still be very different given other relations.

TransR

TransR [2] improves TransE by separating entity space and relation space as shown in Fig. A.1c, where the entity representations $\mathbf{e}_i \in \mathbb{R}^d$ and $\mathbf{e}_j \in \mathbb{R}^d$ and the relation

© The Author(s), under exclusive license to Springer Nature Switzerland AG 2025
K. Cheng and Y. Sun, *Knowledge Graph Reasoning*, Synthesis Lectures on Data, Semantics, and Knowledge, https://doi.org/10.1007/978-3-031-72008-6

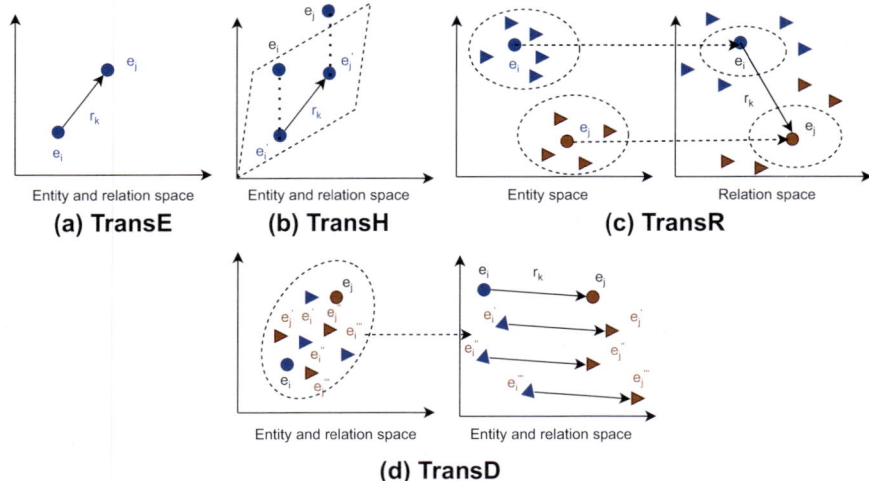

Fig. A.1 Illustrations of representative translation-based models, including TransE, TransH, TransR, and TransD. The core idea of translation-based models is to enforce $\mathbf{e}_i + \mathbf{r}_k \approx \mathbf{e}_j$ when the triple (e_i, r_k, e_j) holds

representation $\mathbf{r}_k \in \mathbb{R}^{d'}$. The entity representations are projected into the relation space $\mathbb{R}^{d'}$ via a relation-specific transformation, denoted as $\mathbf{M}_{r_k} \in \mathbb{R}^{d' \times d}$:

$$
\begin{aligned}
\mathbf{e}'_i &= \mathbf{M}_{r_k} \mathbf{e}_i \\
\mathbf{e}'_j &= \mathbf{M}_{r_k} \mathbf{e}_j
\end{aligned}
\tag{A.3}
$$

Similarly, the score function for a triple (e_i, r_k, e_j) can be defined as:

$$
f_{r_k}(e_i, e_j) = -\left\| \mathbf{e}'_i + \mathbf{r}_k - \mathbf{e}'_j \right\|_2^2.
\tag{A.4}
$$

TransR allows relation-specific projection and thus can accommodate reflexive, 1-to-N, N-to-1, and N-to-N relations.

TransD

In TransR, the projection matrices are only related to the relations. As illustrated in Fig. A.1d, TransD [3] proposes to replace the projection matrix $\mathbf{M}_{r_k} \in \mathbb{R}^{d' \times d}$ in TransR with the product of two projection vectors $\mathbf{w}_{r_k} \in \mathbb{R}^{d'}$ and $\mathbf{w}_e \in \mathbb{R}^{d}$, which correspond to both the relation and the entity. The new entity representations are then defined as:

$$
\begin{aligned}
\mathbf{e}'_i &= (\mathbf{w}_{r_k} \mathbf{w}_{e_i}^\mathsf{T} + \mathbf{I}^{d' \times d}) \mathbf{e}_i \\
\mathbf{e}'_j &= (\mathbf{w}_{r_k} \mathbf{w}_{e_j}^\mathsf{T} + \mathbf{I}^{d' \times d}) \mathbf{e}_j
\end{aligned}
\tag{A.5}
$$

Table A.1 Summary of geometric operation-based embedding models

Method	Ent. and Rel. Embed.	Score function $f_{r_k}(e_i, e_j)$
TransE [4]	$\mathbf{e}_i, \mathbf{e}_j \in \mathbb{R}^d, \mathbf{r}_k \in \mathbb{R}^d$	$-\|\mathbf{e}_i + \mathbf{r}_k - \mathbf{e}_j\|_{1/2}$
TransH [1]	$\mathbf{e}_i, \mathbf{e}_j \in \mathbb{R}^d, \mathbf{r}_k, \mathbf{w}_{r_k} \in \mathbb{R}^{d'}$	$-\|(\mathbf{e}_i - \mathbf{w}_{r_k}^\mathsf{T}\mathbf{e}_i\mathbf{w}_{r_k}) + \mathbf{r}_k - (\mathbf{e}_j - \mathbf{w}_{r_k}^\mathsf{T}\mathbf{e}_j\mathbf{w}_{r_k})\|_2^2$
TransR [2]	$\mathbf{e}_i, \mathbf{e}_j \in \mathbb{R}^d, \mathbf{r}_k \in \mathbb{R}^{d'}, \mathbf{M}_{r_k} \in \mathbb{R}^{d' \times d}$	$-\|\mathbf{M}_{r_k}\mathbf{e}_i + \mathbf{r}_k - \mathbf{M}_{r_k}\mathbf{e}_j\|_2^2$
TransD [3]	$\mathbf{e}_i, \mathbf{w}_{e_i}, \mathbf{e}_j, \mathbf{w}_{e_j} \in \mathbb{R}^d, \mathbf{r}_k, \mathbf{w}_{r_k} \in \mathbb{R}^{d'}$	$-\|((\mathbf{w}_{r_k}\mathbf{w}_{e_i}^\mathsf{T} + \mathbf{I})\mathbf{e}_i + \mathbf{r}_k - (\mathbf{w}_{r_k}\mathbf{w}_{e_j}^\mathsf{T} + \mathbf{I})\mathbf{e}_j)\|_2^2$
RotatE [5]	$\mathbf{e}_i, \mathbf{e}_j \in \mathbb{C}^d, \mathbf{r}_k \in \mathbb{C}^d$	$-\|\mathbf{e}_i \circ \mathbf{r}_k - \mathbf{e}_j\|$

Table A.2 Summary of the abilities of geometric operation-based embedding models in modeling different relation properties

Method	Symmetry	Asymmetric	Reflexivity	Transitivity	Inversion	Composition	1–1	1–N/N–1	N–N
TransE [4]	✗	✓	✗	✗	✓	✓	✓	✗	✗
TransH [1]	✓	✓	✗	✗	✓	✓	✓	✓	✓
TransR [2]	✓	✓	✓	✗	✓	✓	✓	✓	✓
TransD [3]	✓	✓	✓	✗	✓	✓	✓	✓	✓
RotatE [5]	✓	✓	✗	✗	✓	✓	✓	✗	✗

where $\mathbf{I}^{d' \times d}$ is an extended version of the identity matrix for the rectangular matrix. In addition to increasing the capacity of the model by allowing both entity and relation to play a role in the transformation matrix, it can also enhance efficiency due to parameter reduction.

Summary

Table A.1 summarizes entity and relation embeddings and score functions of geometric operation-based models. In addition, we also provide an analysis of these models on their abilities in modeling different relation properties in Table A.2.

A.1.2 Variants of Bilinear Models

SimplE

Different from all the above methods which associate each entity with only one vector, SimplE [6] allows two embeddings of each entity to be learned. SimplE associates each entity e_i with two vectors $\mathbf{h}_{e_i}, \mathbf{t}_{e_i} \in \mathbb{R}^d$ where $\mathbf{h}_{e_i}$ captures e_i's behavior as the head and $\mathbf{t}_{e_i}$ captures e_i's behavior as the tail. To take advantage of the inverse of relations to associate two vectors for each entity, SimplE also learns two embeddings for each relation $\mathbf{v}_{r_k}, \mathbf{v}_{r_k^{-1}} \in \mathbb{R}^d$, where $\mathbf{v}_{r_k}$ captures the relation r_k and $\mathbf{v}_{r_k^{-1}}$ captures the inverse of the relation r_k. The score function of SimplE for a triple (e_i, r_k, e_j) is defined as the average canonical polyadic (CP) score of (e_i, r_k, e_j) and (e_j, r_k^{-1}, e_i):

$$f_{r_k}(e_i, e_j) = \frac{1}{2}((\mathbf{h}_{e_i} \circ \mathbf{v}_{r_k})^\mathsf{T}\mathbf{t}_{e_j} + (\mathbf{h}_{e_j} \circ \mathbf{v}_{r_k^{-1}})^\mathsf{T}\mathbf{t}_{e_i})$$

where ∘ is the element-wise multiplication.

HolE

HolE [7] simplifies RESCAL by proposing a circular correlation operation to compose the head and tail entities at first, then matched with the relation representation to define the score as follows:

$$f_{r_k}(e_i, e_j) = \mathbf{r}_k^\mathsf{T}(\mathbf{e}_i * \mathbf{e}_j)$$

where $* : \mathbb{R}^d \times \mathbb{R}^d \to \mathbb{R}^d$ represents the circular correlation operation and

$$[\mathbf{e}_i * \mathbf{e}_j]_q = \sum_{p=1}^{d}[\mathbf{e}_i]_p[\mathbf{e}_j]_{(q+p) \bmod d}$$

Because in general $\mathbf{e}_i * \mathbf{e}_j \neq \mathbf{e}_j * \mathbf{e}_i$, HolE can model asymmetric relations. Meanwhile, each relation in HolE is only associated with one d-dimensional vector, which is more efficient compared to RESCAL and SimplE.

Summary

Table A.3 presents a summary of entity and relation embeddings and score functions of various bilinear models such as RESCAL, DistMult, ComplEx, HolE, and ANALOGY. It is important to note that these models can be transformed into each other with certain constraints.

Table A.3 Summary of bilinear models

Method	Ent. and Rel. Embed.	Score function $f_{r_k}(e_i, e_j)$
RESCAL [8]	$\mathbf{e}_i, \mathbf{e}_j \in \mathbb{R}^d, \mathbf{M}_{r_k} \in \mathbb{R}^{d \times d}$	$\mathbf{e}_i^\mathsf{T}\mathbf{M}_{r_k}\mathbf{e}_j$
DistMult [9]	$\mathbf{e}_i, \mathbf{e}_j \in \mathbb{R}^d, \mathbf{r}_k \in \mathbb{R}^d$	$\mathbf{e}_i^\mathsf{T}\mathrm{diag}(\mathbf{r}_k)\mathbf{e}_j$
ComplEx [10]	$\mathbf{e}_i, \mathbf{e}_j \in \mathbb{C}^d, \mathbf{r}_k \in \mathbb{C}^d$	$\mathrm{Re}(\mathbf{e}_i^\mathsf{T}\mathrm{diag}(\mathbf{r}_k)\overline{\mathbf{e}}_j)$
SimplE [6]†	$\mathbf{h}_{e_i}, \mathbf{t}_{e_i}, \mathbf{h}_{e_j}, \mathbf{t}_{e_j} \in \mathbb{R}^d$ $\mathbf{v}_{r_k}, \mathbf{v}_{r_k^{-1}} \in \mathbb{R}^d$	$\frac{1}{2}((\mathbf{h}_{e_i} \circ \mathbf{v}_{r_k})^\mathsf{T}\mathbf{t}_{e_j} + (\mathbf{h}_{e_j} \circ \mathbf{v}_{r_k}^{-1})^\mathsf{T}\mathbf{t}_{e_i})$
HolE [7]‡	$\mathbf{e}_i, \mathbf{e}_j \in \mathbb{R}^d, \mathbf{r}_k \in \mathbb{R}^d$	$\mathbf{r}_k^\mathsf{T}(\mathbf{e}_i * \mathbf{e}_j)$
ANALOGY [11]	$\mathbf{e}_i, \mathbf{e}_j \in \mathbb{R}^d, \mathbf{M}_{r_k} \in \mathbb{R}^{d \times d}$ s.t., $\mathbf{M}_{r_k}\mathbf{M}_{r_k}^\mathsf{T} = \mathbf{M}_{r_k}^\mathsf{T}\mathbf{M}_{r_k}$ $\mathbf{M}_{r_k}\mathbf{M}_{r_k'} = \mathbf{M}_{r_k'}\mathbf{M}_{r_k}$	$\mathbf{e}_i^\mathsf{T}\mathbf{M}_{r_k}\mathbf{e}_j$

† r_k^{-1} represents the inverse of relation r_k, ∘ represents Hadamard product
‡ $*$ denotes circular-correlation

A.1.3 Deep Representation Learning-Based KGE Models

Semantic Matching Energy (SME)

Semantic Matching Energy (SME) [12] makes the first attempt to utilize neural networks for learning the confidence of triples in KGs. Given a fact (e_i, r_k, e_j), SME combines the relation $\mathbf{r}_k$ with the head entity $\mathbf{e}_i$ to get $g_u(\mathbf{e}_i, \mathbf{r}_k)$, and combines the relation $\mathbf{r}_k$ with the tail entity $\mathbf{e}_j$ to get $g_v(\mathbf{e}_j, \mathbf{r}_k)$. The score of a fact is defined as matching g_u and g_v by their dot product.

$$f_{r_k}(e_i, e_j) = g_u(\mathbf{e}_i, \mathbf{r}_k)^\mathsf{T} g_v(\mathbf{e}_j, \mathbf{r}_k)$$

There are two versions of SME: a linear version as well as a bilinear version. SME(linear) is defined as:

$$g_u(\mathbf{e}_i, \mathbf{r}_k) = \mathbf{M}_u^1 \mathbf{e}_i + \mathbf{M}_u^2 \mathbf{r}_k + \mathbf{b}_u$$
$$g_v(\mathbf{e}_j, \mathbf{r}_k) = \mathbf{M}_v^1 \mathbf{e}_j + \mathbf{M}_v^2 \mathbf{r}_k + \mathbf{b}_v$$

where $\mathbf{M}_u^1, \mathbf{M}_u^2, \mathbf{M}_v^1, \mathbf{M}_v^2 \in \mathbb{R}^{d \times d}$ and $\mathbf{b}_u, \mathbf{b}_v \in \mathbb{R}^d$.

SME(bilinear) is defined as:

$$g_u(\mathbf{e}_i, \mathbf{r}_k) = \mathbf{M}_u^1 \mathbf{e}_i \circ \mathbf{M}_u^2 \mathbf{r}_k + \mathbf{b}_u$$
$$g_v(\mathbf{e}_j, \mathbf{r}_k) = \mathbf{M}_v^1 \mathbf{e}_j \circ \mathbf{M}_v^2 \mathbf{r}_k + \mathbf{b}_v$$

where $\mathbf{M}_u^1, \mathbf{M}_u^2, \mathbf{M}_v^1, \mathbf{M}_v^2 \in \mathbb{R}^{d \times d}$ and $\mathbf{b}_u, \mathbf{b}_v \in \mathbb{R}^d$.

ConvKB

To simplify *2D ConvE*, ConvKB [13] captures relationship in a triple with *1D convolution* over the concatenated embeddings of the head entity, relation, and tail entity together. Specifically, it represents a fact (e_i, r_k, e_j) as a three-row matrix $[\mathbf{e}_i; \mathbf{r}_k; \mathbf{e}_j] \in \mathbb{R}^{d \times 3}$, in which each element is corresponding to a row vector. The filter $\omega \in \mathbb{R}^{3 \times 1}$ is used to obtain a feature map $[f_1, \ldots, f_d] \in \mathbb{R}^d$. A convolution layer yields multiple feature maps, which are then concatenated and projected to a final score as below

$$f_{r_k}(e_i, e_j) = \text{concat}(g([\mathbf{e}_i; \mathbf{r}_k; \mathbf{e}_j] * \omega))\mathbf{W},$$

where $\mathbf{W}$ denotes the projection matrix.

ConvR

ConvR [14] extends the global filters in ConvE to relation-specific filters. Similar to ConvE, it reshapes the head entities into 2D matrix $\overline{\mathbf{e}_i}$ to extract more feature interactions. Then, it splits the relation vector $\mathbf{r}_k$ into different blocks $\mathbf{r}_k(1), \ldots, \mathbf{r}_k(c)$ with equal size, and each block is reshaped into a 2D convolution filter $\overline{\mathbf{r}_k(1)}, \ldots, \overline{\mathbf{r}_k(c)}$. ConvR convolves across the input 2D matrix of head entities $\mathbf{S}$ using adaptively constructed, relation-specific filters. For each filter $\mathbf{R}^{(l)}$, a convolutional feature map $\mathbf{C}^{(l)}$ will be generated, with the mnth entry calculated as:

$$c_{m,n}^{(l)} = f\left(\sum_{i,j} s_{m+i-1,n+j-1} \times r_{i,j}^{(l)}\right)$$

By flattening and stack the convolutional feature maps $\mathbf{C}^{(1)}, \ldots, \mathbf{C}^{(c)}$ into $\mathbf{c}$, the score of a triple can be computed as:

$$f_{r_k}(e_i, e_j) = f(\mathbf{W}\mathbf{c} + b)^\mathsf{T}\mathbf{e}_j$$

InteractE

InteractE [15] alleviates the limitations of ConvE by capturing additional heterogeneous feature interactions. InteractE is able to achieve this by utilizing three central ideas, namely feature permutation, checkered feature reshaping, and circular convolution. The score function used in InteractE is defined as follows:

$$f_{r_k}(e_i, e_j) = g(\text{vec}(f(\phi(\mathcal{P}_k) \circledast w))\mathbf{W})\mathbf{e}_j$$

where $\phi(\mathcal{P}_k) = [\phi(\mathbf{e}_i^1, \mathbf{r}_k^1), \ldots, \phi(\mathbf{e}_i^t, \mathbf{r}_k^t)]$ and $[(\mathbf{e}_i^1, \mathbf{r}_k^1), \ldots, (\mathbf{e}_i^t, \mathbf{r}_k^t)]$ are t-random permutations of both $\mathbf{e}_i$ and $\mathbf{r}_k$. $\circledast$ denotes depth-wise circular convolution, $\text{vec}(\cdot)$ denotes vector concatenation. Functions f and g are chosen to be ReLU and sigmoid respectively.

Table A.4 summarizes entity and relation embeddings as well as the score functions of these CNNs-based models.

Table A.4 Summary of General Neural Networks-based Model and CNNs-based Model

Method	Ent. and Rel. Embed.	Score function $f_{r_k}(e_i, e_j)$
SME [12]	$\mathbf{e}_i, \mathbf{e}_j \in \mathbb{R}^d, \mathbf{r}_k \in \mathbb{R}^d$	$g_u(\mathbf{e}_i, \mathbf{r}_k)^\mathsf{T} g_v(\mathbf{e}_j, \mathbf{r}_k)$
NTN [16]	$\mathbf{e}_i, \mathbf{e}_j \in \mathbb{R}^d, \mathbf{r}_k, \mathbf{b}_{r_k} \in \mathbb{R}^k$ $\underline{\mathbf{M}}_{r_k} \in \mathbb{R}^{d \times d \times k}, \mathbf{M}_{r_k}^1, \mathbf{M}_{r_k}^2 \in \mathbb{R}^{k \times d}$	$\mathbf{r}_k^\mathsf{T} \tanh(\mathbf{e}_i^\mathsf{T} \underline{\mathbf{M}}_{r_k} \mathbf{e}_j + \mathbf{M}_{r_k}^1 \mathbf{e}_i + \mathbf{M}_{r_k}^2 \mathbf{e}_j + \mathbf{b}_{r_k})$
MLP [17]	$\mathbf{e}_i, \mathbf{e}_j \in \mathbb{R}^d, \mathbf{r}_k \in \mathbb{R}^d$ $\mathbf{M} \in \mathbb{R}^{k \times 3d}, \mathbf{w} \in \mathbb{R}^{k \times 1}$	$\sigma(\mathbf{w}^\mathsf{T} \tanh(\mathbf{M}[\mathbf{e}_i; \mathbf{r}_k; \mathbf{e}_j]))$
ConvE [18]†	$\mathbf{e}_i, \mathbf{e}_j \in \mathbb{R}^d, \mathbf{r}_k \in \mathbb{R}^d$ $\overline{\mathbf{e}_i}, \overline{\mathbf{r}_k} \in \mathbb{R}^{d_w \times d_h}$ where $d = d_w d_h$	$f(\text{vec}(f([\overline{\mathbf{e}_i}; \overline{\mathbf{r}_k}] * \omega))\mathbf{W})\mathbf{e}_j$
ConvKB [13]†	$\mathbf{e}_i, \mathbf{e}_j \in \mathbb{R}^d, \mathbf{r}_k \in \mathbb{R}^d$	$\text{concat}(g([\mathbf{e}_i; \mathbf{r}_k; \mathbf{e}_j] * \omega))\mathbf{w}$
ConvR [14]	$\mathbf{e}_i \in \mathbb{R}^d, \mathbf{e}_j \in \mathbb{R}^d, \mathbf{M}_{r_k} \in \mathbb{R}^{d \times d}$	$f(\mathbf{W}\mathbf{c} + b)^\mathsf{T}\mathbf{e}_j$
InteractE [15]‡	$\mathbf{e}_i, \mathbf{e}_j \in \mathbb{R}^d, \mathbf{r}_k \in \mathbb{R}^d$	$g(\text{vec}(f\phi(\mathcal{P}_k) \circledast w)\mathbf{W})\mathbf{e}_j$

† $*$ Denotes convolution

‡ $\circledast$ Denotes depth-wise circular convolution. $\phi(\cdot)$ is a reshaping function

SACN

SACN [19] takes the benefit of GCN and ConvE together, which consists of an encoder of a weighted graph convolutional network (WGCN), and a decoder of a convolutional network called Conv-TransE. The encoder WGCN utilizes node structure, node attributes, and relation types to define the strength of two adjacent nodes with the same relation type while the decoder Conv-TransE enables the ConvE to be translational between entities and relations, which scores a triple as follows:

$$f_{r_k}(e_i, e_j) = g(\text{vec}(\mathbf{M}(\mathbf{e}_i, \mathbf{r}_k)W))\mathbf{e}_j$$

where $\mathbf{M}(\mathbf{e}_i, \mathbf{r}_k) \in \mathbf{R}^{C \times d}$ and C is denoted to C different kernels M-GNN [20] replaces the mean aggregator in each graph convolution layer in R-GCN with a multi-layer perceptron (MLP) to support the injective property, (i.e., to map two entities to the same location only if they have identical neighborhood structures with identical embeddings on the corresponding neighbors).

A.2   Neuro-Symbolic Integration for KG Completion

A.2.1   Extension of pLogicNet with the Graph Neural Network (GNN) as the KG Embedding Model

The triple independence assumption made in pLogicNet for the variational distribution design might be overly simplified. To address the limitation, several attempts are proposed to use GNNs to provide a variational distribution that takes the dependency suggested by the graph structure into consideration, which leads to more effective relational data modeling.

Algorithm 1: GNN Encoder of ExpressGNN

Input: Initialize entity embedding $\{\mathbf{e}^{(0)}\}$

Output: Updated entity embedding $\{\mathbf{e}^{(T)}\}$

1 **for** $t = 0$ *to* $T - 1$ **do**

2 | # Compute message

3 | $m_{e' \to e}^{(t)} = \text{MLP}_1(\mathbf{e}'^{(t)})$

4 | # Aggregate message

5 | $m_e^{(t+1)} = \text{AGG}(\{m_{e' \to e}^{(t)}\}_{e' \in \mathcal{N}_e})$

6 | # Update embedding

7 | $\mathbf{e}^{(t+1)} = \text{MLP}_2(\mathbf{e}^{(t)}, m_e^{(t+1)})$

8 **end**

9 **return** entity embedding $\{\mathbf{e}^{(T)}\}$

ExpressGNN

ExpressGNN [21] proposed to use the Graph Neural Networks (GNN) to design the inference network. The learning process of the GNN is given in Algorithm 1. ExpressGNN uses learned embeddings of entity e_i and e_j to define the variational posterior. In particular, the score of each triple is computed as follows:

$$f_{r_k}(e_i, e_j) = \sigma(\text{MLP}_3(\mathbf{e}_i, \mathbf{r}_k, \mathbf{e}_j)) \tag{A.6}$$

where $\sigma(x) = \frac{1}{1+\exp(-x)}$. We use the notation MLP_1, MLP_2, and MLP_3 to refer to three distinct multilayer perceptrons. In Algorithm 1, MLP_1 and MLP_2 are employed for message computation and embedding updates, respectively while MLP_3 in Eq. (A.6) is utilized for computing the score of a triple.

pGAT

In addition to GNN, graph attention networks such as KBAT [22] also lead to more effective knowledge graph embeddings. pGAT [23] leverages KBAT [22] for as a knowledge embedding component instead. KBAT takes node embeddings as well as relation embeddings as input. The feature associated with each triple (e_i, r_k, e_j) can be represented as $\mathbf{t}_{ijk} = \mathbf{W}_t[\mathbf{e}_i||\mathbf{e}_j||\mathbf{r}_k]$, where $\mathbf{W}_t$ is the weight matrix of a linear transformation and $[\mathbf{e}_i||\mathbf{e}_j||\mathbf{r}_k]$ is the concatenation of entity embeddings and relation embeddings. Each triple is assigned an attention score α_{ijk} by normalized LeakyRelu($\mathbf{W}_\alpha \mathbf{t}_{ijk}$) through a softmax function over the neighbors of entity e_i. The new embedding of entities can be updated via graph neural network as the weighted sum of all its connected triple weighted by the attention values:

$$\hat{\mathbf{e}}_i = \sigma\left(\frac{1}{C} \sum_{c=1}^{C} \sum_{(e_i, r_k, e_j) \in \mathcal{N}_i} \alpha_{ijk}^c \mathbf{t}_{ijk}\right) \tag{A.7}$$

A multi-head attention mechanism is used to update the embedding, where C is the number of head attentions and $\mathcal{N}_i$ is the set of connected triples of entity e_i. The final embedding matrices for entities e_i, and for relations r_k are computed as:

$$\begin{aligned} \tilde{\mathbf{e}}_i &= \mathbf{W}_e \mathbf{e}_i + \hat{\mathbf{e}}_i \\ \tilde{\mathbf{r}}_k &= \mathbf{W}_r \mathbf{r}_k \end{aligned} \tag{A.8}$$

where $\mathbf{W}_e$, $\mathbf{W}_r$ are both parameters of linear transformations. Following the common setting of KGE methods, KBAT is trained by minimizing the pairwise ranking loss:

$$\sum_{(e_i, r_k, e_j) \in O} \sum_{(e_i', r_k, e_j') \in H} \max(\gamma + \left\|\tilde{\mathbf{e}}_i + \tilde{\mathbf{r}}_k - \tilde{\mathbf{e}}_j\right\|_1 - \left\|\tilde{\mathbf{e}}_i' + \tilde{\mathbf{r}}_k - \tilde{\mathbf{e}}_j'\right\|_1, 0) \tag{A.9}$$

References

1. Z. Wang, J. Zhang, J. Feng, and Z. Chen. Knowledge graph embedding by translating on hyperplanes. In *Proceedings of AAAI Conference on Artificial Intelligence (AAAI)*, pages 1112–1119. AAAI Press, 2014.

2. Y. Lin, Z. Liu, M. Sun, Y. Liu, and X. Zhu. Learning entity and relation embeddings for knowledge graph completion. In *Proceedings of AAAI Conference on Artificial Intelligence (AAAI)*, 2015.

3. G. Ji, S. He, L. Xu, K. Liu, and J. Zhao. Knowledge graph embedding via dynamic mapping matrix. In *Proceedings of the Annual Meeting of Associations for Computational Linguistics (ACL)*, pages 687–696. The Association for Computer Linguistics, 2015.

4. A. Bordes, N. Usunier, A. Garcia-Duran, J. Weston, and O. Yakhnenko. Translating embeddings for modeling multi-relational data. In *Advances in Neural Information Processing Systems (NeurIPS)*, pages 2787–2795, 2013.

5. Z. Sun, Z.-H. Deng, J.-Y. Nie, and J. Tang. Rotate: Knowledge graph embedding by relational rotation in complex space. In *International Conference on Learning Representations (ICLR)*, 2018.

6. S. M. Kazemi and D. Poole. Simple embedding for link prediction in knowledge graphs. In *Advances in Neural Information Processing Systems (NeurIPS)*, pages 4284–4295, 2018.

7. M. Nickel, L. Rosasco, T. A. Poggio, et al. Holographic embeddings of knowledge graphs. In *Proceedings of AAAI Conference on Artificial Intelligence (AAAI)*, pages 1955–1961. AAAI Press, 2016.

8. M. Nickel, V. Tresp, and H.-P. Kriegel. A three-way model for collective learning on multi-relational data. In *International Conference on Machine Learning (ICML)*, pages 809–816. Omnipress, 2011.

9. B. Yang, W.-t. Yih, X. He, J. Gao, and L. Deng. Embedding entities and relations for learning and inference in knowledge bases. *arXiv preprint* arXiv:1412.6575, 2014.

10. T. Trouillon, J. Welbl, S. Riedel, É. Gaussier, and G. Bouchard. Complex embeddings for simple link prediction. In *International Conference on Machine Learning (ICML)*, pages 2071–2080, 2016.

11. H. Liu, Y. Wu, and Y. Yang. Analogical inference for multi-relational embeddings. In *International Conference on Machine Learning (ICML)*, pages 2168–2178. PMLR, 2017.

12. A. Bordes, X. Glorot, J. Weston, and Y. Bengio. A semantic matching energy function for learning with multi-relational data. *Machine Learning*, 94(2):233–259, 2014.

13. D. Q. Nguyen, T. D. Nguyen, D. Q. Nguyen, and D. Phung. A novel embedding model for knowledge base completion based on convolutional neural network. *arXiv preprint* arXiv:1712.02121, 2017.

14. X. Jiang, Q. Wang, and B. Wang. Adaptive convolution for multi-relational learning. In *Proceedings of the Conference of the North American Chapter of the Association for Computational Linguistics: Human Language Technologies (NAACL-HLT)*, pages 978–987, 2019.

15. S. Vashishth, S. Sanyal, V. Nitin, N. Agrawal, and P. Talukdar. Interacte: Improving convolution-based knowledge graph embeddings by increasing feature interactions. In *Proceedings of AAAI Conference on Artificial Intelligence (AAAI)*, volume 34, pages 3009–3016, 2020.

16. R. Socher, D. Chen, C. D. Manning, and A. Ng. Reasoning with neural tensor networks for knowledge base completion. In *Advances in Neural Information Processing Systems (NIPS)*, 2013.

17. X. Dong, E. Gabrilovich, G. Heitz, W. Horn, N. Lao, K. Murphy, T. Strohmann, S. Sun, and W. Zhang. Knowledge vault: A web-scale approach to probabilistic knowledge fusion. In *Proceedings of the ACM SIGKDD International Conference on Knowledge Discovery and Data Mining (KDD)*, pages 601–610, 2014.
18. T. Dettmers, P. Minervini, P. Stenetorp, and S. Riedel. Convolutional 2d knowledge graph embeddings. In *Proceedings of AAAI Conference on Artificial Intelligence (AAAI)*, 2018.
19. C. Shang, Y. Tang, J. Huang, J. Bi, X. He, and B. Zhou. End-to-end structure-aware convolutional networks for knowledge base completion. In *Proceedings of AAAI Conference on Artificial Intelligence (AAAI)*, volume 33, pages 3060–3067, 2019.
20. M. Grassia, M. De Domenico, and G. Mangioni. mgnn: Generalizing the graph neural networks to the multilayer case. *arXiv preprint* arXiv:2109.10119, 2021.
21. Y. Zhang, X. Chen, Y. Yang, A. Ramamurthy, B. Li, Y. Qi, and L. Song. Can graph neural networks help logic reasoning? *arXiv preprint* arXiv:1906.02111, 2019.
22. D. Nathani, J. Chauhan, C. Sharma, and M. Kaul. Learning attention-based embeddings for relation prediction in knowledge graphs. *arXiv preprint* arXiv:1906.01195, 2019.
23. L. V. Harsha Vardhan, G. Jia, and S. Kok. Probabilistic logic graph attention networks for reasoning. In *Companion Proceedings of the Web Conference 2020*, pages 669–673, 2020.